AFGHANISTAN

Afghanistan: Dynamic for Survival

ISBN: 81-[illegible]

Jagmohan Meher

Published in 2008 in India by
Kalpaz Publications
[illegible] Satyawati Nagar, Delhi-110052
E-mail: kalpaz@hotmail.com

[illegible] Master Computers, Delhi
[illegible]

AFGHANISTAN
Dynamics of Survival

Edited by
Jagmohan Meher

Publications

KALPAZ PUBLICATIONS
DELHI-110052

Afghanistan : Dynamics of Survival

ISBN : 81-7835-640-6

Published in 2008 in India by
Kalpaz Publications
C-30, Satyawati Nagar, Delhi-110052
E-mail : Kalpaz@hotmail.com

Laser Typesetting at : Master Computers, Delhi
Printed at : Singhal Print Media, Delhi

Contents

Preface

Even after a quarter century of anarchy, civil war and blood-bath, Afghanistan continues to be on international lime light not because the international community does not want peace, but because they want peace in their own terms and conditions. Those terms and conditions are unacceptable to the Afghans who themselves are polarized on ethnic divisions and marred by their tribal loyalties. Therefore, the warring factions in this war-torn country are yet to agree on a stable political process. The Bonn agreement of 2001 promised a new era of hope, peace and prosperity, but within six years the ground reality of the situation of war and insurgency changed and distorted. It shows that the country's stabilization and reconstruction process has been stuck with the curve of national security and Taliban insurgency moving down ward. Afghanistan may yet again witness another round of instability and anarchy if the neighbouring countries and the international community leave this war-torn country fends for itself.

At this critical juncture of Afghanistan's turbulent history, this volume is a small attempt to clarify some perceptions/misperceptions about the country, and to contribute to the Dynamics of Survival of this great nation. I sincerely hope that the efforts of the contributors will be well received by those who evince interests on this land-locked, but strategically significant, landmass.

I am grateful to all the contributors, who, despite their hard pressed schedule, met the dead-line in putting forward their chapters.

I wish to thank Prof. L.N. Misra, my former Ph.D. guide and presently Vice Chancellor of Utkal University, Orissa, for all his love and blessings bestowed on me throughout my career. I am also thankful to Prof. B. Ramesh Babu, Prof. P.M. Kamath and Prof. P.L. Dash for their time to time encouragement to move on academic pursuit.

I am grateful to Mr Amit Garg and senior members of Kalpaz Publications, New Delhi for readily agreeing to publish this manuscript.

Last but not least, I wish to thank my wife and life long friend Nivedita for all her love and motivation in completing this work.

National Defence Academy, **Jagmohan Meher**
Khadakwasla, Pune, India
The 16th July 2007

List of Contributors

1. *Dr. P M Kamath,* emeritus Professor of Politics, Mumbai University, has specialized in International Relations, foreign Policy and National Security. He has authored or edited 13 books and guided over 17 students in their research. Currently, he is the Hon. Director of VPMs Centre for International Studies, Mumbai.

2. *Vaishali Singh* is a Researcher at the Institute for Defence Studies and Analysis, New Delhi. Her area of expertise includes US Strategic Policy and Indo-US Relations. She was attached as Research Officer to the National Security Council Secretariat's 'Task Force on Global Strategic Developments' from November 2005 to May 2006.

3. *Dr. P.L. Dash,* Professor and Director, Centre for Central Eurasian Studies, University of Mumbai. He was educated in Moscow as a Government of India scholar between 1974-1984. Prof. Dash has more than 110 publications in journals and edited volumes and six books on related Soviet/post Soviet affairs.

4. *Dr. Sheel K. Asopa,* is a retired professor of International Politics (Third World & Development). Prof. Asopa has specialized in international politics with special reference to West Asia and Central Asia.

She has written extensively on International politics, West Asian and Central Asian affairs, environmental and women-related issues, Human Rights and Child Labour in news paper and academic journals.

5. *Dr. Uttara Sahasrabuddhe* is a Reader in the Department of Civics and Politics of the University of Mumbai. Her research interests are Indian Foreign Policy, International Relations, IR Theory, and current Indian politics. She has published many articles on these themes in scholarly journals as well as edited books. She has co-suthored a book (with Dr. Aruna Pendse) on International Relations in Marathi, which is being published by Orient Longman Ltd., Mumbai.

6. *Dr. Sudha Mohan*, a former Fulbright Fellow at Columbia University, New York, is a Reader in the Department of Civics and Politics, University of Mumbai. She has published in the areas of urban governance, role and relevance of civil society, decentralisation and citizen participation, civil society activism in the era of globalization.

7. *Dr. Anand P. Mavalankar*, Professor, Department of Political Science, The Maharaja Sayajirao University of Baroda. He specialises on North South divide and the problems of the Third World Countries.

8. *Dr. [Mrs] Salini Saxena* is a specialist in Modern Indian and Modern Chinese history with interest in international relations. After her retirement from teaching profession, she is adjunct faculty, Department of History, University of Mumbai.

9. *General Eustace D'souza (Retd)* is a military historian and an expert on India's national security. He is a recipient of the Polish Army Gold Medal for "his significant contribution to the history and traditions

of the Army," and is the only non Australian to be made a Honorary Life Member of the Royal United Services Institution Queensland Australia for his contributions to its Quarterly Bulletins. Currently, he is working on a four volume Coffee Table Book on the Indian Army post 1947 to date.

10. *Dr. Jagmohan Meher* teaches Political Sciences, International Relations, and Area Studies at National Defence Academy, Khadakwasla, Pune. He is a former Fulbright Fellow at the University of Illinois, and has visited Maison Des Sciences De L'Homme, Paris as a research scholar under the Indo-French Cultural Exchange Programme. He has published books and articles in the field of international relations, including on Afghanistan, Indo-US Relations and India's Foreign Policy.

1

Introduction

Jagmohan Meher

Three years after the ouster of the fundamentalist Taliban regime following the 9/11 terrorist attacks on the United States, the Bush administration boasted of a "success story" in Afghanistan. Afghanistan was portrayed as a foreign policy accomplishment while US troops faced daily turmoil in Iraq. American optimism was generated by the adoption of a new constitution, a fragile political stability including the country's first Presidential elections with direct voting, creation of a national army and national police force, dismantling major factional militia units, and a slow pace of economic growth. Later in 2005, the country also witnessed its first Parliamentary elections; thus completing the agenda of the Bonn process.[1] Majority of the Afghans also seemed to be supportive of the ongoing political and military developments in the country. A 2005 ABC News survey in Afghanistan indicates that 77 percent of Afghans believe their country is heading in the right direction, 91 percent prefer the current Afghan government to the Taliban regime, and 87 percent call the US-led overthrow of the Taliban good for their country.[2]

But despite these claims of "success," and "accomplishments," Afghanistan seems to be tilting towards another round of precariousness, insurgency and instability. The Taliban appear to be on the move once again with the same Pakistani backing. Islamabad is now supporting the Taliban in a manner similar to the way it supported the Afghan mujahiddin against the Soviets two decades ago. And this is notwithstanding the presence of the US and multi-national forces and the international nation-building efforts which are solid impediments to the Taliban's design in this war-torn country. Members of American and Canadian Special Forces have already admitted that they were "not winning against the Taliban,"[3] and the Taliban have claimed that they are now getting more weapons, more recruits and that "any fear the people may have had of helping the Taliban has vanished."[4] The situation is becoming so volatile that analysts who saw Afghanistan as a success and treated it as a model for other trouble spots in the world had to forcefully retract and reevaluate their positions.

The presence of nearly 40,000 foreign troops to hunt down the remnants of Taliban/Al Qaeda elements and to stabilize the country has clearly failed to bring peace to this country ravaged by twenty-seven years of war.[5] Although the American invasion of the country dethroned the fundamentalist regime, the unending military presence of the US and Western forces and billions of dollars of reconstruction efforts has not ended Afghanistan's woes. The country seems to be heading towards yet another quagmire if proper precautions are not taken in time. And therefore, any sense of optimism generated by the adoption of a new constitution and the holding of elections in Afghanistan may prove short-lived.

For the Americans, the "war against terrorism" remains a war, but for many Afghans, the United States is increasingly being looked upon as an "occupying power." American forces were initially greeted as liberators as they ousted the fundamentalist Taliban regime. But the longer they linger, the more they are likely to be viewed as an occupying imperial power. It would certainly be a wrong way for the Americans to follow up with what a Canadian writer; Michael Ignatieff called "empire lite" in Afghanistan.[6] Failure to develop an independent time bound political strategy to bring about genuine peace in the country and, an open convincing policy of withdrawing from Afghanistan might lead to more antagonism from the common people. Present American insensitivity to human rights is also strong reminiscent of the mistakes the US policy makers made in the 1980's and early 1990s. For its permanent peace and stability, Afghanistan does not need more American troops, but a political system more responsible to its ethnic diversity and more protective of civil and religious rights.

Empires are beaten very badly in Afghanistan. The British in the 19th century and the Soviets in the 20th century made that painful discovery. There is no doubt that the situation in the country is altogether different today. But Afghans have a tradition of opposing foreign occupation. In the long run, it will not matter much whether it is Gulbuddin Hekmatyar or Mullah Omar in the helm of affairs; it will only be of importance with who are they actually fighting and why. If proper preventions are not contemplated, the current imbroglio may well be the turn for the Americans.

The most desirable outcome from the current fragility would be: a hundred percent honesty and sincerity on the part of the United States in the ongoing reconstruction efforts and on disarming the warlords in a steady process without being looked like an occupying foreign power which the Afghans will not accept. Peace in Afghanistan also requires that the neighbouring countries are convinced of America's good intensions and that in turn, they abandon plans for hegemony and interference in Afghanistan's internal affairs. American focus on its "war against terrorism" in Afghanistan should not overshadow the threats emanating from warlords and drug traffickers which are more damaging to the population than terrorist violence. Bringing about such a situation in this war-ravaged country will depend on how the United States acted upon in the coming days. The present trend does not look conducive to permanent peace in the country.

The American peace efforts so far appear fragile, and the country is passing through a thin edge of instability as it is still being haunted by so many divisive and centrifugal forces.

The current Afghan situation shows that (1) A sense of xenophobia against the Americans is intensifying, (2) The attacks within Afghanistan were up 20 percent between 2004 and 2005, suicide bombings increased "almost fourfold" and use of makeshift bombs, similar to those used in Iraq, had "more than doubled," (3) A sustained offensive by Taliban and counter attacks by the coalition forces has caused about 4,000 violent deaths in 2006.[7] (4) The Taliban attacks have terrorize local people, and the perilous security across the south has halted virtually all development and reconstruction projects and more significantly helped turned the population against the Afghan government and its foreign backers.

From all indications, it could be easily inferred that peace is a distant dream in Afghanistan. In a clear reminiscence of the Soviet occupation of the country in the 1980's,[8] today, as stated above, a "not winning" view is gaining momentum among the foreign troops. But at the same time, so far, the Taliban are not powerful enough to create road blocks. What they intend to do is to disrupt the situation in Afghanistan toward achieving their stated goal: the withdrawal of the US and other foreign troops from the country and the establishment of what they believe to be a genuine Islamic state there. Secondly, the Taliban also do not seem to have enough hard-core fighters to allow them to open several fronts against the Afghan government troops (ANA) and the multi-national forces.

However, as long as present conditions continue the insurgency will not be defeated and the insurgents will continue to exploit vulnerable points caused by the country's fragmented centers of power. While the rebels do not yet have the capacity to pose strategic threats to the government, they create a sense of insecurity, hinder economic reconstruction and weaken government influence in remote areas. This may eventually lead to much stronger insurgency capable of challenging the government. In many parts of the country, the resurgence of Taliban violence is caused more by the lack of government presence than the ability of the insurgents. The country is therefore, most likely to remain a volatile place for a long time to come.

What is going wrong in Afghanistan? How and why is the current state of insurgency emerging as a formidable force? And why are anti-American feelings gradually increasing despite the fact that the United States and the international community are spending billions in Afghan reconstruction to stabilize the country? What are the options for Afghanistan and international community? Above all, what are the dynamics of survival of this unfortunate land-locked landmass?

This book is an attempt to answer these questions in proper prospective and to suggest developmental strategies for a peaceful and prosperous Afghanistan. The study focuses upon the different aspects of Afghanistan's current problems and highlights the various forces that are at work in this war-torn country. The study analyzes the post 9/11 Afghan war and concludes by professing that the present US entanglement in the country is going to be a long term one and that the American attempts at transforming the present tragedy into its geo-political advantage in the region would fail.

The book contains twelve chapters.

General Eustace D'souza (Retd), a military historian, looks at Afghanistan's historical and geo-political dimensions in order to understand the country's dynamics of change and survival. This brief historical background highlights some of the forgotten facts of Afghanistan's turbulent past.

Dr. Shalini Saksena in his study on "Afghanistan: The Anglo-Russian Rivalry," looks at the "Great Game" phase of the country's turbulent history to show the vulnerability of this land-locked landmass to out side powers. She underlines how Afghanistan falls prey to the imperialistic designs but at the same time enhances it strategic importance before the regional and international players.

The present study would probably look incomplete if it does not touch upon the recent big event in the history of Afghanistan, i.e., the Soviet invasion of the country in December 1979. Prof. P.M. Kamath, an authority on national security and security policy-making in the US and India gives a new perspective of the events and highlights the Indian response

Prof. Sheel K. Asopa, an expert in international relations, focuses on both the internal and external political dynamics about the turmoil of Afghanistan. She underlines the role played by Pakistan, Saudi Arabia and the United States. Her study suggests that much of Afghanistan's woes can be attributed to its location, having linkages with the people inhabiting the neighbouring countries, and almost total absence of a centralized power structure which commands authority over its people and territory.

Dr. Uttara Sahasrabuddhe, in her essay dwells upon the question "who decides when and where to intervene" and focuses upon "intervention" in the post-World War II international order and within the purview of the UN system. She argues that a strong case exists for the liberal international agenda of promotion of democracy, respect for international law and strengthening international organisations like the UN.

Dr. Sudha Mohan, in her scholarly piece suggests that Afghanistan is one country that has found itself embroiled in crisis, clashes and confrontation without really being responsible for it directly. It is engaged in a great struggle to determine its national identity in a more complex, evolving and very changed world. In her concluding remarks she puts forward the views that "the path leading to sustainable development, functioning democracy and lasting peace requires an interface between state, non-state and international agencies."

Prof. P.L. Dash argues that a single factor that differentiates Afghanistan from rest of the countries of the region is the direct Soviet and American military and political involvement in that country for successive long years. He hypothesizes that "an asymmetrical political configuration emerges when a big power engages a small and weak state in its pursuits of international relations with not so well defined regional objectives." Prof. Dash views that current Afghan instability is the saga of these two militarily potential powers and the lingering impact they continue to exert on Afghanistan and its neighbours.

Prof. Mavalankar's essay looks at the present crisis in Afghanistan from a broader framework of the internal balance of forces within the country as well as evolution of the wider international environment since 9/11. He suggests that the distinct religious character of Taliban and Al-Qaeda network has to be understood for the purposes of determining the prospects of 'liberal' model in reconstituting the political authority in contemporary Afghanistan.

Vaishali Singh, a defence and security expert focuses upon the impact of the American War on Terrorism on Afghanistan beginning October 2001 and the subsequent developments there. She argues Afghanistan as a post-conflict society which faces numerous intricacies in terms of its national security as well as nation building process. The analysis delves around the crucial question whether the US will prioritize the long-term commitment to stabilization in Afghanistan over the hunt for Bin Laden, and engage in nation-building?

There are two other studies; one of which looks at the US invasion of Afghanistan in terms of its strategic ramifications for India and Russia and peeps into its future geo-political trends. It argues that the sense of "clear and present danger" in Jammu and Kashmir, and Central Asia and Chechnya respectively made India and Russia feel like they are on the front lines of the America's anti-Taliban war. But as the war in Afghanistan winds down, resentment and apprehension about the continued and protracted American military presence in the region came to the fore in both the countries. The article shows that the US-backed Afghanistan is seen by the two countries as empowering, as well as constraining at the same time.

The other study underlines Pakistan's current Afghan policy under General Musharraf and focuses upon how the Pakistani dictator is playing tricks under the shadow of the United States. The article highlights that the 9/11 terrorists attacks in the United States and the subsequent American invasion of Afghanistan provided a great opportunity to Pakistan's military dictator to legitimize his rule and be a 'friend' of the Bush administration.

It is hoped that this book would be found useful to the students, teachers, diplomats, military officials, members of the Afghan government and other researchers and members of so many Non-governmental Organizations (NGO's) who are working hard to bring about peace and stability to this war-torn country.

Notes

1. See the text of Bonn Agreement in Appendix A of this book.
2. See Gary Langer, "Poll: Four Years After the Fall of the Taliban, Afghans Optimistic About the Future," ABC News, http://abcnews.go.com/international/pollvaults/story?id=1363276
3. As quoted in Carlotta Gall, "Taliban Surges as U.S. Shifts Some Tasks to NATO," *The New York Times,* 11 June 2006.
4. See Ron Moreau, Sami Yousafzai and Joe Cochrane, "Afghanistan: A Violent Wake-Up Call," *Newsweek,* 12 June 2006, p. 28-30, and "Afghanistan: The Taliban Resurgent," *The Economist,* 10-16 June 2006, pp. 25-26.
5. In the first week of October 2006, out of about 20,000 US troops, 12,000 in eastern Afghanistan were transferred to the 31-nation International Security Assistance Force (ISAF) which was created under UN Security Council resolution 1386 in December 2001. With this, the strength

of NATO goes up to 31,000 in all, which marks the largest deployment of the Alliance's troops since its formation in 1949 to defend Western Europe.

6. The term "empire lite" has been quoted in "Show me the way to go home," *The Economist,* 16 August 2003, p. 9.
7. See Pamela Constable, "Scores of Insurgents Killed in Afghan Border Area," *The Washington Post,* 12 January 2007, p. A10.
8. After four years of their invasion, Soviet Union had concluded that they were not winning in Afghanistan. For a comprehensive study on the subject, see Jagmohan Meher, *America's Afghanistan War: The Success That Failed,* Kalpaz Publications, New Delhi, 2004, pp. 160-161.

2

A Brief Historical Survey of Afghanistan from its Inception to 2001

General Eustace D'souza (Retd)

Introduction

It is common knowledge that the central government's authority under Hamid Karzai, propped up by the US and NATO, is restricted to the confines of Kabul and its outskirts. The presence of the US led NATO and the ever looming presence of the Taliban, (and Osama Bin Laden allegedly hiding in the North West Frontier region of Pakistan), the situation in Afghanistan remains volatile. To understand the present chaotic conditions, this article will discuss the geo-strategic location of the country and a brief history of Afghanistan till the US invasion of the country in 2001. By so doing a clearer picture will emerge as to why fierce tribal loyalties and the growing Shia-Sunni divide continue to call the tune and the Taliban attempts to regain control much to the discomfiture of the US and NATO and surrounding nations in West, South and Central Asia.

The Geo-strategic Dimension

As of date, Afghanistan occupies a unique geographical location in Asia, standing as it does at the cross roads of

Central, West and South Asia described by historian Arnold Toynbee as 'a roundabout of the ancient world' leaving behind a legacy of a mosaic of ethnic and linguistic groups. Among the first European travelers to traverse it was Marco Polo and his silk route. Since then, because of this unique geographical location, vast armies of the world have passed through it leaving their imprint in antiquity and modern times as will become manifest subsequently.

Afghanistan today shares borders with China to the East-76 kms, Iran to the West (936 kms), Pakistan to the South and South East (2430 kms, the longest of all), to the North, Tajikistan (1206 kms), Turkmenistan (744 kms), and Uzbekistan (137 kms). Significantly all these countries except China are Muslim dominated. The lowest elevation of this rugged land is the Amu Darya and the highest Nowshak (7485 kms). It has rugged mountains including the forbidden land mass of the Hindu Kush Mountains, with plains in the North and South. Yet it has been subject to invasions mainly from the Northern and Southern plains and from the West.

Resources wise Afghanistan has deposits of Natural Gas and Petroleum sufficient for its internal needs. Other natural resources include coal, copper, zinc, iron ore, salt, and precious and semi precious stones. 12.1% of its land mass is arable capable of producing only 0.20% of permanent crops. Its purchasing power in the international arms market is derived from poppy (opium) production representing 1/3rd of its meager GDP. Being landlocked and the lack of adequate natural resources make it a poor country for its population of 31 million consisting of a number of ethnic groups: Pashtuns (42%), Tajiks (27 %), Hazaras (9%), Aimaks (4%), Turkmen (3%), and Balooch (2%). A number of languages are spoken viz Dari (50%), Pashtu (35%), Turko comprising Uzbek and Turkmen (11%) and 30 other minor languages like Baluch etc.. Thus ethnicity and language contribute largely to its fiercely tribal culture. Today, 80% of its population is Sunni and a mere 12% Shia, surrounded as it is by Islamic States. This is one of the major reasons why till today no foreign power has been able to dominate it or hold it for any length of time as will become evident as the story unfolds. Thus its geostrategic location and landlocked position has contributed largely to the present chaos in the country.

The Influence of History

The fact that the Dari and Pashto languages continue to survive testify to the legacy left by the Iranians evident from the distinct and noticeable cultural traits even today. This retention of Iranian Culture is best explained by an expert historian on Asian Affairs, Sir Olaf Caroe, in his definitive and scholarly work *The Pathans* where he states: "... *There is indeed a sense in which all the upland (*the Iranian Plateau) from *the Tigris* (*in* ancient Mesopotamia now Iraq) *to India is one country. The spirit of Persia has breathed over it, bringing an awareness of one background, one culture, one way of expression, a unity of spirit as far away as Quetta and Peshawar,"* and may well explain why Afghanistan is insisting that Baluchistan and Pasthunistan up to the Khyber Pass be part of it. It is therefore not a matter of surprise that it is this Iranian past and subsequent Islamic invasion that have defined modern Afghanistan and that the Buddhist influence and Zoroastrian past have long since vanished.

Because of its unique location between Central and South Asia and East and West Asia, in the hoary past it was the scene of great empires and flourishing trade for over 2 millennia, resulting in the area's heterogeneous groups not bound by a single political entity as evident even today with tribal groups fiercely guarding their individual identities. This state of affairs continued till 1747 when Ahmed Shah Durrani founded a monarchy that continued until as long as 1973. In the subsequent power struggles in Asia and because of its strategic importance to the two competing world powers Great Britain and Tsarist Russia, Afghanistan, located as it is lay between these two great competing powers; Great Britain determined to prevent Russian expansion to South Asia and likewise Russia attempting to assert its authority and gain access to the warm water ports in the North Arabian Sea. This caused the 'Iron Amir', Abdur Rehman Khan to remark that *"his country stood like a goat between these lions (Great Britain and Tsarist Russia) or like a grain of wheat between two millstones of the grinding mill"* and wondered how it could do so without being ground to dust.

It was also around this time that Islam began to play a key role in the formation of Afghan society as it does even today; hence its title as the Islamic Republic of Afghanistan. The Mongol invasion led by Genghiz Khan, despite its brutality, had failed to uproot the well entrenched Islamic civilization. It is not generally realized that an important event in shaping Afghanistan's future occurred in the 10th century through the Ghaznavids who ensured the Sunni dynasty gained from strength, preventing the spread of Shiite Islam from Iran. This would explain the preponderance of Sunnis in the demographic make up even today. The Ghorids who followed were largely responsible for creating Afghanistan into a major medieval power and a recognised center of learning that threw up intellectual of the caliber of Firdausi, Al-Biruni and Khushal Khan Khattak.

The Pre Islamic Period

This period in its history is dominated by Alexander the Great of Greece fighting the Persian Monarch Darius. The Aryan invasion of this cockpit of Asia began as early as the year 2000 BC and continued over the years through inroads made by, in turn, the Persian, Median, Greek, Mauryan, Bactrian and other civilizations each in turn leaving traces of their culture. Alexander the Great crossed the borders of present day Afghanistan from the West leading to the capture of Bactria (Balkh of today). This intrusion was followed by invasions by the Sycthians, White Huns and Gok Turks, all from the West. It was during this period that Afghanistan and Gandhara became centres of culture and learning. Prior to the Islamic conquest of this landmass (642 to 1747), Afghanistan was ruled by the Sassanids and other Iranian powers and may well explain why the Dari language and Farsi continue to be spoken in some pockets of the country even today.

Islam Enters Afghanistan (642 to 1747)

It was the Arabs who introduced Islam into Afghanistan when they invaded it in its entirety, at a period when the country had local rulers. It was the Khorasam-Persian-Arabs who controlled Afghanistan with the emergence of the Ghaznavids in 998, during which period Mohamud of Ghazni (998-1030) became the consolidator. He was responsible for establishing the historically well known Ghazni into a known cultural centre and a base for his forays into Hindustan. However the Ghaznavids were defeated by the Ghors in 1146. Be that as it may, the Ghaznavid Khans continued to live in Ghazni as the 'Nosher' until the early twentieth century but did not regain their once vast power until 500 years later when Ghilzai Mir Wais Khan Hotaki defeated the Persians at Kandahar and assumed the mantle of the Persian Shah. By 1219, the country had fallen to the Mongols. The legendary Genghiz Khan led the invasion and resorted to mass slaughter of the population and destruction of the historic towns of Herat, Ghazni and Balkh. What is worse is that he ruthlessly despoiled scarce fertile agricultural farmland (in modern terminology, a scorched earth policy) to subjugate the hapless population. On his death in1227, a succession of petty Chiefs and Princes fought among themselves and this internecine struggle continued until the late 14th century. It was one of Genghis Khan's descendants Timur Lenk (Lane) who incorporated what we know today as Afghanistan into one vast Asian empire. It was then left to a well known descendant Babur (Babar) the founder of India's Moghul Empire, who in the early part of the 16th century made Kabul the capital of an Afghan principality. For the ease of governance this principality was followed by the division of Afghanistan into three parts for better governance and tribal dictates. To the North were the Uzbeks, Persia in the West and the Moghul Empire to the East. This was followed by yet anther upheaval. The Afghans, or more specifically the Ghilzai Pashtuns under Nasher, rose against the Persian Army. In the ding-dong battles that followed, Nadir Shah of Persia, in 1721, in turn defeated the Afghans in the battle of Damgham. The Afghans were driven out of Persia. In 1738, Nadir Shah conquered Kandahar and in the same year occupied Ghazni, Kabul, and Lahore. In this continuing power struggle Nadir Shah was assassinated. As a result, the Durrani Pashtuns became rulers of Afghanistan. These rival factions continued to fight against each other and continued doing so until the 20th century.

The Durrani Empire (1747 to 1826)

In 1747, Ahmed Shah Durrani, an important player in the Afghan history, known as the founder of modern day Afghanistan, established himself as the ruler of Afghanistan. He was a Pashtun and was elected to office by the first ever Loya Jirga after the assassination of the Persian ruler Nadir Shah at Kharbushan the same year. Durrani established his credentials as a ruler by consolidating the numerous Chiefs, many petty principalities and the fragmented provinces, his writ extending from Mashad (Meshed) in the West to Kashmir and Delhi in the East, and from the Amu Darya (Oxus) in the North to the Arabian Sea in the South. With the exception of a short 9 month period in 1929 until the Marxist coup in 1978, all Afghanistan's rulers hailed from Durrani's Pashtun confederation, belonging to the tribe's Mohammedzai clan.

European Powers with Interest in the Region Enter the Fray

In the eternal power struggles in this cockpit of Asia, Dost Mohammed Khan had gained control in Kabul at a time when "The Great Game" between two European Powers; Great Britain in India and the Russians entered the arena. Great Britain, an imperial power was wary of any attempted Russian imperialist designs to dominate this region and gain a land corridor to the North Arabian Sea through Afghanistan and influence to get a foothold into Persia. As a result, the British launched two ill fated expeditionary forces into

Afghanistan culminating in the Afghan Wars. The first between 1839 and 1842 ended in the rout of the British Indian Army. It would appear that the British underestimated the fighting qualities of the Afghans and their resistance to foreign rule.

The second Afghan War between 1878 and 1880 was sparked off by Amir Sher Ali's refusal to accept a British mission in Kabul to keep a watch on the Russians. This conflict brought Amir Abdur Rahman Khan to the throne and he ruled from 1880 to 1901 during which the British and Russians officially established the boundaries of modern Afghanistan as it is today and retaining control over Kabul's foreign affairs to put off any designs of the Russians. Yet, Afghan remained neutral during World War I notwithstanding attempts of Kaiser's Germany to stir up anti British feelings in this sensitive area along the border with British India. The Afghans by and large resented the King's attitude of neutrality presumably to get rid Afghanistan of any foreign interference. Habibullah, Abdur Rahman's son and successor was assassinated in 1919 by family members who resented British influence. However, the third son Amanullah regained control of Afghanistan's foreign policy after launching the third Afghan War with an attack against British India weakened by World War I. The treaty of Rawalpindi resulted in the war weary British relinquishing control of Afghanistan's foreign affairs. As the treaty was signed on 19th August, the Afghans celebrate the date as their Independence Day.

Reforms of Amanullah and the Civil War (1919-1929)

King Amanullah, during his reign, sought to end his country's traditional isolation in the years following the Third Anglo-Afghan War. To this end he established diplomatic relations with most major powers. During his tour of Europe and Turkey in 1927, he was struck by the reforms of Kemal Ataturk in modernizing and secularizing Turkey, a predominantly Muslim country. He decided to emulate Kemal Ataturk by modernizing his own country. However, this laudable attempt in abolishing the Chador and burqa worn by Afghan women and establishing coeducational institutions, angered many conservative tribal and religious leaders. He was forced to abdicate in the face of overwhelming armed opposition in January 1929 after the capital Kabul fell to forces led by the Tajik brigand Bacha-i-Saquo. The close knit Islamic society succeeded in preventing such reforms.

Nadir Shah and Zahir Shah Enter the Scene (1929-1973)

The brigand Bacha-i-Saqao did not survive for long and was defeated by Prince Mohammed Nadir Khan, a cousin of the deposed King Amanullah with considerable Pashtun tribal support and succeeded in installing himself on the throne as King Nadir Shah. He addressed himself to consolidating his hold and regenerating his hapless country. He set about his task by instituting reforms of modernization in a more gradual manner. Yet, this was resented and he was assassinated in a revenge killing by a Kabul student. He was succeeded by his 19 years old son Mohammed Zahir Shah and he had a long reign from 1933 to 1973. Until 1946 he sought the guidance in governance from his Uncle Sardar Mohammed Hashim Khan who held the post of Prime Minister. He was responsible for continuing the policies of King Nadir Shah. In 1946 another of King Zahir Shah's Uncles, Sardar Shah Mohammed Khan was appointed Prime Minister. He was forced to reverse his policy of greater political freedom when it went further than he had planned. In 1953 he was replaced by Mohammed Daoud Khan, the King's cousin. Dauod sought closer links with the Soviet Union, its immediate northern neighbour and a more hostile one towards its eastern neighbour Pakistan, the main gateway for trade. The dispute with Pakistan led to his resignation in 1963 and thereafter from that date for the next 10 years King Zahir Shah assumed a more active role in governance.

He was responsible for introducing a bicameral legislature in which the King appointed one third of the deputies, the people elected one third and the remainder were selected individually by provincial assemblies. This experiment in democracy did produce a few lasting reforms but also permitted the unofficial growth of extremist parties, both right and left. One of the parties it threw up was the People's Democratic Party of Afghanistan (PDPA) which had close ideological ties with the USSR. In 1967, the PDPA further split up into two factions-the Kahlq (masses) faction headed by Nur Mohammed Taraki and Hafizullah Amin and supported by elements of the military. The second faction was the Parcham (Banner) led by Babrak Kamal. As would have been deduced, this split was based on ethnic, class and ideological divisions within the basically tribal society and reflected the fact that heads of state were Ghilzai (Taraki, Amin, Najib and Mullah Omar) attempting to wrest power from the Durrani Clan.

Daoud's Republic of Afghanistan (1973-1978)

Soon charges of corruption and malformation were made against the Royal Family. These factors, resulting from the severe 1971-72 drought caused former Prime Minister Mohammed Daoud Khan to seize power through a military coup in July 1973 when the King was on a trip to Italy, Daoud abolished the monarchy, abrogated the 1964 Constitution and declared Afghanistan a Republic and assumed the roles of both President and Prime Minister. However, political instability in this traditionally volatile country resulted in failure of his attempted efforts to introduce economic and social reforms in this tradition based society and the end result was that his efforts to introduce the new constitution failed to subdue political instability. Disillusionment set in April 1978. In a bloody coup Daoud and most of his family were murdered and Nur Muhammed Taraki of the PDPA became the President of the Revolutionary Council and Prime Minister of the newly constituted Democratic Republic of Afghanistan with strong ties with the USSR. This resulted eventually in Soviet intervention in Afghanistan.

The Expected Soviet Intervention (1978-1992)

As mentioned earlier, the presence of the PDPA Government with strong ideological ties with the USSR, and the power struggle to control the oil rich Caspian Basin and the increasing US interest in West Asia to ensure an uninterrupted supply of hydrocarbons to keep the economy on the move, it would not be long before the Soviets entered Afghanistan. As a pro-communist socialist party, the PDPA implemented a socialist agenda that included abolition of usury, banning of forced marriages, women's rights, replacement of the Shariat law with secular and Marxist ones, abolishment of tribal courts and land reforms created a situation ripe enough for the Soviets to make their presence felt. Males were required to do away with beards, women with the burqa, and mosque visiting were frowned upon and not passé with the PDPA regime. The PDPA went a step further by inviting the Soviet Union to assist in developing the economic infrastructure which was at best mediocre, help in exploration of the nation's mineral deposits and exploration of natural gas deposits. To make its presence stronger, the Soviets sent contractors to construct roads, hospitals, schools and locate water resources. More importantly, they also trained and equipped the Afghan Army and fledgling Air Force. As expected, these measures met with a violent backlash by the tradition bound establishment. A movement was initiated, no doubt with the tacit approval of the US and Pakistan, to reverse this growing dependence on Soviet aid. Expectedly, there was a reaction where sabotage of these efforts to industry and infrastructure became the order of the day. The PDPA Government reacted heavy handedly by invoking the military and those involved were apprehended, arrested, executed and exiled, especially the Afghan mujahedin. But by 1979, it became increasingly difficult for the Afghan Army to handle the growing unrest and expectedly the Russians moved in ostensibly to help the PDPA Government to maintain law and order. Also the Soviets were to install a pro Moscow Government and support the new Government. The Soviet entered Kabul from the north and this heralded the starting point for the Soviet occupation of Afghanistan. For 9 long years the Soviet Army conducted operations against the Afghan mujahedin rebels who were aided, abetted and supplied by the CIA, Pakistan and Saudi Arabia. At this point of time Osama Bin Laden entered the scene and helped the mujahedin as an organizer and financier through his Maktab al Khadamat (MAK). The MAK ensured a steady flow of money, arms, and Muslim fighters from around the Islamic world, with assistance from the US through Pakistan. The rest is history. The Soviet Army was compelled to withdraw its presence from Afghanistan in February 1989 but continued to support the Government of Mohammed Najibullah. At the same time massive aid continued to flow to the mujahedin from the CIA and Saudi Arabia, the later keen to protect Islam. As a result of the spirited resistance of the mujahedin and the collapse of the Soviet Union, the Najibullah Government was overturned in April 1992 when military commander Abdul Rashid Dostum mutinied and allied himself and his followers with Ahmed Shah Massoud. The control of Kabul was affected and the Islamic State of Afghanistan was declared.

The Writ of the Taliban (1994 to 2001)

This phase deals primarily with the entry of the Taliban on the scene after the Soviet withdrawal. When the victorious mujahidin entered Kabul to assume control over the city, predictably, internecine fighting between the various factions and militias that had coexisted uneasily during the Soviet occupation, erupted. And predictably, with the exit of the Russians and the availability of arms supplied to the Taliban by the CIA through Pakistan, fell into their hands. Civil war continued as ethnic, clan, tribal, religious and personality differences surfaced. It was at this stage that an Islamic Jihad Council was formed, first led by Sibghatullah Mojadeddi followed two months later by Burhanuddin Rabbani. This change signaled an increase in intensity of inter faction rivalry. Expectedly, this warlordism and anarchy and the lack of Pashtun representation in Kabul resulted in a movement of Islamic scholars, some belonging to the former mujahedin, to band together. The Taliban, with the availability of arms and war material, took over control of 90 % of the country, limiting the opposition to a small largely Tajik corner of the country in the Northeast and the Panjshir Valley. An Afghan Northern Alliance was born and recognized by the UN as the Government of Afghanistan. The rationale behind this acceptance is debatable as it represented a mere 10% of the Afghans. After the 9/11 attacks on the United States, the US and its coalition allies invaded Afghanistan to oust the Taliban Government. Afghan factions met in Bonn and chose a 30 member interim authority led by Hamid Karzai who was pro US. After Karzai governed for 6 months, King Zahir Shah who returned to Afghanistan after his exile in Italy, held a Loya Jirga and elected Hamid Karzai as President with authority to govern the country for 2 years. In October 2004, Karzai was elected President of Afghanistan in the first ever Presidential elections. His writ was restricted and he was able to rule because of the support of the US and UN.

Concluding Remarks

This brief historical background highlights some of the forgotten facts. The strong influence of Islam and the reintroduction of the Shariat by the Taliban in an attempt to enforce traditional Afghanistan conservatism keeping beards, banning women working and coeducation, reintroduction of the burqa for women and so on. The fierce tribal loyalties that have surfaced and existed for centuries making it impossible for foreigners or outsiders to rule this rugged country, which for centuries, has never ever been governed; not by the British or the Russians or any foreign power. It is doubtful therefore whether the US/UN/NATO combine will achieve its objective, a situation that may well worsen should the US decide to attack Iran.

3

Afghanistan: The Anglo-Russian Rivalry

Shalini Saxena

A Buffer State

A mountainous and landlocked Afghanistan is strategically located in Central and south west Asia. Rich in natural resources, it lies at the crossroads of trade and cultural exchanges, thus enhancing its geopolitical importance. Situated between the empires of the Britain and Russia, Afghanistan was caught up in a web of their political and economic rivalries. It had the possibility of falling a prey to their imperialistic designs. However their rivalry not only left her free from subjugation but also made Afghanistan assume a position of pivotal importance in Anglo-Russian rivalry in central Asia.[1] Afghanistan emerged as an object of their colonial contest. It formed a buffer between the two empires, Great Britain in the south and Czarist Russia in the north. Geography placed this central Asian kingdom precariously between the imperial designs of the two. Russian ambition to push southwards and British desire to protect her Indian empire made animosity between the two inevitable. Central Asia was turned into a venue of Anglo-Russian rivalry that had its roots in their earlier antagonism.

A united Afghanistan under the firm grip of the British could serve as a constraint to Russian expansion in Central Asia. Herat, the most northwestern province of Afghanistan was the main vulnerable point from where the armies of all the great conquerors of India from Alexander to Ahmed Shah Abdali assembled and invaded. British policy therefore aimed at making Afghanistan a buffer state between the Russian and British possessions in the East. Two major wars were fought with the Afghans to prevent Afghanistan from falling under Russian influence. Both the Afghans and the Russians were given to understand that the British would not tolerate Russian predominance in Afghanistan. This policy worked out well throughout the British rule in India but it also meant that Russia was permitted to do what she pleased north of the Hindukush.[1a]

Russian Expansionism

A brief background of Russian history will reveal how over a period of time Russia got involved with the Central Asian Khanates and Afghanistan. Till the 18th century Russia was considered backward and barbarian with practically no significant influence on European politics. Though race and religion [Slav and Orthodox Christian] connected her to Europe, she was Asiatic and oriental in manners and civilization including a despotic government. The coming of the Romanoff Dynasty, particularly Peter the Great [1689-1725] changed the direction in which Russia was moving and thus her destiny. Peter wanted to modernize Russia and bring her at par in eminence and influence with other European countries and extend her borders to the south and west in order to have access to the sea. If Russia had to develop as a commercial and naval power it was essential to acquire an ice free port. Sweden barred her access to the Baltic and Turkey to the Black Sea. Peter dreamt of extending his influence towards the Oxus and the Indus to partake in the trade from which the British and the French benefited.[2] With vision and energy, Tsarina Catherine II [1762–1796] continued Russia in the Europeanising process and successfully enlarged her role in international politics making her a power to be reckoned with. She obtained a firm footing on the northern coast of the Black Sea, acquiring Crimea with the right to navigate the sea and an ambiguous protectorate over the Christians in Turkey. This gave birth to the Eastern Question in the 19th century.[3] Catherine launched a policy of southward expansion with a view to capturing Constantinople. Britain considered this imperial trend in Russian policy a threat to the balance of power in Europe and her dominant position in the Levant and the Mediterranean. Britain made an unsuccessful attempt to have Russia give up the Ochakov fortress on the Black Sea to Turkey. To disarm British opposition to her designs in possessing the Straits of Bosphorus and the Dardanelles, Russia resorted to a policy of threatening India with invasion through the Central Asian routes. Tsar Paul I along with Napoleon mooted the idea of a joint expedition to overthrow Britain in India. A Russian army would descend on India from Khiva and Bokhara while the French army would proceed by the Herat-Kandahar route. Though this did not materialise, Franco-Russian collabouration against the British did not cease. At the treaty of Tilsit Napoleon won Tsar Alexander's recognition as Emperor of the West in return for a future possibility of Alexander as the Emperor of the East. The only obstacle to both was the stubborn resistance of Britain, which barred Napoleon's path to the west as she checked Alexander's expansion towards Turkey, Persia, Afghanistan and India.[4] Thus the Eastern Question gave rise to the Indian question, which in turn became part of the Central Asian problem with both Britain and Russia directing their expansionist effort towards Kabul.[5]

British Interests in Central Asia

The expansion of the British Empire in India in the late 18th and early 19th centuries made her the target of the rival

European powers like France and Russia having imperialistic aspirations. British Government's interests were two fold, the expansion of commerce and the protection of the empire. Acquisition of new territories and extension of sphere of influence followed from these, but economic motive was perhaps more dominant. The impending threat of the Kabul ruler Zaman Shah's invasion from the north west led to the emergence of British interests in Asian kingdoms beyond India's north western frontier and the foundations of a far reaching Central Asian policy which became a dominant feature of India's foreign policy in the subsequent period. The rapid advance of Russia in Central Asia up to the frontiers of Afghanistan and Persia became a constant source of anxiety to the British in India. Russian position in Central Asia was poised, not only to threaten the integrity of Afghanistan but was a menace to the security of India.[6] Suspicious of Franco-Russian design the British in India moved swiftly and established friendly relations with Persia, Punjab, Sind and Afghanistan. The Shah of Persia went further in his support and assured that no European force will be allowed to pass through Persia and that he would not enter into any treaty disadvantageous to the British territories in India.[7] The British Governor General of India Lord Wellesley even invoked Persian aid as a perpetual check on the adventurous impulses of the Afghan prince. The coming together of Napoleon and the Russian Tsar could not humble the imperial pride of Britain; Russian interest in India continued unabated even when Napoleon's strength was broken, rather it assumed the form of a permanent irritant for the British in Asia.[8]

Early 19th Century Developments

Afghanistan provided the arteries of communication between the military bases in India and the Russian bases in Central Asia. It was the gateway through which the British citadel in India could be approached. This made the British Government in India extremely sensitive to alien encroachment on Afghanistan. The British dispatched a diplomatic mission under Elphinstone to discuss with Shah Shuja, the Amir of Afghanistan, measures of mutual defence against the Franco-Russian threat to Afghanistan and British India. The mission succeeded in concluding an Alliance in 1809 by which the two governments pledged eternal friendship and agreed not to interfere in each others country.[9] Britain also concluded the treaty of Tehran with the Shah of Persia in 1814 according to which 'all alliances between Persia and European nations hostile to Great Britain were made null and void and all European armies were to be prevented from entering Persia if hostile to Great Britain.[10] However the new Shah of Persia Mohammad Mirza, who ascended the throne in 1833 turned out to be a friend of Russia and Russian influence became predominant at the Persian court. Russia instigated the Shah to lay siege on Herat [Nov. 1837 to Sept 1838] which occupied a strategic position vis-à-vis the Indian empire. The future Central Asian policy of the British was therefore to preserve the independence and secure the friendship of the government of Afghanistan. British Viceroy Lord William Bentick sent experienced officers like Alexander Burnes and Connolly to Sind, Punjab and Central Asia with a double object of gathering information about these unknown tracts and to explore the navigational possibility of Indus and it's role in the future commercial intercourse in Central Asia. Such a reconnaissance cum diplomatic mission would help the British judge the future course of action.[11] Amir Dost Mohammad was willing to accept friendly overtures of the English provided they put pressure on Maharaja Ranjit Singh of Punjab to restore Peshawar to him. The refusal of the British under Governor General Lord Auckland destroyed all hopes of an Anglo-Afghan alliance, and the Amir turned to Persia and Russia for friendship. This led to the disastrous first Afghan War, which deposed Dost Mohammad and restored the exiled Shah Shuja on the throne of Kabul with the support of Ranjit Singh. For the British the war was a disaster, a folly and a crime. Shah Shuja, the puppet installed by the British was murdered and Dost Mohammad once again ascended the throne of Kabul. In 1844 the Russian

Tsar Nicholas I visited Queen Victoria and came to an understanding that Bukhara, Khive and Samarkand should be left as neutral zone between the two empires.[12] The British proceeded to complete the conquest of northwest India by annexing Sind in 1843 and the Punjab in 1849. They then turned their attention to fixing and defining their northwest frontier and the problems of its defence.

British Policy and Afghan Civil War

The latter half of the 19th century witnessed developments having far reaching implications on Afghanistan. The Russian defeat in the Crimean War frustrated her march in south eastern Europe and she therefore recommenced her forward policy in Central Asia deepening British anxiety. Post 1858, the British Government in England dictated by European conditions conducted India's foreign policy. The question that British statesmen and policy framers pondered over was whether to go ahead and annex Afghanistan in order to secure a 'scientific frontier' or to halt any further expansion. The former policy was advocated by the 'forward' school and the Conservative Party and the latter by the 'non intervention' school led by the Liberals.[13] John Lawrence created the policy of 'masterly inactivity' in 1858 recommending the modification of the frontier boundary to coincide with the Indus. This was rejected by British Viceroy in India Lord Canning on the ground that military opinion does not consider a river as a good line of defence. Russian position in Central Asia poised a threat to the integrity of Afghanistan and a menace to the security of India. The fear about Russian ambition or Russo phobia is reflected in the policy of the British Government in the late 19th century.

Amir Dost Mohammad maintained friendly relations with the British. When Persia threatened Herat and Kandahar, the Amir sought help from the British and a treaty was concluded in 1855.[14] John Lawrence who negotiated the treaty was convinced that it was dangerous to meddle with the independence of Afghanistan and that they will resent interference in their internal affairs. Thus the integrity and independence of Afghanistan became the basis of friendship, with non-interference in domestic matters. The death of Dost Mohammad in 1863, created a new situation. A struggle for succession broke out among his 16 sons. For five years Afghanistan was a scene of fratricidal wars. Lawrence, now Governor General of India, adopted a policy of strict neutrality, recognizing the de facto ruler of Afghanistan and refusing aid to any of the contenders. At times more than one ruler was recognized as they held slices of the country. Finally when Sher Ali proved successful in the contest Lawrence recognized him and sent him succour to consolidate his position. Lawrence's policy of 'masterly inactivity' has been criticized on the ground that Sher Ali was dissatisfied with the British stance of neutrality and that he could not be expected to be friendly to them when he received no support at the most critical moment of his life. The British tried not to antagonize and alienate Sher Ali but the later clearly realized that the British looked to nothing but their own interest. The policy is however commendable that it helped prevent Russian and Persian intervention on behalf of the contenders to the Afghan throne, isolated the Afghan civil war and prevented any international complications.

Russian Counter Moves

The political and territorial expansion of Russia proceeded rapidly after 1865 increasing their strategic bases and influence beyond the Oxus. Britain's hope of supplanting Russian influence in Central Asia enhanced considerably when the Khanates of Bokhara, Khiva and Khokand were incorporated in the Russian Empire. In 1868 the Khan of Khokand signed a treaty with Russia, under threat of force, to accord the Russians preferential treatment in relation to other foreigners and extraterritorial rights. It gave fillip to their trade and the Khanate became a stepping-stone for commercial and political expansion of Russia. The fall of Khokand alarmed the Amir of

Bokhara who attempted a coalition of Muslim states of Kashgar, Khokand, Khiva and Afghanistan. They appealed to the British for help, which was refused. Russian General Kauffmann captured and occupied Samarkand in May 1868. The Khanate of Bokhara became a Russian vassal and Khiva was annexed in 1873, without any resistance.[15] Britain could have helped and supported the formation of a confederacy of the Central Asian states against Russian encroachments. However Britain refrained from supporting these Khanates against Russian thrust and establishing cordial relations with the British in India. But they kept intelligence information regarding Russian movements in Central Asia–political, commercial or military, by pressing into service native agents disguised as merchants or mendicants.[16] Russia had succeeded in forestalling British chances of acquiring even an economic foothold in Central Asia and Russian established herself as a paramount power by 1878.

Deterioration of Sher Ali's Relations with British

Sher Ali was anxious to secure the support of the British who failed to give him a firm assurance for future patronage and an unequivocal guarantee of support in case of external attack. This was due to the continuation of the policy of "masterly inactivity" by Lord Mayo, the successor of Lawrence in India. Alarmed at the occupation of Khiva in 1873 Sher Ali again asked the British for a written commitment for arms, money and if necessary troops to repel aggression by Russia or her dependencies. The then Governor General of India Lord Northbrook was willing to accede to the Amirs request but the British Government rejected the proposal and continued the existing policy.[17] The Amir realized that he could not rely on British protection against Russia. The relations further deteriorated when the British accepted to arbitrate a boundary dispute between the Amir and the Shah of Persia over Seistan. The award in some respects went against Afghanistan. The British even refused to recognize Abdulla Jan as heir apparent to Sher Ali. The Amir still continued friendly contact with the

British and sent his Prime Minister Syed Noor Mohammad to Simla to meet the Viceroy in the hope of removing mutual misunderstandings. Disgusted with the British attitude Sher Ali was driven to Russian arms who seized the opportunity to gain favour in Kabul.

Second Afghan War

In March 1874 Lord Disraeli became the Prime Minister in England and Lord Lytton replaced Northbrook in India. A more active and spirited foreign policy replaced "masterly inactivity." The British wanted to depute their agents to Kabul and Kandahar. It fell on Lytton to reverse the earlier policy and adopt a forward policy, which led to the second Afghan war. The Afghan problem became more complex when viewed from the angle of Anglo-Russian politics in Europe and Russian ambitions in the Balkans. Moving towards the Black Sea and the Dardanelles, Russia fought a war against Turkey in 1877 and imposed the stringent Treaty of San Stefano. England and Austria protested and asked the German Chancellor Bismark to convene a congress at Berlin to settle the Eastern Question. Several issues came into focus. If Russia's prime interest was in the Black Sea region, was she just posing a threat in Afghanistan to engage Britain in Central Asia so that she may have a free hand in Europe? Was Russian threat to Afghanistan a work of British imagination so that she may herself interfere in Afghan affairs?

Disraeli suffered from "Russo phobia" and his protégé Lytton was an exponent of the aggressive and forward school of frontier policy. With a view to improving relations with Sher Ali, Lytton persistently asked for stationing of a British envoy at Kabul which the Amir refused saying that in such a case, he could not refuse a similar request from Russia. Lytton's ulterior motive was to have a subordinate Sher Ali who would acquiesce into British demands and thus allow the British to checkmate Russian advance in Central Asia. A Russian officer Stolietoff left for Kabul bearing a draft treaty conceding the terms the Amir had asked the British under Northbrook. In 1878 Lytton was ready to concede to the Amir's request and dispatched a British Mission under Sir Neville Chamberlain with a threat of war if the mission was refused. In the mean time the Treaty of Berlin settled the Eastern Question and the Russian emissary withdrew from Kabul. However the British troops invaded Kabul and the Amir's authority collapsed. He sought Russian help, which was not forthcoming, as they did not want to embroil in a fruitless war against the British for the sake of the Amir. Sher Ali died brokenhearted and was succeeded by Yakub Khan who concluded the treaty of Gandamak in 1879.[18] It deprived Afghanistan of its traditional character of a buffer state and the Amir became a feudatory of the British crown. The Amir agreed to a permanent envoy at Kabul, and the control of foreign policy was vested in the British Government. The districts of Pishin, Kurram and Sibi were ceded to the British along with permanent control of the Khyber and Michni passes. The British government was to support the Amir against foreign aggression with arms, money and troops and pay him and his successors an annual subsidy of Rs. 600,000.

On the conclusion of the war, Disraeli remarked that they had secured an adequate frontier for their Indian empire. The British Government of India was in complete command over Afghan destiny. The Prime minister and the Viceroy apparently forgot the remarks of the Duke of Wellington made to Lord Auckland in 1839, 'In Asia, where victories cease, difficulties begin'[19]. Louis Cavagnari the British envoy to Afghanistan was murdered along with his staff. The collapse of the scientific frontier made the situation serious, Yakub Khan abdicated and the future of Afghanistan was in peril. The options open to Lytton was either to annex Afghanistan or dismember it; he preferred the latter, offered Herat to Persia and recognized Kandahar as an independent state. But before any decision could be effected Gladstone replaced Disraeli as Prime Minister of England and Lord Ripon took over as Viceroy of India. It was left to Ripon to secure the scientific frontier and negotiate with the new Amir Abdur Rehman a nephew of Sher Ali who lived as a refugee under Russian protection in Samarqand. Afghanistan owes a tremendous debt of gratitude to him for having guided her destiny with remarkable political perception and diplomatic shrewdness.[20] Abdur Rehman proved to be a capable and strong ruler and a firm friend of the British. The entire episode of the Afghan war and forward policy could be justified as it achieved the aim of securing a firm grip in Afghanistan for the British and removing Russian menace which could jeopardize British empire in India.

Durand Line and Its Aftermath

Though the Russian policy received a set back when British preponderance was established in Afghanistan, Russia kept nagging on the frontier outposts, causing aggressive actions while professing pacific intentions. In 1884 they occupied Merv strengthening Russian grip on the Oxus region. The British protests yielded a positive result and the British and Russians agreed to delimit the Russo-Afghan borders. Before a settlement could be reached Russia occupied a small village of Panjdeh in 1885. A warlike situation developed but British Prime Minister Gladstone diffused the matter. Finally in 1887 the border was demarcated; Russia retained Panjdeh and the Amir was given the Zulfikar pass.[21] The southern boundary of Afghanistan was still a source of contention. The unruly tribes, which lived in the region lying between the Afghan and British territories, owed allegiance to neither. The British desired to extend power over them. The Afghan boundary commission under Sir Mortimer Durand formally defined Indo-Afghan boundary from Chitral and Baluchistan. The Amir agreed not to interfere with the tribes on the Indian side of the frontier and the British Government of India would not interfere in the territories lying on the side of Afghanistan. When it seemed that all outstanding problems between India and Afghanistan were resolved, fresh issues emerged. [22] The turbulent tribesmen often rose in revolt and punitive expeditions were required against them. The tribal problem is in fact inseparably linked to the Afghan policy. Between 1893 and 1897 several revolts including those of the Mohmands and Afridis kept the British engaged. As a counter measure roads and railways were built in frontier districts, troops were redistributed to be more effective and a new North West Province was created out of the Punjab. Till the turn of the century relations continued to be normal only to be reviewed by Lord Curzon who was the British Viceroy of India at the turn of the century and the new Amir Habibullah Khan who ascended in 1901.

Amir Habibullah 1901-1919

When Habibullah the son and heir designate of Abdur Rehman succeeded peacefully, it was a thing hitherto unknown in Afghan history. Curzon expected that sooner or later some tribes will challenge his authority but nothing happened which could give Curzon a pretext to initiate any action.[23] The British regarded all treaties and engagements with Abdur Rehman as personal and not binding upon Indian authorities to continue them with his successors. Habibullah ignored the invitation of Curzon for a conference in Peshawar. Curzon then tried to pressurize and coerce the Amir by suspending his subsidy and detaining a consignment of ammunition purchased by the Amir, but to no avail. Habibullah insisted that the old agreement with his father was valid and did not require a renewal. Curzon probably desired to initiate a new and stronger Central Asian policy in view of the political, commercial and constructional activities of Russia in the Persian Gulf and Central Asia.[24] Curzon could not appreciate that it was not possible for Habibullah to leave his kingdom without consolidating his position. Moreover being sovereign in his state he claimed the title of His Majesty even if it was irksome to Curzon. And he was perfectly justified in not wanting to meet a representative to a king, however powerful. The Amirs reluctance to meet and Russia's moves in Afghanistan increased Curzons anxiety. The situation had changed since the creation in 1885 of a coterminous Russo-Afghan frontier and the completion of the trans-Caspian railway. The extension of Russian railroad system from Tashkent to Khushk on the Afghan border made the British realize the importance of Afghan friendship, an indefinite postponement of which would be injurious to the British. They therefore decided to dispatch Sir Louis Dane, Foreign Secretary to the British Government of India to Kabul to discuss all questions concerning joint mutual interests of India and Afghanistan and conclude a treaty. The British government was against any rupture with Habibullah, overruled Curzons objections and signed a treaty in March 1905. The arrangements with Abdur Rehman were renewed and the British retained control over foreign affairs, which was the focal point of British policy in respect of Russian expansion in Central Asia. The Amir styled himself as His Majesty and the arrears of his subsidy was also released. The treaty was a clear triumph of Habibullah and a repudiation of Curzon's policy. It put an end to mutual distrust and suspicion and a closer friendship was strengthened when the Amir visited India in 1907.

In the context of European diplomacy, Anglo Russian rivalry in Afghanistan took a different turn. The Anglo-Russian Convention of 1907 settled their differences over Tibet, Persia and Afghanistan. The Russians accepted Afghanistan to be outside their sphere of influence. The British on their part assured that they would not modify the political status of the Amir. Both powers were provided equal commercial facilities. Though the Amir regarded this union of his two neighbours with suspicion it stood the test of time. During the First World War Habibullah rendered the English valuable service by maintaining a policy of strict neutrality.[25] The fall of Tsarist Russia in 1917, the consequent end of Anglo-Russian friendship, the defeat of Turkey and the popular unrest in Afghanistan due to the introduction of Western civilization, had serious repercussions. The Amir wanted the recognition of Afghan independence at the Paris Peace Conference. Before any decision could be reached, Habibullah who was becoming unpopular due to his Europeanizing policy was assassinated in February 1919.

Third Afghan War

Amir Amanullah who succeeded Habibullah was the leader of the emerging anti-British movement in Afghanistan and a propagator to the cause of Afghan freedom. Generally opposed to the British and under pressure due to internal troubles, he embarked on a war against the British to secure complete independence for Afghanistan. He even posed as a friend of the freedom fighters in India.[26] Amanullah was severely and decisively defeated and a peace treaty signed at Rawalpindi in August 1919. The British recognised the complete independence of Afghanistan and agreed not to attempt any hold over their foreign policy. An accredited British minister was henceforth to reside at Kabul and the Amir was to be represented by one of his own ministers in London. In spite of having lost the war, Afghanistan won favourable terms in the peace treaty, so much so that the Afghan delegate at the Paris Peace Conference announced that Afghanistan won the war.[27] The British did not react because they were still reeling under the shock of the World War and conditions in India were uncertain with the emergence of Mahatma Gandhi on the scene. In the final analysis, it may be mentioned that a strong, friendly and independent Afghanistan was beneficial to the British. During the Khilafat movement in India nearly 25,000 Muslims migrated to Afghanistan. It caused alarm as Afghanistan would have to feed and accommodate these Indians. In 1927 Amir Amanullah went to England and on his return wanted to introduce far reaching reforms on the lines of Turkey under Kemal Pasha. There was serious opposition leading to a civil war. The orthodox Mullahs exploited the mass resentment and compelled Amanullah to abdicate in January 1929. During the period of uncertainty, the Government of India maintained a policy of neutrality. Nadir Khan, born and brought up in India crossed over to Kabul and was proclaimed the new ruler of Afghanistan. The treaty of friendship signed in 1921 was renewed and reaffirmed. Schemes of modernization and reform were cautiously undertaken. Yet in November 1933 a fanatic assassinated Amir Nadir Khan and his son Muhammad Zahir ascended the throne peacefully.[28] He maintained friendly relations with both England and Russia, which made Afghanistan a stable buffer between them. During the Second World War, Afghanistan maintained neutrality in spite of Hitler's offer to join them.

Thus Afghanistan remained sand-witched between the imperial Great Britain and an expansionist Russia for about one and half century. Even during the bipolar cold war era till 1990, Afghanistan had to very carefully handle its foreign and defence policies taking into consideration both the American and Soviet interests in the country and the region. Even today, the buffer status of the country remains its soul determinant of survival in the changing geo-political contours of this land-locked nation.

Notes

1. Anuradha Sareen, *India and Afghanistan: British Imperialism Vs Afghan Nationalism 1907–1921*, Seema Publications, Delhi, 1981, p. 1.
2. Mohammad Anwar Khan, *England, Russia and Central Asia [A Study in diplomacy] 1857–1878*, University Book Agency, Peshawar, 1963, pp. 307-8.
2. C. S. Samra, *India and Anglo Soviet Relations 1917–1947*, Asia Publishing House, Bombay, 1959, p. 4.
3. L. Mukherjee, *A hand book of Modern Europe*, Mondal Brothers & Co, Calcutta, p. 198.
4. David Thompson, *Europe Since Napoleon*, Penguin Books, Longmans Reprint, 1973, p. 64.
5. C. S. Samra, *op ci*, p. 7.
6. Bisheswar Prasad, *Foundations of India's Foreign Policy, Volume I 1860–82*, Calcutta, 1955.

7. C. S. Samra, *Ibid,* p. 6.
8. Bisheswar Prasad, *Our foreign policy Legacy,* Peoples Publishing House, New Delhi, 1965, p. 2.
9. Anuradha Sareen, *op cit* pp. 2-3.
10. Majumdar, Dutta and Ray Choudhry, *Advanced History of India,* p. 751.
11. Warikoo K., *Central Asia and Kashmir: A Study in the Context of Anglo Russian Rivalry,* Gyan Publishing House, New Delhi, 1989, pp. 121 & 127.
12. Advanced History, *op cit,* p. 829.
13. C. S. Samra, *op cit,* pp. 8-9.
14. Advanced History, *op cit,* p. 830.
15. Bisheswar Prasad, *Foundations of India's Foreign Policy.*
16. Warikoo, *op cit,* p. 129.
17. Anuradha Sareen, *op cit* pp. 8-9; Advanced History *op cit* pp. 832-833; G.P Tripathi *Indo Afghan Relations* Kumar Brothers, New Delhi, 1973, p. 11.
18. D. P. Singhal, *India and Afghanistan 1876–1907,* Queensland, Australia, 1963, p. 49.
19. Quoted by C. S. Samra, p. 12.
20. D. P. Singhal, *op cit.*
21. Anuradha Sareen, *op cit,* pp. 12–13; Advanced history, *op cit.* p. 836.
22. Hassan Ali Shah Jafari, *Indo Afghan relations 1947–67,* Sterling Publishers Pvt Ltd, New Delhi, 1976, p. 10; Advanced History, *op cit,* p. 837.
23. *Ibid,*.pp. 902-903.
24. Anuradha Sareen, op *cit* pp16–17, D.P Singhal *op cit.*
25. Advanced History, op *cit,* p. 904.
26. *Ibid,* Hassan Ali, *op cit* p. 15.
27. *Ibid,* p. 16.
28. Advanced History, *op cit.*905, Hassan Ali, *op cit* p. 21.

4

The Soviet Intervention in Afghanistan: The Indian Response

Padmanabh M. Kamath

On 27 December 1979 the Soviet Union militarily intervened in Afghanistan, a non-aligned country on its southern border, with about a 90,000-strong force. This was the first time it was militarily intervening outside its own sphere of influence. Unlike the American incremental intervention in Vietnam, the Soviets intervened with a massive force right in the beginning. The Soviet troops clashed with Hafizul Amin's loyal troops, and Amin was killed in the clash. The invaders then put up a puppet Government for Afghanistan headed by Babrak Karmal of the Parcham faction of the National Democratic Party of Afghanistan. To a world stunned by their massive military intervention, the Soviets said that they had been invited to intervene by the Kabul Government under the Peace and Friendship Treaty of December 1978 signed by the two Governments after the Saur Revolution of April 1978. They never clarified which one of the two Governments–the one deposed by them or the one installed by them–extended the invitation! It is one of the ironies of the Afghan Revolution that Amin, who signed the treaty on behalf of his Government in 1978, was done away with, in 1979, under the same instrumentality.

Reasons behind the Intervention

Why did the Soviet Union decide upon military intervention in a neighbouring country, which, by any stretch of imagination, did not pose a security threat to it? This is one of those questions of foreign-policy formulation where the knowledge of foreign-policy-makers and that of foreign-policy analysts do not differ very much.[1] There is no firm answer to the question why the Soviets decided to intervene militarily. One line of argument is that Hafizul Amin, because of his excessive zeal in pushing through the programme of communization, had become unpopular with the Soviet leaders and was, in their perception, jeopardizing the gains of the Saur Revolution. The Soviets felt that he was responsible for an increase in the hostility of the freedom fighters and the consequent international attention and criticism of the Afghan ruling clique. They, therefore, sought to get him out of power in September 1979, but in vain. Instead Taraki, the then President, was killed in the palace shoot-out. Amin's realization of the Soviet role in the September 1979 incident made him an anti-Soviet nationalist-Communist. The Soviets in their turn feared lest personal ambition should make him repudiate the Soviet connexion.[2]

Another explanation relates to the growing Islamic fundamentalism in Afghanistan and in the region around it. Any success of Islamic fundamentalism, which was already ruling high in Iran, would have far-reaching repercussions in the Soviet Union, for the simple reason that there were 43 million Muslims in that country. Between September 1979 and the military intervention of 27 December 1979 Amin had attempted to make his regime more broad-based by reaching some accommodation with religious leaders and nationalists.

Externally, he was probably willing to co-operate with the West. He was scheduled to receive the then Foreign Minister of Pakistan, Agha Shahi, on 30 September 1979, only three days before his assassination. Even a partial accommodation with the fundamentalists internally, and with the West externally, would have been a retrogressive step for the Soviets from the standpoint of bringing off a Communist revolution. Brezhnev's description of Amin as an abettor of aggression against Afghanistan and the *Pravda* editorial declaring him "an imperialist stooge ... who was an agent of U.S. intelligence services" are significant in this context.[3]

Thirdly, there is the old theory of the ambition of the Tsars to expand the Russian Empire right up to the warm waters of the Indian Ocean. The Soviet rulers, it is argued, have not given up the old dream of the Tsarist rulers. The military occupation of Afghanistan, it is said, is a result of that ambition. Hard-line anti-Soviet thinkers particularly hold this view and by US policy-makers, past, like Zbigniew Brzezinski.

Fourthly, it is argued that the Soviets wanted not only to gain better control over Afghanistan and thereby get closer to the warm waters of the Indian Ocean but also to command the rich deposits of important strategic minerals like copper, oil, gas, bauxite, and chrome, which, according to them, Afghanistan possesses in plenty.[4] If the political goals are unattainable by their military presence, they might decide to annex the whole of Afghanistan or at least a part of it to their growing empire.

Apart from these general explanations, some US policy-makers then believed that the growing fear in the Soviet Union of being surrounded by hostile forces contributed to their final decision to intervene. The Soviets perceived the United States as leaning towards the People's Republic of China (PRC) in military relations and as strengthening its NATO buildup at the same time. This perception was reinforced by the NATO decision of 12 December 1979 to place 572 intermediate-range Cruise and Pershing II missiles in Western Europe in reaction to the Soviet deployment of SS 20s. With the uncertainty of the Senate approval of the SALT II Treaty, US-Soviet relations had deteriorated sharply, and the Soviets felt that any military intervention by them in Afghanistan was unlikely to damage those relations any further.[5] Iran was passing through a fundamentalist revolutionary turmoil. Intervention in Afghanistan could, the Soviets probably argued, help them influence policies not only in Iran but in Pakistan and India as well. There was also the strategic advantage of countering, through their occupation of Afghanistan, the American presence at the Diego Garcia base in the Indian Ocean.

On all accounts it seems reasonable to argue that the Soviets thought of a quick fix in Afghanistan: their objective was to enable their puppet Government of Babrak Karmal to take root and then withdraw their forces. The Soviet military intervention in Afghanistan is similar to the US military intervention in the Dominican Republic in 1965 or the US military intervention in Grenada in October 1983. However, whereas the US military intervened in the Dominican Republic and in Grenada to prevent an alleged Communist take-over in those countries, the Soviet military intervention in Afghanistan was to prevent the failure of the Communist revolution.

India's Perception of the Crisis

How did Indian government perceive the crisis? What was its initial response to the Soviet intervention in Afghanistan? What were the implications of the Soviet presence in Afghanistan for India's national security? What changes came about in India's initial response to the crisis? What was the US response as a Super Power? How far the US response complicated and influenced the Indian perception of the Soviet threat? Was there a way out for the Soviet troops from Afghanistan? These issues are discussed in this article.

The first ever-Soviet decision to militarily intervene outside its sphere of influence then showed a growing confidence on its part in its ability to commit its armed forces to achieve foreign-policy goals. It could be, as has been argued in some quarters, an indication of its growing sense of insecurity, a feeling of being surrounded by hostile states. These observations need not be mutually exclusive. If, however, the timing is an important factor in the success of a foreign-policy decision, the Soviets could not have chosen a better time for the military intervention. The United States was totally preoccupied with the hostage crisis in Tehran, which only compounded and confirmed the then prevailing perception of President Carter as indecisive and incompetent. In view of the impending Presidential elections in November 1980, the hostage crisis was an obsession with the Carter Administration. The domestic situation in India in its own way was no better. For the first time in the history of independent India, it had a caretaker Government led by Charan Singh. It was, in fact, no Government, not one capable of taking care of India's national security. All political parties were busy going through the electoral process to elect a new Lok Sabha.

India's Initial Reaction

India's response to the Afghan crisis may be analyzed in two parts–the initial reaction of the caretaker Government of Charan Singh and then the response of Indira Gandhi's Government from the middle of January 1980. A spokesman of the Government of India stated on 28 December 1979 that India had always opposed outside interference in the internal affairs of one country by another. Any situation, which qualitatively changes the political structure of a society, is significant, and naturally India was concerned about it.[6] Later

Charan Singh called the Soviet Ambassador to his office and expressed India's concern at the Soviet military intervention and asked for an early withdrawal of its troops. He also told the Ambassador that India would like Afghanistan's independence and non-aligned status to be restored.[7]

However, it was clear that Indira Gandhi was to be the next Prime Minister. She was due to take office on the "auspicious" day of 14 January 1980. In such a situation the incoming Prime Minister has greater influence from outside, than the outgoing Prime Minister from within, on the process of policy formulation. This was revealed in the UN General Assembly. Thus, in view of the incoming Prime Minister's well-known leaning towards the Soviet Union, Brajesh Mishra, then India's Permanent Representative in the United Nations, reiterated during the debate on Afghanistan on 12 January 1980 India's opposition to the presence of foreign troops and bases in any country. What, however, sent a shock wave in diplomatic circles was his observation that the Soviet Union in the case of Afghanistan had assured India that it would withdraw its troops whenever the Kabul Government asked it to do so: "We have no reason to doubt the assurances, particularly from a friendly country like the Soviet Union, with whom we have close ties."[8] Jawaharlal Nehru, the co-founder of India's non-aligned policy, would not have accepted such assurances from Britain on its invasion of the Suez Canal. Indira Gandhi did not accept the US justification that the Organization of East Caribbean States had invited it to invade Grenada.

Thus, India's stand was that it was opposed to all kinds of intervention but that in this particular case there were special reasons for not considering the Soviet action publicly unjustified. The UN resolution asking for the unconditional and immediate withdrawal of the Soviet troops was passed with 104 to 18 votes. In all, eighteen nations abstained, and India was one of them. It is significant to note that sixty out of a total of ninety-six non-aligned countries voted for the resolution. Iraq, another non-aligned country with a Peace and Friendship Treaty with the Soviet Union, similar to the one India signed in 1971, also voted for the resolution. If the Indian stand was decided in consultation with Indira Gandhi, there was a change in her own perception of the Soviet threat to India's security in 1979 during and after the elections. As a candidate for the office of Prime Minister, Indira Gandhi had said, in an interview to France's Europe Radio Station, that the Soviet Intervention in Afghanistan was "a danger to India."[9]

American Factor

The Indian response to the Afghan crisis and the implications of the Soviet presence in Afghanistan for Indian security were complicated by the US response to the Afghan crisis. As a Super Power the United States is the only nation that was in a position to check the growing interventionist policies of the Soviet Union. Often the US policies are determined mainly by the requirements of the need to maintain the balance of power *vis-à-vis* the Soviet Union in disregard of the regional consequences of those policies. Then the United States saw every issue through the prism of the Soviet equation. Thus the American response, not only in this case but also in most regional crises in South Asia, directly or indirectly affected policy formulation by regional Powers like India. The US response to the Afghan crisis was typically in the style of the Cold War as though there had been a sudden realization of the Soviet threat. President Carter declared the Soviet invasion of Afghanistan as the greatest threat to world peace since the Second World War. Within a few days of the Soviet intervention, the United States imposed a grain embargo, cut off all sales of high technology, and announced a boycott of the Moscow Olympics of 1980. It justified all these steps on the ground that it must make the Soviet Union pay for its aggression."

What surprised the Soviets were not so much the steps that the United States proposed to take as the intensity of the hostility underlying them. The United States had not made it publicly clear to the Soviets earlier that their intervention in Afghanistan would be an unacceptable security threat.[11] It had sufficient information on the possibility of a Soviet intervention in Afghanistan. Brzezinski, President Carter's National Security Adviser, had even informed the Press that the Soviets were amassing troops on the Afghan borders.[12] Vance records in his memoirs that on 20 December 1979 the United States had information that '*elite* Soviet paratroopers had moved into Afghanistan."[13]

However, Brzezinski is of the opinion that the United States did not react to the Soviet intervention in advance as it possessed no effective means to prevent it.[14] Though the Rapid Deployment Force (RDF) had been conceived before the Afghan crisis, it had not taken shape until then. It can, however, be argued that if the United States had come up with the Carter Doctrine, which Brzezinski claims to be similar to the Truman Doctrine, before the Soviet intervention rather than after the event, the Soviets would possibly have given a second look to their plans.[15] A parallel in President Reagan's response to the developing crisis in Poland in 1981 cannot be missed. Though a number of other factors deterred the Soviets from directly intervening in Poland, including their entanglement in Afghanistan, Reagan's "Hands Off" warning to the Soviets did play a part.

It was a clear case of failure on the part of the top-level foreign-policy-makers of the United States correctly to assess the information in their possession as to Soviet intentions. In retrospect, Cyrus Vance also writes "Soviet activities received less top-level attention" than was necessary.[16] It was a major failure of US foreign policy. It is possible that a decisive response from the United States would have prevented the tragedy in Afghanistan. The Carter Doctrine, which came after the Soviet intervention in Afghanistan, did not include Afghanistan within the operational purview of the doctrine.

Soviet Occupation a Security Threat to India

India's response was not the kind that could give much comfort in the West, especially in the USA. A typical reaction was that of President Carter. He said: "The Indian representative's speech in the United Nations was as strongly supportive of the Soviet invasion as were those of Czechoslovakia and Vietnam. Even Cuba was more reticent in its praise than India."[17] India's policy was to abstain from the vote on a resolution demanding immediate and unconditional withdrawal of the Soviet troops from Afghanistan, and the Indian representative need not have said what he did say in the UN General Assembly; for the 'Afghan intervention was not on the pattern of the old military interventions by the Soviet Union in its own sphere of influence in Eastern Europe, far away from India's immediate neighbourhood. Afghanistan was a non-aligned country, next door to India's northwest frontier. The conflict between the Super Powers had come close to its borders. If India could not choose its neighbours, it should at least have responded differently from the way it had responded to the Soviet interventions in the past–in Hungary and Czechoslovakia–in view of the fact that the Soviet power had moved closer to its borders. India's policy ought to have aimed at keeping the Soviet power away from its borders.[18]

Afghanistan and Pakistan were the two buffer states between the massive Soviet power and India. By their military intervention, the Soviets removed one of these buffers at one stroke and threatened the other by bringing their power closer to the Indian borders. India's policy had to be one that aims not only at preserving Pakistan as a buffer state but also at restoring the non-aligned status and independence of Afghanistan so that it continues to be a buffer. Then only can it ensure that the Soviet Union, which is a land-based Power, does not extend its borders up to Kanyakumari.

Further, a dangerous doctrine had been expounded by the Soviets since their military intervention in Afghanistan. They say that their intervention acquires legitimacy if the victim is territorially contiguous with their country. Brezhnev's chief spokesman on foreign affairs, Leonid Zamyatin, said: "The USSR's vital interests in Afghanistan are certainly higher than America's because their country lies on our southern borders, but is thousands of kilometers away from the USA."[19] This means that just because a state has common borders with another, it gets the right to intervene militarily in the affairs of its neighbour. When such a doctrine comes from a Super Power it poses a threat to others as well. If the Soviets had decided not to leave Afghanistan, they could have eventually posed a security threat to Pakistan and even to India. Unfortunately India's policy-makers did not show any awareness of this fact, at least publicly.[20]

India's stand on the crisis is not liked by a large number of intellectuals. Opposition parties like the Bharatiya Janata Party, the Janata Party, and the Lok Dal did not approve of the government stand. Afghanistan has traditionally been a friend of India. But after the Soviet military intervention, the ordinary people in Afghanistan, and for that matter even Babrak Karmal's Government, were not too happy with the stand of the Government of India for different reasons. J.D. Singh of the *Times of India,* after a visit to Kabul, filed this report about six weeks after the Soviets entered Afghanistan:

> The Government of Afghanistan would have liked India to take a positive stand in favour of Kabul's known position that the Soviet army came to Afghanistan on an invitation to repel internal and external threats. The ordinary man in Kabul on the other hand is critical of India for adopting a pro-

> Moscow stand not exercising pressure for vacation of the Soviet occupation of his country.[21]

The stand that India took was not in keeping with the general trend within the non-aligned movement (NAM); nor was it in keeping with the stand of its neighbours. The Islamic countries also found India's stand contrary to their own. Normally India sides with the Islamic countries in their disputes with the Western countries–as, for instance, on the Palestine question. Of course, whether India's response is pro-Moscow or not depends on what one expects from India. Those who wish India to be more forthright in condemning the Soviet intervention looked upon its response as pro-Moscow; and those who wished India to condone the Soviet action and toe the Soviet line did not consider it to be pro-Moscow.

Though India has abstained from public criticism of the Soviet intervention, it has not condoned it. Since the beginning all talks with the Soviet leaders have been aimed at convincing them of the wrong they have committed by intervening in Afghanistan and at persuading them to withdraw their troops. Gromyko in February 1980 and Brezhnev in December 1980 were informed in clear terms that they must resolve the Afghan crisis. In September 1982, during a visit to the Soviet Union, Indira Gandhi made it clear at a Press conference that she wanted the people of Afghanistan to be left alone to decide their own destiny.

Under the pressure of domestic and international opinion India also has started manifesting a greater balance in its approach to the crisis than in the beginning. In June 1980, after his visit to Moscow, P.V. Narasimha Rao, the then Minister for External Affairs, informed the Lok Sabha that the Soviet presence in Afghanistan would not be "limited in time" as the Government had originally presumed.[22] In February 1981 India endorsed the Delhi Declaration of the NAM Foreign Minister's Conference, which asked for the withdrawal of all foreign troops from Afghanistan. The appeal was repeated at the NAM Summit in March 1983.

Muteness of India's Response

What is the explanation for India's reluctance openly to demand unconditional and immediate withdrawal of the Soviet troops from Afghanistan? A variety of explanations have been offered. One explanation is that Indira Gandhi felt obliged to the Soviet Union for its support during the Bangladesh War of 1971. If that was so, she not only personalized domestic affairs, but foreign affairs as well. But it is also said that she was a shrewd politician not known to sacrifice national interests as she perceived them. She knew that in international relations, nations had neither permanent friends nor permanent enemies but only permanent interests. And it was evidently in India's national interest to see that the Soviet troops were withdrawn from India's immediate neighbourhood. If it was a concern for India's long and consistent friendship with the Soviet Union, it can be argued that in international relations the Soviet Union needed India's friendship more than India needed the friendship of the Soviet Union; for, in the non-Communist world, the Soviet Union had very few reliable friends.

Similarly it is pointed out that India's muted response is due to the Indo-Soviet Treaty of Peace and Friendship of 1971. Whenever there is a treaty between a Super Power and a small or even a major Power like India, the implementation of the treaty is normally in favour of the stronger Power (possibly with the exception of the initial purpose which compelled the weaker one to get into a treaty relationship with the stronger). Thus, for instance, the Soviets did not inform India in advance as to the threat, if any, created by the Afghan situation before they decided militarily to intervene. Even when the Soviets decided to withdraw a small contingent of their troops from Kabul soon after the Indian External Affairs Minister's visit in

June 1980, they chose to inform the former French President, Valery Giscard d'Estaing, rather than India. As a matter of fact, the withdrawal announcement was aimed at Europe, as President Giscard d'Estaing was to meet President Carter in Venice. Its purpose was not to pacify the anti-Soviet insurgency in Afghanistan or world public opinion. That India was not consulted is clear from the words of the Government spokesman when he said that the announcement of withdrawal of troops came as a "pleasant surprise" to India.[23]

Hence the explanation for India's muted response has to be found elsewhere, in two of its foreign-policy concerns. First, the Soviet Union was India's principal arms supplier; and, secondly, India's security was threatened by Pakistan and China. India was dependent on the Soviet Union to the extent of seventy per cent for its arms supplies. Until the goal of diversification of sources for arms procurement is achieved, India does not want to antagonize the Soviet Union. The experience of Egypt should not be lost sight of in this context. After the late President Sadat asked Soviet advisers to quit his country, Egypt was unable to get spare parts for its Soviet MiGs. Egypt's request for those spare parts from India was politely turned down on grounds of "contractual commitments."[25]

Pakistani Factor

India's problems with Pakistan are very complex. Their significance in India's decision-making is further enhanced by the US actions in the region. In reality the Afghan crisis generated in India a tremendous amount of sympathy for Pakistan. For the first time even political parties of the Right, which had generally seen the partition of undivided India as artificial, showed themselves to be sensitive to the security concerns and the survival of Pakistan as an independent nation. Pakistan suddenly became a buffer state of great importance to Indian security. There was similar awareness in Pakistan on the need for Indo-Pakistani amity in the wake of the security threat from the Soviet Union.[26] Unfortunately the goodwill generated in each country was not fully exploited to improve Indo-Pakistani relations. The blame lies with both the countries.

Soon after Indira's return to power, India sent its then Foreign Secretary, Ram Sathe, to Islamabad, to express India's concern over the developments in Afghanistan. Sathe reassured Pakistan that it need not worry over its eastern front and that India would not take advantage of its security concerns. He offered a 'No War Pact' to Pakistan, which Pakistan rejected. Unfortunately, Pakistan's military rulers saw the crisis not so much in terms of the survival of Pakistan as in terms of their own survival. The subsequent developments in Pakistan, especially the demand for the restoration of democratic government–the Movement for the Restoration of Democracy (MRD)–indicated very clearly that in the absence of the Afghan crisis, the military rule of General Zia ul Haq would have by then been a part of history. The crisis helped Zia to defuse the domestic political opposition and to prolong his rule. The subsequent abortive *coup* against Zia further confirms this view.

However, it is the American response that has really complicated Indian thinking on the crisis. Beyond the steps taken to impose direct sanctions against the Soviet Union, the Carter Administration behaved in typical Cold War style as in the 1950s. As a matter of fact, the Soviet intervention in Afghanistan ushered in the second phase of the Cold War. The Carter Administration decided to respond militarily to the crisis by accepting Pakistan as a frontline state and offering to it military and economic aid of the order of $400 million. Pakistan, however, had become wiser after the two wars with India in 1965 and 1971, when, according to the Pakistanis, in spite of Pakistan's membership of the US-sponsored military alliances, the United States did not come to its aid. It, therefore, demanded a higher economic and strategic price for its co-operation against the Soviets. The price, militarily, was a security pact with the United States, which would cover not only a threat from the Soviet Union, but also from India.[27] The economic price was a larger package than $400 million. Owing, however, to the policy uncertainties of the Carter Administration, the proposals fell through. General Zia rejected the US offer. He described it as "peanuts", hurting the personal feelings of Carter.

With the inauguration of the Reagan Administration in 1981, as a part of its overall policy of confrontation with the Soviet Union and raising its military capabilities, the United States offered to raise the earlier Carter package of military and economic assistance to $ 3.2 billion. When "peanuts" became "walnuts" they were acceptable to Pakistan. Under this package, the United States agreed to provide forty F-16 aircraft to Pakistan (these have since been delivered). Additionally, ignoring Indian protests, it inducted sophisticated weapons in the region. Later, it even agreed to provide Harpoon missiles to the Pakistani Navy. The F-16s are not suitable for mountain warfare and hence irrelevant to the security challenge to Pakistan from the Soviet backed Afghanistan. Even if one is to accept the US argument that the F-16s are meant to create a sense of confidence in Pakistan against the formidable threat from across the Afghan side, the Harpoon missiles can only be used against the Indian navy! These developments only confirm the initial reactions of India that the Pakistani rulers are trying to re-equip themselves not to face Afghanistan but to attack India. This was not unknown to the Americans. Many American policy-makers privately admitted that the US perceptions of the need for them to provide arms to Pakistan do not coincide with the Pakistani perceptions of their need to take those arms from the United States. But then, for the United States, its global concerns are far more important than the regional concerns.

With the acquisition of sophisticated weapons on the pretext of the threat from the Soviet Union, Pakistan could and would eventually pose a threat to Indian security. The F-16 planes, in the possession of Pakistan, have, for the first time, given it the necessary capability to reach New Delhi, the Indian nuclear complex in Mumbai and the oil exploration installations of Mumbai High as well. Pakistan, reduced to size in 1971, would only be committing *hara-kiri* in attacking India. It is irrational; therefore, to say that there is no threat to India's security from Pakistan.[28] But though it is irrational, it is only human for the Pakistanis close to power, to speak in terms of avenging the defeat of 1971. It is such talk, which made India condition its response to the Afghan crisis, not on the basis of the Soviet action, but on the basis of the US reaction to it.

This security threat has to be seen in the context of Pakistan's plans to go nuclear within a short time and to possess the first Islamic nuclear bomb. Professor Stephen Cohen, an expert on South Asia, said after a visit to Pakistan in December 1982 that when he asked a military general why Pakistan was planning to go nuclear, the answer was that it might be able to take Kashmir through a swift military action.[29] While General Zia had gone through the formalities of denying any intention to go nuclear, Dr. Abdul Qadir Khan, Pakistan's leading nuclear scientist, then had declared that Pakistan did succeed in a short span of seven years in processing enriched uranium, which is essential for building nuclear weapons, and has left India far behind.[30] In his view, what stood between nuclear capability and the actual possession of the bomb was a political decision.

Kashmir and the Soviet Support

So Pakistan's claim to Kashmir is the key explanation for the muted Indian response to the Soviet intervention in Afghanistan. Kashmir is a symbol, which unifies Pakistan's

Islamic nationalism, especially *vis-à-vis* India. It enables the decision-makers in Pakistan, whether elected leaders or military dictators, to argue that the formation of an Islamic state is incomplete until Kashmir forms part of it.[31] In the absence of a deliberate emphasis on Islamic separatism, there is hardly anything to distinguish the Pakistanis from the Indians. Kashmir is also a symbol of Indian secularism. If India admits the claim of Pakistan to Kashmir on grounds of Kashmir's Muslim majority, similar demands could be heard from many other parts of India endangering the very unit of the nation.

Thus, so long as Pakistan keeps Kashmir a live issue, India needed diplomatic support from a Super Power in war and peace. The Bangladesh War of 1971 demonstrated that non-aligned India would not be able to win a decisive victory in a war without diplomatic support from a Super Power. There is always the possibility of Pakistan raising the Kashmir issue in the UN Security Council. If it does so, India would need a permanent member of the Security Council to use veto in its favour. Such an exercise of the veto cannot be expected from the United States or from the two other Western nations, France and the United Kingdom. In the past these nations had unduly favoured Pakistan in the matter of Kashmir. Such an exercise of the veto cannot be expected from the PRC either for reasons to be discussed later. The Soviet Union, a permanent member of the Security Council, had consistently supported India on the Kashmir question, and India expected it to do so in future also. In fact, it is this consideration which first compelled India in the 1950s to move closer to the Soviet Union in diplomatic affairs because Pakistan, by virtue of its membership of the US-led military alliances, started raising the Kashmir question in the United Nations, and other international forums. In the absence of any assurance from the Western countries, especially the United States, that their tilt towards Pakistan cannot be taken for granted on the issue,

India could not afford to lose the diplomatic support of the Soviet Union.

The diplomatic support of the Soviet Union was vital in yet another matter. Although India's relations with the PRC were improving, the border problem, which caused the war of October 1962 between the two, is still outstanding. So long as the border problem is not solved to its satisfaction, and so long as a Sino-Soviet *détente* did not develop, India needed Soviet support. That is why India went in for a Peace and Friendship Treaty with the Soviet Union in the wake of the Bangladesh War in 1971; for China was then threatening to intervene on behalf of Pakistan. If the PRC should ever turn aggressive in its dealings with India, India can rely on Soviet support to activate the Sino-soviet border conflict and deter the PRC from supporting Pakistan. In fact this was what happened during the Bangladesh War. The PRC had also been a consistent supporter of Pakistan in international affairs. In the perception of Pakistan the support it has received from the PRC has been even better than the support it has received from the United States. Thus there is no possibility of the PRC extending support to India over the Kashmir question, whether in times of peace (in the UN Security Council) or during a period of war.

The need for Soviet support was vital also in view of the fact that during the Bangladesh War, the United States made it clear to India that unlike in 1962, India should not bank upon US support in the event of an intervention by the PRC on the side of Pakistan.[32] It may appear strange, but it is a fact, that Kissinger fully coordinated US moves in and out of the United Nations over the Bangladesh War in 1971 with the PRC representative, Huang Hua. His anguish at the inaction of the PRC is clear when he describes his mistaken belief that the PRC would intervene militarily in the war even at that late stage.[33] The subsequent normalization of Sino-US relations, the US use of the China card against the Soviet Union, and frequent talk by US policy-makers of entering into a military relationship with the PRC further complicated the Indian dilemma; for, if Pakistan could use the weapons given to it by the United States for the ostensible purpose of facing the Soviet threat against India, so could the PRC divert any sophisticated military hardware that the United States might give it as part of a triangular military strategy for use against India.

Conclusions

It is clear from the above analysis that India's muted response to the Afghan crisis is due mainly to Pakistan's claim to Kashmir and the involvement of the Super Powers in the Kashmir question. What could then have been done to resolve the Afghan crisis? It must be said that there was no easy military solution to the crisis. The leaders of Pakistan had said more than once that they were not going to take on the Soviet Union, or the Soviet-backed Afghan Government, and commit suicide. At the same time it was cruel of the Soviets to have ignored the existence of the refugees or to call the refugees nomads; they cannot call the freedom fighters mere bandits armed by Pakistan and the United States and ignore the existence of the problem of Afghan insurgency. While it was undeniable that the PRC, the United States, and others were arming the freedom fighters of Afghanistan, no one would pull a trigger without a nationalist cause, and take on the mighty Soviet Union just because somebody offered a gun free.

Hence the need was to find a political solution to the Afghan crisis that is acceptable to the main actors. The primary aim was to see that the three million or more refugees then in Pakistan were enabled to return to their homes in Afghanistan with honour and a sense of security. This they were unlikely to do until they had a reasonable guarantee that they would have a Government that is not bent on destroying their age-old customs, which enjoyed their confidence. It had to be a broad-based Government acceptable to the freedom fighters. It may or may not be a democracy, though democracy is not the exclusive preserve of a few developed societies or a value peculiar is not the exclusive preserve of a few developed societies or a value peculiar to Indian culture.

At the same time it must be remembered that the Soviet Union had proved its ability militarily to intervene in Afghanistan to secure its foreign-policy goals. It must also be recognized that the Soviet Union demonstrated that Moscow would not tolerate a Government hostile to its interests on its southern border. Not that the Soviet Union had a right to impose its will as to the form of government that its small neighbours must live under. (US intervention in Grenada to undo the Marxist take-over of that country only confirmed that essentially the behaviour of the Super Powers is similar in spite of their being two totally different societies.)

Thus the establishment of a broad-based Government in Afghanistan and the restoration of the non-aligned character of Afghanistan were imperative to resolve the crisis not only in theory, but also in a practical sense. It may serve world peace better if the neighbours of the Super Powers follow the policy of non-alignment. In the case of Afghanistan this ought to have been acceptable to the United States on two counts. First, US interests in Afghanistan were only minimal, mainly arising from the desire to check the growth of the Soviet power. Secondly, even prior to the Soviet military invasion, the Americans had perceived Afghanistan as a country falling mainly within the Soviet sphere of influence.

The Soviets, however, needed a face-saving device, as any Power needs. One device was to station UN troops on the Afghan-Pakistani and Afghan-Iranian borders so as to prevent any attacks by insurgents from those sides. Indeed this device could have been used even at an early stage of the crisis. Since the alibi given by the Soviet Union for its presence in Kabul was the external threat to the Karmal Government, the presence of UN troops would have removed such a threat. With the disappearance of the alibi the Soviet Union could have been persuaded to return with honour. But having allowed the crisis to prolong for years, that option might have become unworkable. It was also feared that if the Soviet troops were withdrawn, the Karmal Government would have collapsed any time.

Yet a political solution to the crisis had to be found within the UN framework. It may be recalled that the efforts made by the UN Secretary General's Special Representative, Dieogo Cordovez, in June 1983 had helped in the form of indirect negotiations in arriving at some tentative principles for the withdrawal of the Soviet troops. He had in fact evolved a 4-point formula.[34] These four points were: (1) The Soviets would withdraw their troops from Afghanistan, (2) All external help to the insurgents would cease. (3) The return of the refugees would be facilitated and (4) There would be an international guarantee on the observance of the terms.

There were differences over details. The Soviets wanted to spread troop withdrawals over a period of eighteen months, but Pakistan wanted the process to be completed within six months. Pakistan was also reluctant to accept the Karmal Government; it insisted on a broad-based government. The Soviets were reportedly not averse to changing the Karmal Government in the interest of facilitating a compromise. The prospects of the Soviets staging their first-ever withdrawal of troops from a country that they had chosen to invade were, therefore, seen as very bright.[35] The UN Secretary-General too was very optimistic. However, the West is reported to have dragged its feet. And instead of facilitating the withdrawal of the Soviet troops the United States stepped up its aid to the insurgents and reportedly pressurized Pakistan not to agree to any solution.[36] Obviously it cared more for its power politics than for the return of peace and tranquility to war-torn Afghanistan.

It was felt that the movement to restore democracy in Pakistan when succeeds, it is possible that the Pakistan People's Party (PPP) would emerge as the dominant voice. The PPP had indicated that while it wants the Soviet troops to be withdrawn from Afghanistan, it is not hostile to the continuance of the Karmal Government. Whenever the United States withdraws from Grenada completely, it would set an example for the other Super Power to change its behaviour. The United States was also expected not to place any obstacles in the way of a political solution in Afghanistan.

What could India have done to find a solution? Indira Gandhi was quick to deplore, and rightly, the US-led invasion of Grenada and to demand the withdrawal of all foreign troops from the Caribbean island. But on the Soviet invasion of Afghanistan, India's public stand has not changed. India abstained for the fifth time (1984) on a UN General Assembly resolution demanding the withdrawal of "foreign troops" and urging a political solution of the Afghan crisis.[37] Though for the first time the UN resolution did not specifically name the Soviet Union,[38] the Indian vote continued to be what it was when the UN General Assembly passed its first resolution on the subject early in 1980.

Pakistan had a crucial role. As is well known, it proposed a No War Pact with India under the US pressure in the context of the Congressional consideration of US military assistance. If it had pursued this proposal unreservedly, and not merely as a tactic, India could have been well assured that Pakistan does not believe in a military solution of the Kashmir question. The stage would then be set for India and Pakistan developing a joint approach to the Afghan crisis. India and its six neighbours, which had then formed the South Asian Regional Co-operation (SARC), could have played an important role in the resolution of the Afghan crisis. When the two Super Powers fight for supremacy, it is the small and weak Powers which suffer–just as, when two elephants fight it is the grass that gets destroyed. India is a dominant regional Power. Power has its own responsibilities. India could not have abdicated its responsibility as a dominant Power to tell the Soviet Union to leave the nations in the region alone to decide their internal affairs as they think best. During its ethnic trouble in July 1983 Sri Lanka requested outside Powers for military help. India told foreign Powers to keep their hands off. It could have similarly told the Soviets publicly to leave the countries of the region to themselves. At the meetings of SARC India could have also fallen in line with other members of the group, which publicly had demanded the unconditional and immediate withdrawal of the Soviet troops from Afghanistan.

Notes

1. That is the conclusion that the present author reached after his discussions with some of the top foreign-policy advisers of President Carter as well as Indian diplomats and after listening to Pakistan's Foreign Minister, Sahibzada Yaqub Khan, and other participants present at the conference on "Pakistan and South-West Asia Security" (organized by the Center for Strategic and International Studies, Georgetown University, in Washington, D.C., on 1 December 1982).
2. Cf.Jagat S. Mehta, "Afghanistan: A Neutral Solution," *Foreign Policy*, summer 1982, pp. 142-3.
3. See the text of "President Brezhnev's Answers to Questions by a Pravda Correspondent," USSR Information Branch Press Release (Bombay), 13 January 1980. The Soviets accused Amin of being a CIA agent. See *Times of India* (Bombay), 23 June 1980.
4. "An Underlying Impetus for Soviet Invasion," *Business Week* (New York), 29 September 1980, p. 62.
5. See, for instance, Cyrus Vance, *Hard choices: Critical Years in America's foreign Policy* (New York, 1980), p. 388.

6. *Times of India* (Bombay,) 29 December 1979.
7. *Ibid,* 1 January 1980
8. *Ibid,* 13 January 1980.
9. *Ibid,* 9 January 1980.
10. Vance, n.5, p. 389.
11. However, Carter records that early in October 1979 he had sent several messages warning Brezhnev against any direct intervention in Afghanistan. See his *Keeping Faith: Memoirs of a President* (New York, 1962), p. 264.
12. See Zbigniew Brzezinski, *Power and Principle: Memoirs of the National Security Adviser, 1977-81* (New York, 1983), p. 483.
13. Vance, n. 5, p. 387
14. The present author's interview with Brzezinski, 14 June 1983.
15. Brzezinski says, in the context of the Truman Doctrine: "When President Truman made these commitments to Greece and Turkey, the United States did not have the capacity to defend those areas. The purpose of the commitment ... was to make clear to the Soviets that an intrusion into any one of these designated vital areas would precipitate a massive engagement with the United States." "East Asia and Global Security: Implications for Japan," *Journal of International Affairs,* Vol. 37, No. 1, summer 1983, p. 6.
16. Vance, n.5, p. 367. Some other participants in formulation of foreign policy during the period have confirmed this view, but they wish to remain anonymous.
17. Carter, n. 11, p. 479.
18. See P.M. Kamath, "India in International affairs: Twin Challenges of '80s". *Radical Humanist* (New Delhi), October 1980.
19. "The Kremlin answers Carter," *Newsweek* (New York), 4 February 1980, p. 145.

20. Asked about Afghanistan her apparent unconcern about the Soviet occupation of Afghanistan especially when, in the past, she had been so critical of the United States in Vietnam, Mrs. Indira Gandhi said: "We don't like foreign presences in Afghanistan. But there is a very big difference. Afghanistan happens to be on the Soviet border. It's a neighbour." "Indira Gandhi Tells Why She is Sour on U.S." *U.S. News & World Report,* 15 February 1982, p. 26.

21. *Times of India (*Bombay), 13 February 1980.

22. India, Lok Sabha, *Debates,* 17 June 1980, p. 195.

23. He elabourated to say that it was "pleasant" because that was what India had been seeking. But it was a "surprise" because External Affairs Minister Narasimha Rao had been told during his talks in Moscow (3-8 June 1980) that the Soviet Union would not consider a withdrawal as long as foreign interference on the borders of Afghanistan continued. *Times of India* (Bombay), 23 June 1980.

24. *Indian and Foreign Review (*New Delhi), 15 April 1976, p. 27.

25. Cf. Ian Clarke, "Autonomy and Dependence in Recent Indo-soviet Relations," *Australian Outlook* (Melbourne), Vol. 31, No. 1, April 1977, pp. 155-6.

26. Writing in the *Pakistan Economist,* a senior Pakistani journalist, M.B. Naqvi, called for a rethinking on Pakistan's relations with India in view of the perilous situation created by the Soviet occupation of Afghanistan. See *Times of India* (Bombay) 14 May 1980.

27. Brzezinski says in his memoir that while the Carter Administration was willing to guarantee Pakistan's security *vis-à-vis* the Soviets, it was unwilling to cover any threat from India. See Brzezinski, n. 12, p. 449.

28. Major General (retd) M. Pasricha said in an interview to the *Sunday Observer* (Bombay) that did not see any threat from Pakistan in the next two years. *Sunday Observer,* 27 November 1983. A former US ambassador to Afghanistan, Robert Neuman, said, "Pakistan does not pose a military

threat to India". Ibid., 19 February 1984.

29. Author's talk with Professor Stephen Cohen, University of Illinois, 18 May 1983. Also see *Times of India* (New Delhi), 2 October 1982.

30. *Times of India* (Bombay), 10 February 1984.

31. For instance, Bhutto said in his election broadcast to the nation on 18 November 1970: "Pakistan without Kashmir is like a body without head. The ideology of Pakistan ... will find its logical articulation from our party in its drive for the liberation of Jammu and Kashmir." See *Foreign Affairs Reports* (New Delhi). January 1971, pp. 20-21.

32. Christopher Van Hollen, "The Tilt Policy Revisited: Nixon-Kissinger Geopolitics and South Asia," *Asian Survey* (Berkeley, Calif.), Vol. 20, No. 4, April 1980, p. 348.

33. Henry A. Kissinger, *The White House Years* (Boston, Mass., 1979), pp. 906-7.

34. *New York times,* 16 June 1983, p. 46.

35. *Ibid,* 25 June 1983, p. 3. Cordovez insisted that the Geneva talks had made "further progress" in resolving the Afghan crisis "in spite of hurdles."

36. See Fred Halliday, "The New Cold War: Entering a most Dangerous Phase," *Times of India* (Bombay), 31 October 1983. This has, of course, been denied by Pakistan. *Ibid,* 11 January 1984. A confirmation of this view comes in a interview of Karmal. Says he: "When we came close to resolving the issue last year, Pakistan changed its position after its foreign minister visited the United States for his orders." See "Karmal: I'm Not a Puppet," *Newsweek,* 11 June 1984, p. 10.

37. The thrust of the resolution is similar to that of the Delhi Declaration of 1982 and the NAM summit of March 1983. *Times of India* (Bombay), 25 November 1983.

38. Zia and his aides have often said that the No War Pact cannot apply to Kashmir, which, in their view, is a disputed territory.

5

The Turmoil of Afghanistan: Role of Pakistan, Saudi Arabia and the United States

Sheel K. Asopa

Afghanistan appears to be a perpetually tormented state. Much of its woes can be attributed to its location, topography, natural resources, climatic conditions, historical backgrounds, heterogeneity of population which is a mosaic of varied ethnicities having linkages with the people inhabiting the neighbouring countries, and almost total absence of a centralized power structure which commands authority over its people and territory.

The Setting

Afghanistan is a large country with an area of about 2,52,000 sq. miles dominated at the centre by Hindukush mountains. It is the gateway to oil-rich Central Asia. Its four major cities are Herat in the west, which is also a gateway to Iran, Kandahar in the southeast linking it to Quetta and Mazar-e-sharif in the north with roads to Turkmenistan, Uzbekistan and Kazakhstan. Kabul lies in the east as the western end of the road to the great Pushtun city Peshawar, which runs through Jalalabad and Khyber Pass. It lies in the region which had been the arena of conflict between the three imperial powers-Iran, Britain and Russia. It has been a traditional invasion route for the sub-continent.

This intricate structure of Afghanistan has not been shaped so much by the nature as much by the British and the Russians who in the era of "Great Game" determined the borders of the state keeping their own interest in mind.

The Durand Line Agreement (1893) is a glaring example of thoughtlessness of the British imperialists who arbitrarily divided Afghanistan's Pushtun population in two parts-placing one part in Afghanistan and other in Pakistan. This arrangement was further confirmed by the subsequent treaties in 1905, 1921 and 1930. The area between the Durand line and British India was declared to be a free tribal territory where tribal inhabitants are given complete autonomy. Notwithstanding this arrangement, Afghans are constantly trying for the unification of the two parts and wish to have Pushtunistan as a distinct political entity for themselves. Durand line is a highly sensitive matter between Afghanistan and Pakistan. Afghanistan had refused to recognize Pakistan as an independent state in 1947 and it was the only country which voted against membership of Pakistan in the United Nations. However, the demand of Pushtunistan has been opposed by Pakistan and its supporters in the west and they tend to overlook the emotional and psychological strain caused to the Pushtuns living in Afghanistan (13 million i.e. about 50 % of the population of Afghanistan) and Pakistan (14 million).

Afghanistan's current population is estimated to be 26 million which does not include the four million Afghan refugees belonging to the various ethnicities living in Pakistan. The Afghan population besides 13 million Pushtuns, consists of Tajiks (25 %), Hazaras (19 %) and Uzbeks (6 %). In addition to these there are Turkmen, Aimaq, Baluch, Nuristani and Kizilbashi groups which are despite being small are quite effectively active. After the Saur revolution in 1978, role of Islam in Afghanistan politics has been seen as something very important. In reality Afghanistan had never been under influence of any religious leaders. The separation of state and religion was an important component of Afghan politics. Most Afghans are Sunni Muslims while the Shias are mostly concentrated among the Hazaras.

The economy of Afghanistan is primarily agricultural; growing cereals like wheat, rice and barley. It also produces fruits, raisins, almonds and pistachios. But these are not sufficient for the population of Afghanistan. The economy largely depends on foreign aid given by the international agencies of the United Nations and the European community. However, the mother of all agricultural crops is opium (poppy). In 2006, its production was estimated to be around 6000 tons of opium, enough to produce 600 tons of heroin. Infact, it is the main business of Afghans not withstanding the declared ban on the production of opium and its export from Afghanistan.

A well known commentator[1] has observed that "opium and foreign aid keep the Afghan economy chugging (GDP approx. 30.5 billion PPP). While the drug money at least reaches down to the people, little of the aid percolates down. "It is commonly held that more than 80 % of the aid is actually consumed by the NGOs who are mostly American and European. There are several hundred western NGOs operating in Afghanistan intending to increase the level of education, health, sanitation, human rights, condition of women and children and improving the standard of living of the people there. However, the actual condition of Afghan population speaks openly "how successful these NGOs have been in their jobs?"

The tribals keep selling the opium / heroin secretly and also doing odd jobs for the armed forces of Pakistan and others for money and small arms. The foreign activity in Afghanistan increased during the period of cold war, especially after the exile of King Zahir Shah and Mohammad Daoud's coming to power in 1973. Since Afghanistan formed a buffer state between the Soviet Union and the South-West and South Asia, the United States through its allies in the region–Pakistan and Iran–tried to draw Afghanistan into the US-sponsored Baghdad pact (renamed CENTO in 1958). However, Afghanistan having the experience of British imperialists' tactics of exploiting the interests of the country, continued to maintain the status of "neutrality" all through the cold war period.

Owing to Afghanistan's lack of trust in the West, Soviet Union was the only external power it could rely upon. The USSR respecting the Soviet–Afghan Treaty of Friendship (1921) extended economic help and co-operated in the development projects initiated in Afghanistan. Several western scholars and political analysts viewed the growing friendship between the two countries as a process of "Sovietization" of Afghanistan and raised false alarms provoking the US Administration to enhance anti-Soviet activities in the region.

A brief look at the political developments that took place in Afghanistan during and in between the two *coup d' etat* (1973 and 1978) may be helpful in understanding the situations that led to re–enactment of the "Great game" in Afghanistan played clandestinely in the religious garb provided and financed by Pakistan and Saudi Arabia and sponsored by the United States.

Mohammad Daoud came to power for the first time in 1953 but soon he was ousted by the King Zahir Shah. He was replaced by Mohammad Yusuf but Yusuf too proved a failure and situation in Afghanistan went from bad to worse. Mohammad Daoud again seized power in 1973 by staging a bloodless *coup* against the King. Daoud embarked upon the programme of economic reforms and associated the People's Democratic Party of Afghanistan (PDPA, a leftist party launched in Yusuf's regime) and Perchmites in these reforms projects. Gradually he initiated a process distancing from the Soviet Union and started improving relations with Iran and Pakistan. Later, he dropped some of the PDPA ministers from the cabinet and arrested the leftist leaders (1977) who have been critical of Daoud's policy.

The increasing US interest in Daoud's regime and its indirect relations through Pakistan and Iran was an indication of the preparation for destabilizing the Soviet position in Afghanistan. A South Asian expert in a dispassionate analysis has said:

> Whatever grand schemes Soviet policy makers had for Afghanistan prior to 1978 (Saur revolution), they had never conceived of the country as ripe for a socialist revolution and, indeed, their doubts persisted even after the *coup* (1978) which bought a Marxist regime to power. The ideologues in Moscow viewed Afghanistan as a backward, feudal country, which in its traditional heroic role, would stand as a buffer against the West.[2]

Notwithstanding such balanced observations, the United States continued with its policy of promoting anti-Soviet forces in Afghanistan and drawing them closer to the pro-west countries by offering money, arms and moral support backed by the Islamic clergies raised in Saudi Arabia.

The Saur Revolution: Soviet, US-Pak–Saudi Activities in Afghanistan

The Saur revolution (April 1978) turned the scenario upside down by dethroning Daoud and appointing Noor Mahammad Taraki of the PDPA as President and Prime

Minister of the Democratic Republic of Afghanistan. Selig Harisson in one of his articles (Foreign Policy, winter 1980-81) commented that the "overthrow of Afghan monarchy by Daoud in 1973 was a reaction to American machinations against the Soviet Union in South West Asia. It was also responsible for enhancing the Soviet activity in Afghanistan after the coup of 1973. The US was actively supported by Iran, Pakistan and the Gulf states in its campaign against the Soviet Union". Prior to his dismissal, Daoud was visiting several West Asian countries. He invited the Shah of Iran to visit Kabul. He was planning to visit the US when suddenly on 17 April 1978 the murder of a Paracham leader Mir Akbar Khaiber sparked off a confrontation between the communists and Daoud.

The Saur revolution was an outbreak of several volatile situations like the Shia Revolution in Iran led by Ayatollah R. Khomeini against the US protégé Shah of Iran, Khomeini's threat to spread the Shia Revolution in the Gulf countries and Iraq. Soviet Central Asia had only Afghanistan as a buffer state between the Soviet Union and Iran. The outbreak of Iraq-Iran war, concentration of America's Central Command and Rapid Deployment Force (RDF) in the Arabian Sea and near the Gulf further aggravated the risk to Soviet security in the region.

The new regime under Noor Mahammad Taraki was trying to consolidate its power but it did not have mass following and had a narrow base of support in the Afghan army. Taraki was a hardliner and after assuming power he embarked upon a number of radical socialist reforms which alienated the country's Islamic tribal groups. The colour of the national flag of Afghanistan was also changed from "Islamic Green" to "Socialist Red" which further antagonized the commonmen.

By March 1979, a series of spontaneous tribal revolts spread in more than half of the 28 provinces of Afghanistan.

The Afghan army was not in a position to handle the situation. Taraki was removed from power in September and his position was taken over by Hafizullah Amin. Taraki died soon after. Amin's regime was also short. Arnold Anthony has observed: "....... Insurgency was everywhere; the Government could control individual cities by dispatching the dwindling military forces.... Not even Kabul was safe from insurgents' attack and military rebellions."[3] In December 25, 1979, Soviet military intervened in Afghanistan.

Hafizullah Amin was assassinated and Babrak Karmal of Parchem faction of the PDPA was installed with the Soviet military help. Soviet occupation of Afghanistan continued for a decade but inspite of several serious measures the Soviet-backed government could not check the increasing strength of the Pak–Saudi trained *Mujahideen* and rising influence of Islamic militants.

Commenting on the Soviet intervention in Afghanistan Robert H. Donaldson has written:

> "From Moscow's standpoint; (collapse of pro-Soviet regime) would have posed a security threat of substantial dimensions since a successor regime would probably had a strong Islamic overtones, blended with anti-Soviet resentment and possible American and Chinese backing. If Afghans were to join Iran and Pakistan as militant Islamic outposts on the borders of the USSR, the combined religious and nationalist lure might well have become irresistible for millions of Soviet Muslims in the region."[4]

Donaldsons' prediction has come true. The Soviet troops withdrew from Afghanistan soon after Geneva Accord of April 1988. They did not make any arrangement for the safety of Soviet-backed Nazibullah government in Afghanistan. The Islamic forces trained in Pakistani *madarssas* and training centers run with the financial support given by Saudi Arabia started taking position in Afghanistan. Islamic militants initiated repressive measures against the leftists and terrorized the masses.

In post-Soviet Afghanistan a number of Islamic parties emerged. They were mostly anti-Shia and adherents of Wahabi ideology. The religions factions reflected the ethno-linguistic overtures or "fault lines" which are in abundance in Afghanistan.

Rise of Islamic Organization and Parties

The Afghan Islamists of the fifties and sixties have been under the influence of Muslim brotherhood's ideology, which is opposed to separation of state of Islam. The Afghan *Jamiat-e-Islami* was formed in Kabul by the teachers of the faculty of Theology at the University of Kabul and (Ghulam Mohammad Niyazi and Burhanuddin Rabbani) and students of faculty of engineering (Hekmatyar and Massoud). The *Jamiat* shared the ideology of Pakistani *Jammat-e-Islami* and participated in revolts against the leftist governments in Afghanistan (1963–1973).

Gulbuddin Hekmatyar's *Hezb-i-Islami* (Party of Islam) was shaped on Stalinist model with a cell structure and pyramidal chain of authority with himself at the top. A splinter group of *Hezb-i-Islami* emerged under Maulana Younis Khalis in 1979. Another Islamic party *Ittehad-i-Islami*, was formed by Abdul Rasul Sayyaf a teacher at the University of Kabul. It was follower of Wahabi anti-Shia ideology propagated by Saudi Arabia *Harkat-i-Inquilab-i-Islami* established by Maulana Nabi Mohammad had undertaken the revolt against the pro-Soviet governments. These parties enjoyed support of Pakistan, Saudi Arabia and patronage of the United States which was too keen to eradicate the Soviet influence from Afghanistan.[5]

After the Soviet withdrawal and later collapse of the Soviet Union all these Islamic parties backed by their mentors entered into the race for grabbing power in Afghanistan. After the fall of Nazibullah government, Nawaz Sharif tried to break coalition government but failed. Gulbuddin Hekmatyar who was under the influence of Pakistan and also enjoyed backing of the United States was opposed to inclusion of Tajik and Uzbek leaders in the coalition government.

Hekmatyar had different plans of his own. Instead of joining the coalition and forming a broad based transitional government, from his bases south and east of Kabul, launched a barrage of rockets against the city in 1992 which killed over 2000 civilians. Then he attempted to break the unity of the coalition partners by putting one against other. He provoked anti-Shia's Sayyaf to initiate confrontation between Massoud's government forces and the Shi'ite militants in Kabul, and then with Dostum and Mujaddidi. Hekmatyar succeeded in weakening of the Rabbani government and ultimately assuming power in 1996, but in the process he exacerbated the anarchic conditions which paved the way for success of Taliban. He also lost his credibility in the eyes of Pakistani sponsors as a vehicle for their ambitions in Afghanistan.

Hekmatyar's position was weakened by his disastrous defeat at the hand of the Taliban. He was seen as a great liability by the Kabul coalition which was headed by him. His forces were first to surrender and defect in large numbers before the Taliban forces in Jalalabad and Sarobi. However, he was fortunate enough not to lose the support of the Pakistani rulers and *Jammat-e-Islami* which had been at the back of Hekmatyar in his campaign to raise the Pushtun power base through Pushtun *mujahideen* parties in Afghanistan.

Zia-ul-Haq driven by his intense Islamic zeal and anti-communist mind-set provided maximum assistance to the *Jihadi* elements in Afghanistan. His policy was seen as consistent with long term interests of Pakistan. Because of the cultural affinities of Sunni Muslim, Pushtuns on either side of the border, and through the influence of the Pushtuns in the upper echelons of the army and the bureaucracy, the policy in practice tilted in favour of Pushtun *mujahideen* parties. It was thought that a friendly Pushtun-led post-Soviet government in Kabul would pre-empt the revival of the demand for a "Pushtunistan," which has kept relations between the two countries strained since independence of Pakistan.[6]

Zia-ul-Haq too, favoured Hekmatyar for realizing his ambitions. He was known as effective and charismatic and his links with Pakistan's own *Jammat* and Islamist parties in Afghanistan further strengthened his position. Hekmatyar became the chief beneficiary of the largesse from US and Saudi Arabia. Money and arms channeled through Pakistan Inter Services Agency (ISI) gave him much leverage during the *Jihad* in the traditional patron-client relationship.

The Taliban

Taliban raised by Pakistan and strengthened by Saudi Arabia (for spreading *jihadi* zeal in Afghanistan and Central Asia) and the United States (earlier for eliminating the influence of communists in Afghanistan and later for seeking their assistance in constructing gas pipeline from Turkmenistan to Pakistan via Afghanistan to be exported to European countries and others in the international market) have been the greatest tormentors of Afghans. After coming to power they lost interest in the gas pipeline project of America, stabilizing their own power by crippling down the Afghanistan's entire population and crushing the voices of dissent if at all there were any.

Taliban is a Persian (also Pushtu) plural of Talib (religious student in Arabic) which is used to address the religious students of humble status learning Koran and the Hadith in rural based or privately run *Madarssas* in the Muslim countries of the Sub-continent.[7]

Ahmad Rashid in his well researched and documented book "Taliban" has written in great detail about their origin, growth, development and activities in Afghanistan. According to him the young man were literally "Children of Jihad" most of them born in Pakistan refugee camps, some were war orphans. They received their basic education in the network of *madarssas* run for their benefit in Pakistan's North West Frontier Province and in Baluchistan. Besides Pushtu, the only other language they knew was Urdu and not Persian which is the *lingua franca* of their homeland. They were therefore basically rootless and receptive to their influence to which they were exposed in Pakistan. The chief influence on the ideology of Taliban was the *Jamiat-e-Ulema-Islami* (JUI) who ran their *madarssas.* The JUI was ideologically linked to the Deobandi School in India which has trained generations of Afghan Ulema. The JUI also acts as a political party and had won some seats in Baluchistan Assembly but always remained in opposition to the government.

JUI played an important role after Benazir Bhutto's PPP came to power in 1993 elections. Its leader Maulana Fazlur Rehman was made Chairman of the National Assembly's Committee of Foreign Affairs. It enabled him to influence Pakistan's Afghanistan policy. General Naseerullah Babar who had been the advisor to Benazir's father on Afghanistan affairs also joined Benazir and during that period ISI and the Ministry for Foreign Affairs were relegated to the back seat. Fazlur Rehman who was the main supporter of Taliban advocated their importance in the context of Afghanistan and lobbied in the capitals of Europe and in the United States. He made Gulf States and Saudi Arabia deeply interested in Taliban and drew enormous funds for the Taliban from these oil-rich states of the Muslim world.

The Collapse of the Soviet Union and emergence of independent political entities in the post Soviet Central Asia enhanced Pakistan's interest as well as prospects in the region.

Islamabad started dreaming about its privileged position in Central Asia via Afghanistan which with the help of Islamists parties and Taliban could be made possible. However, internal disorder and civil strife in Afghanistan and outbreak of full scale hostility between various ethnic factions controlled by strong and influential charismatic leaders shattered its dream for a while.

The January 1994 internal war in Afghanistan made the use of traditional northern route from Peshawar via Kabul and the Salang tunnel impracticable. Pakistan's continuing support to Hekmatyar turned the Afghan government hostile to Pakistan. In view of these geo-political difficulties in the way of its dream project of gaining control over the affairs of the Central Asian region, Pakistan started exploring the possibility a new Southern route from Baluchistan to Turkmenistan via Kandahar and Herat. The stakes of Pakistani ambitions were further higher when international competition for carving out spheres of interest in Central Asia between the major powers intensified in mid-nineties. The politics of oil and gas and oil pipelines further drew Pakistan in the region's politics.

The southern route became an obsession with Pakistani rulers. Babar visited the area and surveyed the highway inside Afghanistan and announced the experimental use of the road by Pakistani traders-the convoy was to propel the Taliban onto Afghanistan. In order to raise the funds to rebuild the highway between Kandahar and Herat, Babar took ambassadors of six countries to visit the route. In the meantime, Taliban succeeded in capturing Kandahar. General Babar set up an Afghan trade development cell in his ministry which became a source of considerable logistic and infrastructural support to Taliban–a microwave telephone network for Kandahar linked to the Pakistani grid, and internal wireless network for Taliban field operations, repairs at the Airport of Kandahar and of the captured aircrafts by Pakistani technicians.

The Taliban group headed by Mullah Omar worked to end the activities of ex-*mujahideen* warlords who were preying on local population. The first breakthrough came with the seizure in October 1994 of the major trucking stopover of Spin Boldak and the huge Pasha arms depot near the Pakistani border; earlier these were controlled by Hekmatyar's forces. About 200 Taliban took parts in this event. The famous 30 truck Pakistani convoy was accompanied by ISI officers with the Taliban riding shotguns. They were stopped by warlords' militants for political ransom. On November 3, Taliban reinforcement from the Pakistan freed the convoy and swept into Kandahar and captured the city in two days fighting.

The Taliban acquired planes, helicopters, tanks and armoured vehicles in Kandahar and moved to Uruzgan in the north and to the Zabul in the north west which they could take without having fired any shot. Taliban started taking sides in local conflicts between the warlords but seemingly maintained that they were neutral in the power struggle between Rabbani and Hekmatyar. In the meantime they took Helmand and Gazni and moved toward Kabul. Hekmatyar's forces staged a retreat to Sarobi in February 1995 leaving Kabul to Taliban. The Taliban after capturing Kabul settled down in power and started carving out their own strategies for further expansion of their power and influence in Central Asia.

The Taliban project of taking over Afghanistan and spreading *jihad* were supported by the United States. The US administration saw Taliban as a disciplined, efficient, committed people capable of bringing about law and order and political stability in war-torn country. Besides, the US hoped to get Taliban support in bringing the Turkmen gas pipeline to Pakistan *via* Afghanistan to facilitate gas supply in international markets.

Pakistan still had to find engagements for the *mujahideen* who had been rendered jobless after the Soviet withdrawal from Afghanistan. Some of the *mujahideen* had returned back to their homelands but still in large numbers were there awaiting new assignments. To get rid of them, Pakistan diverted the foreign terrorists to Jammu and Kashmir, Chechnya, Egypt, Philippines, Algeria, Indonesia and Central Asian republic to spread *jihad,* organize Islamic groups and train local terrorists.

Pakistan's strategy in Afghanistan has been successful till Taliban came to power making the Northern Alliance shrunk to a small area. Taliban, who were being financed by Pakistan gradually developed their own interests and strategy. Osama bin Laden's arrival in Afghanistan strengthened their position as he himself could finance the Taliban and the *Jihadi* movement.

Pakistan's position was precarious. It did not wish to leave the company of Taliban and at the same time it did not want to handover the total control over Afghanistan to Osama bin Laden and Taliban alone. Ever since its involvement in Afghanistan since 1978 Pakistan has become a training ground for terrorists of all kinds from different countries of Muslim world. *Jihad* in Afghanistan and its possible export to Central Asia was supported by the United States too.

However, terrorists attack on world Trade Towers and Pentagon changed the scenario. Pakistan invested a lot in its Afghan policy during the decades following the Soviet occupation of Afghanistan. The fall of Taliban and defeat of Osama bin Laden and Mullah Omar in US led war against terrorism in Afghanistan; large number of terrorists crossed the border in Pakistan. Mullah Omar and Osama bin Laden too are hiding into Pakistan. The United States is aware of this fact but for whatever reasons, it tends to pretend that as if inspite of Pakistan's full support the coalition forces were not able to find these two who have been instrumental in terrorist attack on the United States.

There is no dearth of evidence to prove Pakistan's role in creating terrorist-outfits training and financing them and providing help through its intelligence agency.

Recently *National Commission on Terrorists Attack upon the United States Report*[8] has highlighted the role of Pakistan in fostering terrorism and terrorists on its soil. The report has pointed to the involvement of Pakistan with *al Qaida*. Pakistan did not break its connection with *al Qaida* until after 9/11, although it was harbouring Bin Laden. The report also asserts that Pakistan benefited from the Taliban-*al Qaida* relationship as Osama bin Laden's camps trained fighters for Pakistan's ongoing struggle with India over Kashmir. Arnand de Borchgrave commenting on a document of Pakistani origin stated: "the imprints of every major act of international Islamist terrorism invariably passes through Pakistan right from 9/11, where virtually all participants were trained, resided or met in, coordinated with or received funding from or through Pakistan".

The Pakistan-terrorism nexus and its role in spreading terrorism through Taliban is a known fact. In fact this nexus and its role and impact have had America's blessings. The US–led war against terrorism in Afghanistan with the mandate of the United Nations and support of its members was to take revenge for terrorists attack on America and not for eradicating terrorism or punishing those who continue preparing terrorists in their country.

Role of Saudi Arabia and Iran

Iran and Saudi-Arabia are competitors in Afghanistan as both are interested in spreading political and religious influences in this state which has been a gateway to the Soviet Central Asia.

In the Arab world, from the immediate post-war years up to defeat of Nasser in the Arab-Israel war of 1967, Egypt had been the sole unquestioned leader of the Muslim world. Shah of Iran, another powerful leader of the Muslim world was not interested so much in religious influence, as much in strengthening Iran as a bulwark against the expansion of the communism in the northern tier and West Asia.

After the fall of Nasser and Nasserism, Saudi Arabia gained the leverage to position itself as a leader of the Muslim world. However, after the Ayatollah Khomeini's revolution in Iran and Khomeini's call for Shia revolution in Muslim countries where Shia's are in majority or minority came as a deadly challenge to the Saudi kingdom. Khomeini, after throwing away the Iranian monarchy maintained that monarchy is incompatible with Islam and Saudi-Arabia's close relations with the United States are detrimental to the interest of the Muslim world. The Saudi's were genuinely alarmed when a group of zealots challenging the legitimacy of the royal family occupied the great Mosque in Mecca in 1979. Saudi's were eager to join the Pak-US campaign for spreading Islam in Afghanistan to de-stabilize the Soviet Union. Hence they willingly financed the *mujahideen* and later the Taliban in Afghanistan. The move was also to counter balance the Shia revolution in Iran.

Iran which is one of the closest neighbours of Afghanistan, has always taken interest in the policies of Afghanistan. The inhabitants of Hazara are of Iranian origin and the followers of Shi'ite sect of Islam. Anwar-Ul-Haq Ahady has traced the history of Saudi-Iranian interest in Afghanistan against the backdrop of their rivalry for leadership of the Muslim world.[9]

Iran maintained a low profile during the Iraq-Iran war period, which coincided with the period of Soviet occupation of Afghanistan. Checking the Khomeini's revolution at the gate of Afghanistan was the major objective of Moscow which compelled it to make its military presence felt by the revolutionary Iran and also the western forces that have been concentrating around the Gulf and in the Arabian Ocean.

Iranian policy underwent a sea change at the end of the cold war. It became proactive and cultivated relations with the non-Pushtun parties-the *Jamiat* and *Wahdat* and Uzbeks and the Ismailis-to counter the Peshawar based Pushtun parties particularly those with a pro-Saudi bias. The coalition of largely non-Pushtun parties that succeeded Nazibullah was a great triumph for Iran. After the Taliban's ascendancy to power in Kabul, these parties formed the Northern Alliance based in Mazar-e-Sharif which was actively supported by Iran even to the extent of air lifting arms, fuel and other supplies to them.

The reactions of Russia and the Central Asian Republics (CARS) to the Taliban seizure of Kabul were critical. Russia and the five CARS expressed concerns at the Almaty emergency meeting convened on October 4, 1996. Turkmenistan did not participate in this meeting and also the Moscow meeting in May 1997 as it was interested in seeking Taliban's cooperation in exporting the Turkmen oil and gas through Afghanistan. In view of this possibility, Pakistan, Saudi Arabia and the UAR accorded premature recognition to Taliban. Anthony Hymen has observed that the real targets of the statements and communiqués of the CARS and Russia were not the Taliban as such but their Pakistani and Saudi backers.[10]

The Pakistanis, Iranians and the Saudis could not be effective in increasing the woes of Afghans had the US not given support and protection–first to the *mujahideen* and Islamic militants and later to Hekmatyar and then to the

Taliban. It was the US backing that encouraged the Pak-Saudi nexus to takeover the command of Islamic movement and *Jihadi* campaign in Afghanistan and its neighbourhood in the post Soviet period.

The Role of United States

The US policy in Afghanistan since the Soviet invasion was to move in by proxy. The US President Jimmy Carter and later Ronald Reagan had assigned the CIA to spend what was to amount to US $ 3 billion to support anti-Soviet force in Afghanistan. The major decision making was left to Pakistan which had become a front line state in cold war. Even after the arrival of Taliban, the United States continued to act through Pakistan.

The passive US acquiescence in an eventual Taliban take over was gradually engineered by its Pakistani and Saudi allies to facilitate the UNOCAL game plan. UNOCAL, a consortium of US oil companies formed to exploit the hydrocarbon reserves of Central Asian–Caspian region (Turkmenistan has world's third largest gas reserves and potential oil and gas reserves of Kazakhstan and Azerbaijan). UNOCOL and its Saudi partners, *Delta* had hired every available Americans of those involved in Afghan operations during *jihad* years.[11]

The United State was made to believe that Taliban are capable of protecting the oil and gas interest of the west. They would provide security to the roads and for the oil and gas pipelines connecting Central Asian states to the international markets. The pipelines would exclude Iran and pass through Pakistan. However, the stories of atrocities committed by Taliban on Afghans and cruelest possible treatment given to the women and children, total ban on the education and health facilities and entertainment and curbs on individual freedom that reached through the diplomats, journalists, businessman and media reports disillusioned the Americans although it was difficult for them to discard the Taliban or take immediate corrective measures. In 1997, in a policy statement to the Senate, the Assistant Secretary of South Asian Affairs said that "Washington's objective was a Afghan government that is multi-ethnic, broad-based and that observed the international norms of behavior." Later after the visit to some of the Afghan refugee camps Madeline Albright, the US secretary of State told the journalists that: "I think it is clear that why we are opposed to the Taliban, because their approach to the human rights, their despicable treatment of women and children and their general lack of respect for human dignity... that is more reminiscent of the past then the future."

However, not withstanding such candid statements and the mind boggling report on Afghanistan prepared by various agencies of the UN and the NGO's, the United States and its European allies did not stop financial help to Taliban in the name of humanitarian aid. It was given to the country which under Taliban held the world's worst record in infants and maternal mortality, life expectancy, adult and female literacy, access to the safe drinking water, the proportion of mentally and physically disabled people, the danger of landmines and the number of people dependent on food support.[12] During the Taliban regime it is estimated that over a million people were killed, 700,000 women were made widows. Protests by UN agencies and NGO's against the barbarous rule of Taliban went unnoticed.

The human tragedy was further aggravated by Taliban's promotion of drugs trade, heroin labouratories, *mafia* groups smuggling contrabands which, in fact had been the source of revenue for the Taliban rulers of Afghanistan. Pakistani exporters and smugglers have been more than willing to pay transit taxes to Taliban and voluntarily finance their operations.[13]

The rise and fall of Taliban, the event of 9 /11 and its aftermath, the US-led war against terrorism in Afghanistan with effortfully drawn mandate of the UN and through multifarious pressures extracted support of the permanent members of the Security Council, the US first devastated Afghanistan through carpet-bombing in search of Taliban's hideouts and abodes of Osama bin Laden and Mullah Omar and now after the war has undertaken the task of reconstruction of Afghanistan–not only of it roads, buildings, electricity-water facilities, educational and health institutions but revival of law and order, police and civil administration, agencies of day to day supervision of needs of people and review of their difficulties and problems. In US style of thinking, establishment of western–style democracy, restoring respect for human rights of women and children notwithstanding the anti–women practices introduced by conservative Muslims is also given importance.

Raising a strong broad–based national police and Afghans-based national army, restoring unity amongst various tribal groups, bringing warlords to the negotiation table and make them understand the value of putting national interest on the top and keeping tribal differences, rivalries, inequalities etc. at the lowest level in order to construct an integrated and properly adjusted inter-dependent society also needs attention. Economic reconstruction work has already started and the Asian Development Bank (ADB), the UNDP (United Nations Development Program), World Bank and several other international agencies and the NGO's are engaged in the task of economic and social re-building of war-devastated Afghanistan.

However the most important challenge in the way of reconstruction or revival of Afghanistan as an independent sovereign state having total control over its people, territory and resources is how to stop the re-emergence of Taliban which has started sprouting here and there again with the help of same agencies which had contributed to their birth, growth, strength and their coming to power in the past? Who are these agencies? Perhaps it is known to all those who fought the war against terrorism along with America.

The Bush administration mobilized the NATO to take charge of Kabul's security and maintain law and order besides handling the Taliban menace. This move reflects a sense of urgency in Washington that nearly five years after the "ouster" of Taliban, progress towards peace and stability in Afghanistan has been painfully slow. However, Washington is not able to reconcile the deeper tension between the US interest in Afghanistan and those in Pakistan. Despite being genuinely interested in bringing about a rapid normalization of the situation in post 9/11 Afghanistan, the US is unwilling to confront the sources of regional instability in Pakistan. Unless the US comes to terms with this core contradiction in its policy towards South West Asia, strengthening the military, stabilization efforts and committing more economic resources for development in Afghanistan are not likely to bear fruits.

In the immediate post 9/11 years the US aid to Afghanistan was about $ 10 billion per annum but the actual economic disbursement was just one billion dollars. For 2004, this was raised to 1.6 billion dollars to be spent in reconstruction in Afghanistan. However, the key to success lies in America's Pakistan policy. It would remain illusive as long as Washington remains unwilling to squeeze Islamabad into full fledged co operation in isolating and defeating the forces threatening stability and peace in Afghanistan.

Reconstruction of Afghanistan

Afghanistan's problems are awesome and reconstruction is not a straight-forward task. The crushing of Taliban is only the first stage in the return of Afghanistan to international community. To put the country back on its track, it is necessary to accomplish the inter-connected task of reconstructing the state, rebuilding trust at elite and mass level, overcoming the threat of warlordism, redeveloping shattered infrastructure and meeting the urgent needs of the most vulnerable Afghans without disrupting the market mechanisms and norms of reciprocity which have sustained a large proportion of the population through decades of turmoil.

One of the greatest challenges in Afghanistan is rebuilding of appropriate state instrumentalities. The task is much larger than "assembling" a government. The state in Afghanistan ceased to exist years ago. From 1980s, the ruling regimes were dependent for their survival on a flow of resources from the USSR, which occupied Afghanistan in 1979. After the collapse of Soviet Union in 1991, this supply-line was disrupted which created a crisis for the ruling elite. How to keep the state intact in face of rising economic difficulties and mushrooming socio-political problems? On collapse of Taliban regime in 2001, an agreement was signed in Bonn (5 December) between the anti-Taliban Afghan groups to put Afghanistan on a new path of political development directed not at dividing the "spoils of victory" but at reconstructing institutions. The "Interim Administration" headed by Hameed Karzai was charged with steering the process and leading the nation to holding free and fair election in 2004; thus, to reconstitute state's functions and win sufficient legitimacy to sustain them.

In a democratic system people's mandate is secured through elections. "Is democracy feasible in post-Taliban Afghanistan? Despite occasional election processes adopted during Daoud's period and later after the Saur Revolution in 1978, they have not been genuinely democratic neither in nature nor in practice. In the absence of any past experience of living under a democratic system, it is difficult to introduce democracy in its prevalent form. There are many questions: Should the institution of the state be centralized or divided? Should the constitutional structure be monarchical, presidential or parliamentary? Should the voting system be chosen or foster majoritarianism or proportionality? Should the political institutions be designed to bring together ethnic groups in a grand coalition or should they be rather designed to foster cross ethnic alliance formation? How should the institutions of state and civil society relate to each other? This question has to be answered by Afghans because the wisdom which they would find will shape the future of their country."[14] William Maley in his article titled the "Reconstruction of Afghanistan" in *Worlds in Collision* has raised these questions. To him ensuring an adequate degree of elite stability is a major problem. The International Security Assistance Force (ISAF) is there to ensure the security in the state but reconstitution of an indigenous Afghan national army is essential. Equally important is the revival of civilian policing system. The military forces normally used to destroy or deter the external enemy, whereas the civilian police are concerned with the enforcement of law, preferably with the minimal use of force if possible.

Hameed Karzai has often repeated a commitment to eradicating corruption which in the past prior to the Saur Revolution in 1978 had completely delegitimized the state. Maley has reminded about the "three important institutions provided at the Bonn Agreement of December 2001: a Civil Service Commission, a Judicial Service Commission and a Human Rights Commission. They would supply mechanism for a constructive separation of power for 'guarding the guardians.' It would be tragedy if they would wither."[15]

There are some serious threats in reconstruction of Afghanistan. One of the greatest threats comes from the resurgence of warlordism in Afghanistan. The blithe way in which the US funded the anti-Taliban groups in southern and eastern Afghanistan has led to their rapid and effective re-emergence. Secondly, the longer stay of Afghans in refugee camps is leading to unlearning of their entrepreneurial skills and their expertise in forming and looking after the herds. The war related trauma is another difficult challenge to be met with. Large number of Afghans old man, women and children has been made disabled, orphans and widows and having witnessed the brutal killings and tortures they have become psychological wrecks. They need to be given proper treatment, attention and social and financial security which is possible only with the external financial assistance and supervision.

Besides the psychological trauma there is also a kind of fear in the minds of Afghan youth. They think that the moment foreign forces leave Afghanistan they would again be left to be butchered either by Taliban or exploited by the Islamic zealots. The memories of their past experience when in 1990s the US after the Soviet withdrawal from Afghanistan had just walked away leaving the country exposed to Pakistan's clumsy meddling and to the fantasies of the American oil and gas companies.[16] It is important that the wider world does not lose sight of Afghanistan.

The main threat to Afghanistan's reconstruction, stability and survival as an independent sovereign state comes from Pakistan. It is particularly important that Pakistan is made to realize that the days in which it could claim the right to determine who should rule Afghanistan are over. No other country has brought more misery to Afghanistan them Islamabad, although Islamabad's own gains from its years of manipulations have proved negligible.[17] It is not surprising that in his briefing to the UN Security Council on February 6,

2002, Ambassador Lakhdar Brahimi, the Special Representative of the Secretary General for Afghanistan stated that "proposal for expansion of ISAF beyond Kabul to the rest of Afghanistan should receive favourable and urgent consideration by the Security Council."[18] There is an overwhelming support to this proposal in Afghanistan. The interim government too backed this proposal of increasing the size and area of activity of the ISAF in Afghanistan. Ambassador Brahimi remarked to the Security Council that "the road is still very long and fraught with dangers". It is almost a warning that the Afghan people should not be left to tread that road alone.

Notes

1. Guruswamy, Mohan, "Notes from Afghanistan," *World Focus,* Vol. 24, No. 8, August 2003, p. 21.
2. Weinbaum, Marvin G., "The Soviet in Afghanistan: Risks, costs and Opportunities" in Edward A. kolodzieji: & Roger E. Kanet, ed., *The Limits of Soviet Power in the Developing World,* (London: Macmillan, 1989), p. 228.
3. Anthony Arnold, "Afghanistan: The Soviet Invasion in Perspective," (New Delhi, Arnold Heinemann, 1985) p. 86.
4. Donaldson, Robert H. "Soviet Policy in South Asia," in Raymond Duncan, ed., *Soviet Policy in Third World,* (Newyork : Permagon Press, 1980) p. 227.
5. Angelo Rasanayagam, "Taliban Fundamentalism: The Turmoils of Afghanistan." Review article in *World Affairs,* Vol. 3, No. 2 (April–June 1999) p. 125.
6. *Ibid.* p. 127.
7. The 9/11 Commission Report. Final Report of the National Commission on Terrorists attacks upon the United States. Executive summery, p. 7. see in Param Sinha Palit," The 9 /11Report : Reaffirming Pakistan–Terrorism Nexus," Strategic Analysis, (July–Sept. 1994) pp. 265–268.

8. "Pakistan treating Bin Laden for Kidney Disease," July 25, 2004 at http://davinci.dilyiks.com/story/2004/7/25/164937/572 also quoted in Param Sinha Palit. *Op cit.*
9. William Maley, ed., "Fundamentalism Reborn: Afghanistan and Taliban" (New York 1998), pp. 242 (See Ahady's Article in part II of this Volume).
10. *Ibid.*
11. For details see Ahmad Rashid, "Taliban : Islam, oil, and the New Great Game in Central Asia" (I.B. Tauris Publishers, London, New York : 2001).
12. *Ibid.* pp. 105–116.
13. *Ibid,* pp. 117-127.
14. William Maley in "World in Collision" edited by Ken Booth and Tim Dunne (Palgrave Macmillan : New York : 2002.
15. *Ibid,* p. 185-186.
16. *Ibid,* p. 186.
17. *Ibid,* p. 191.
18. *Ibid,* p. 192.

6

Post 9/11 US Intervention in Afghanistan: Some Legal and Political Questions

Uttara Sahasrabuddhe

Background

The roots of current instability in Afghanistan can be traced back to the period much beyond the Soviet invasion of that country in December 1979. The kingdom of Afghanistan has existed since the nineteenth century.[1] In 1973, King Zahir Shah was overthrown in a coup and Afghanistan became a democracy. Mohammad Daoud, the cousin of the dethroned King became the Prime Minister. The coup was followed by many years of instability. The traditional ethnic leaders as well as the leftist People's Democratic Party of Afghanistan (PDPA) opposed Daoud's rule. The leftist military officers led another coup in April 1978 to overthrow the Daoud government. Daoud was killed in this coup. Soon the traditional ethnic leaders and Islamic fundamentalist elements began an armed revolt against the PDPA rule. Confusion prevailed for some time, as much of rural Afghanistan went under the control of traditional leaders. On 25 December 1979, the Soviet forces entered Afghanistan and established control on Kabul. However, the traditional and Islamic elements continued to fight against leftist rule as well as Soviet occupation. For next almost a decade, they were aided in this effort in many ways by external powers like Pakistan and the US. In April 1988, the US, the Soviet Union, Afghanistan and Pakistan signed an agreement, helped by the good offices of the UN Secretary-General, which facilitated the withdrawal of Soviet forces from Afghanistan. The process of Soviet withdrawal was completed in February 1989.

However, various rebel factions in Afghanistan had not signed the agreement; and these factions continued their fight against the Najibullah government. Thus, the civil war in Afghanistan continued even after Soviet withdrawal. The continued struggle led ultimately to the fall of Najibullah government in 1992. On 24 April 1992, leaders of the Mujaheddin forces–except Gulbuddin Hekmatyar–agreed to form a transitional government. In July 1992, Burhannudin Rabbani was declared President of the Islamic State of Afghanistan. According to the agreement–the Peshawar Accord–Rabbani was supposed to relinquish power in October, but he did not do so. In the following year, President Rabbani and eight other Afghan leaders negotiated two peace accords. One was signed in Islamabad on 7 March 1993; and the other was agreed upon in Jalalabad on 18 May 1993. By these accords, the Afghan leaders agreed to form a government for 18 months, to initiate the electoral process, to write new constitution for Afghanistan, and to establish a defence council to set up a national army. However, despite all these positive developments, fighting was soon resumed. Kabul was besieged once again, this time by the Taliban, i.e., the Islamic students' movement. The Taliban was rooted in Kandahar. It comprised mostly of the sons and orphans of the Mujahideen–the religious elements fighting against the Soviet occupation with the support of Pakistan and the US–who were brought up in refugee camps in Pakistan. The Taliban had taken control of much of southern and western Afghanistan, including Kandahar and Herat, by early 1995. In September, the Taliban seized the control of Kabul. Rabbani joined an opposition alliance, which came to be known as the Northern Alliance. The Taliban soon controlled much of Afghanistan, while the Northern Alliance held territory only in the north. Civil war in Afghanistan continued between 1997 and 2000, as the Taliban and the Northern Alliance continued fighting.[2] However, the military positions of the two factions changed very little.

The Islamist regime of the Taliban had given refuge in Afghanistan to Osama bin-Laden, the supreme leader of the terrorist organisation Al Qaeda, and also to some other leaders, since 1996. Al Qaeda was involved in the 7 August 1998 bombing of US embassies in Dar-es-Salam (Tanzania) and Nairobi (Kenya) which claimed hundreds of lives. US President Clinton had responded to these incidents by firing cruise missiles at the al Qaeda training camps in Afghanistan. Following the 9/11 terrorist attacks in the US, the American intelligence agencies collected several proofs of al Qaeda's involvement in the incident. The US Government was determined to retaliate and consequently, Bush administration declared a "war against terrorism". It prepared for an attack on the Taliban-controlled Afghanistan–an operation that came to be known as "Operation Enduring Freedom". Before launching the attack, the US President Bush gave an ultimatum to the Taliban regime, asking them to hand over al-Qaeda leaders located in Afghanistan to the United States; release all imprisoned foreign nationals, including American citizens; protect foreign journalists, diplomats, and aid workers in Afghanistan; close terrorist training camps in Afghanistan and "hand over every terrorist and every person and their support structure to appropriate authorities; and give the United States full access to terrorist training camps to verify their closure. The combined American and British forces began bombing targets in Afghanistan from 7 October 2001.

War in Afghanistan[3]

America began strikes in Afghanistan as a response to the 11 September terrorist arracks. The American strategy was to help the Northern Alliance fight against the Taliban and the al Qaeda. The first wave of attacks was carried out solely by American and British forces. American and British forces began aerial bombing campaign on 7 October 2001, targeting Taliban forces and Al-Qaeda. The capital city of Kabul was attacked, as well as the airport and military nerve-centre of Kandahar, and the city of Jalalabad where many terrorist training camps were located. The Taliban condemned these attacks and called them an "attack on Islam." In a pre-recorded video tape, Osama bin Laden claimed that the United States would fail in Afghanistan and then collapse, just as the Soviet Union did, and called for a jihad against the entire non-Muslim world. In the next stage of the air campaign, the U.S. used cluster bombing against the Taliban defences. Foreign fighters from al-Qaeda took over security in the Afghan cities, demonstrating the instability of the Taliban regime. As the next step in the attack, the Northern Alliance troops planned to capture Mazar-i-Sharif, thereby cutting off Taliban supply lines. The battle for Mazar-i-Sharif began on 9 November 2001 and was over the same day with the Northern Alliance taking the city. Following this, the Northern Alliance forces made rapid advances in northern provinces. The Taliban were forced to flee from Kabul on 12 November. Areas along the Iranian border fell quickly thereafter, including the key city of Herat. Local Pashtun commanders and warlords took over the control throughout northeastern Afghanistan, including Jalalabad where Taliban training camps had existed. By the middle of December, Kandahar too fell in the hands of the allied forces.

The war was far from over, however, and conflict continued in many parts of the country. The Taliban and Al-Qaeda forces continued retaliatory strikes. The NATO forces have overtaken the responsibility of the ISAF since August 2003.[4] For the NATO, this was the first ever operation outside of Europe. They continue to be in Afghanistan and are mainly involved today in post-conflict activity.

UN Role in Afghan crisis[5]

As mentioned above, Soviet withdrawal from Afghanistan was facilitated by the good offices of the then UN Secretary-General. The UN continued to play humanitarian role in crisis-affected Afghanistan ever since. By the mid-1990s, nearly 800,000 persons displaced from Afghanistan and staying in the refugee camps in Pakistan and Iran depended on UN for food and sustenance. As the fighting in Afghanistan intensified in mid-1990s, the UN Security Council got concerned over the developments. In a Presidential statement on 15 February 1996, the Security Council expressed concern about intensified hostilities around the capital city of Kabul, which prevented deliveries of humanitarian aid. It was also deeply concerned that the continuing conflict provided fertile ground for terrorism, arms transfers and drug trafficking, which destabilized the whole region. On 22 October 1996, the UN Security Council adopted resolution 1076, calling upon all Afghan parties to end hostilities and engage in a political dialogue aimed at achieving national reconciliation. It repeated its deep concern that the conflict provided fertile ground for terrorism and drug trafficking and called on the parties to halt such activities. In July of 1997, the UN Secretary-General appointed the former Foreign Minister of Algeria Lakhdar Brahimi, as his Special Envoy for Afghanistan. His job was to conduct consultations with interested and relevant countries and parties and make recommendations on UN peacemaking activities there. In October that year, Brahimi, along with the UN Under-Secretary-General for Political Affairs, convened a series of informal meetings with what came to be known as the "Six plus Two" group-composed of the six states bordering Afghanistan (China, Iran, Pakistan, Tajikistan, Turkmenistan and Uzbekistan) plus the United States and Russia. Following the August 1998 terrorist bomb attacks on United States embassies in Tanzania and Kenya, the UN Security Council adopted Resolution 1193 on 28 August 1998. The Resolution reiterated the concern of the Security Council over the continuing presence of terrorists within the territory of Afghanistan. The Resolution condemned attacks on UN personnel in Taliban-held areas, including the killing of two Afghan staff members of the World Food Programme and the UN High Commissioner for Refugees in Jalalabad, and of the Military Adviser to UNSMA in Kabul. It also condemned the capture of the Consulate-General of Iran in Mazar-e-Sharif. Resolution 1214 of the Security Council adopted on 8 December 1998 demanded that the Taliban stop providing sanctuary and training for international terrorists and their organizations and that all Afghan factions cooperate in bringing indicted terrorists to justice. The Security Council applied broad sanctions on Afghanistan under the enforcement provisions of the UN Charter on 15 October 1999, citing the failure of the Taliban authorities to respond to this demand. Resolution 1267 of 1999 noted that Osama bin Laden had been indicted by the United States for the August 1998 embassy bombings and demanded that the Taliban faction (it was never recognized as Afghanistan's legitimate government) turn him over to the appropriate authorities to be brought to justice. Following non-compliance from the Taliban, sanctions were implemented from 14 November, which included the freezing of all funds and other financial resources owned or controlled by the Taliban, by member-states.

Besides the problem of civil war and terrorism, the UN also addressed the humanitarian issues emerging from the continued conflict in Afghanistan. Particularly after the withdrawal of the Soviet forces from Afghanistan, the UN made strenuous efforts to coordinate humanitarian assistance. The problem of refugees, shelter and food for the displaced people, were among the major humanitarian issues that called UN attention. The United Nations Food and Agriculture Organization (FAO) estimated that the area under agricultural cultivation in Afghanistan fell by 40 per cent between 1979 and 1991. The UNICEF, the UNDP, the UN High Commissioner for Refugees (UNHCR) and the World Food Programme (WFP), along with the Coordinator for United Nations Humanitarian and Economic Assistance Programmes, jointly developed in 1989, a plan of action for Afghanistan. Agricultural assistance, food aid, public and maternal health services and economic recovery programmes were initiated with resources provided to the United Nations by the international community. Other programmes planned included repairing infrastructure, providing shelter and discouraging narcotics production. However, these had to be shelved because of insufficient funds. During the continued civil war, the number of civilians fleeing the country increased steadily, making Afghanistan the world's worst refugee crisis. By 1990, there were 6.3 million civilians in exile, out of which 3.3 million were in Pakistan and 3 million were in Iran. The UNHCR set up a voluntary repatriation project to tackle this crisis. In 1992, more than 1.2 million refugees had returned home from Pakistan. However, the entry of Taliban into the fighting once again led to the displacement of populations. Some 350,000 people fled the Kabul region and took shelter in camps near Jalalabad, bringing the total of internally displaced people dependent on the UN for food and sustenance to 800,000. By 1994, there were an additional 700,000 Afghan refugees, living mostly in camps in Pakistan and Iran.

In 1994, the first of a series of annual consolidated appeals to aid Afghanistan was launched. The appeals detailed the emergency needs of Afghan people and asked for funds to enable non-governmental and UN agencies to address those needs. This first appeal had some success, with donors supplying 75 per cent of the funds requested. Rehabilitation projects focussed on human development and poverty alleviation in rural communities. High quality seed was distributed to farmers-yielding some 80,000 tons of grain-while some 125,000 hectares of land were irrigated and over 8,000 hectares of orchards rehabilitated. From 1995, however, the annual consolidated appeals were less successful in raising the necessary funds. The 1995-1996 appeal, for example, raised only 50 per cent of the amount deemed urgent-of which practically nothing was available for crucial infrastructure repairs. However, the absence of conflict in some parts of the country made it possible to reopen some roads, allowing greater aid distribution by the United Nations and aid agencies. From January to June 1995, WFP distributed more than 53,000 tons of food aid, while the UN Centre for Human Settlements helped some 10,000 families rebuild their homes. During a health campaign in 1995, nearly 2.4 million children under five years of age were immunized against polio and more than 80,000 under two years old were inoculated against measles.

In a statement on 22 October, the Security Council also expressed deep distress over reports of involvement in the fighting, on the Taliban side, of thousands of non-Afghan nationals, some of whom were below the age of 14. It expressed grave concern at the seriously deteriorating humanitarian situation and deplored the worsening human rights situation— including forced displacements of civilian populations, summary executions, abuse and arbitrary detention of civilians, violence against women and girls, and indiscriminate bombing. The capture of Iran's Consulate-General in Mazar-e-Sharif was described as a flagrant violation of international law, along with the murder there of Iranian diplomats and a journalist. Deeply disturbed by a significant increase in the cultivation, production and trafficking of drugs, especially in Taliban-controlled areas, it demanded that such illegal activities be halted.

Post-WW II World Order, the UN and Intervention

The principle of sovereignty is the basis of the modern nation-state system. Post-Second World War international order formally accepted sovereignty and its corollary, i.e., non-intervention, as its core principles. Article 2 (1) of the Charter of the United Nations declares that the Organization is "based on the principle of the sovereign equality of all its members".[6] And Article 2 (4) urges its members to "refrain in their international relations from the threat or use of force against the territorial integrity or political independence of any state". Incidents of intervention have occurred nevertheless, since the end of the Second World War. The US intervention in Vietnam and Soviet intervention in Afghanistan are well-known incidents of super power intervention. India has a history of intervention in different parts of South Asia-crisis in East Pakistan in 1971, Sri Lanka in 1988 and Maldives in 1987. Iraq's invasion of Kuwait in 1991 is a more recent example. In almost all these instances intervention was justified in terms of the interest of the country seeking to intervene.

The contemporary international law draws a distinction between the "internal" and "external" affairs of a state. And the internal behaviour of a state is of no concern to the international order. The first part of Article 2 (7) explicitly says that "Nothing contained in the present Charter shall authorize the United Nations to intervene in matters which are essentially within the domestic jurisdiction of any state or shall require the Members to submit such matters to settlement under the present Charter". Closely linked with this is the idea of international security in the post-WWII international system, where security is synonymous with the status-quo of existing state boundaries. Any "revisionist" attempt to alter this status-quo was, thus, interpreted as a threat to international security. At the same time, any challenge to regime stability in a state was believed to be a matter strictly of internal or domestic affairs of a state, and so also the behaviour of a certain regime towards its own people. For example, protest of people against their own state–legitimate or otherwise–or violations of rights of the people by the regime fall within the domestic jurisdiction of the state. Thus, the international community is not expected to intervene in the matter. This dichotomy between internal and external affairs of states leads to another–perhaps unintended–dichotomy between "internal justice" and "external order;" and the international community is not expected to interfere in the matters related to internal justice in a state. The United Nations was conceived as an international organization primarily performing three roles, viz., facilitating peaceful resolution of international disputes, enforcing collective security and promoting international co-operation in various fields. Chapter VI of the UN Charter makes provisions for peaceful settlement of international disputes and Chapter VII provides for enforcement of collective security upon the "aggressor" or invader state. The stand-off between the two super powers in the Security Council during the Cold War period, however, stalled the use of provisions in Chapter VII. Consequently, "UN Peacekeeping" was developed as an alternative. It is defined as 'an operation involving military personnel, but without enforcement powers, undertaken by the United Nations to help maintain or restore international peace and security in areas of conflict.' "Since there is no charter provision for peacekeeping, it lies in a "grey zone" between the peaceful settlement provisions of Chapter VI and the military enforcement provisions of Chapter VII. Most peacekeeping operations during Cold War had some common characteristics: peacekeeping operations were undertaken with the consent of parties involved, they raised minimum possible troops, these were often stationed between hostile forces to monitor cease-fire or troop withdrawal, or these forces provided a buffer zone in ongoing conflicts, and the UN peacekeepers were authorized to use force only in self-defence.

In the past decade and a half, the nature of the world system and international politics has changed fundamentally. Forces of globalization have led to erosion of "sovereign" power of the state. The boundary between "internal" and "external" is becoming increasingly blurred. Consequently, there is some rethinking on what should cause concern to the international community and when, therefore, the international community can "legitimately" intervene in a state. There is greater acceptance of international intervention in some cases, which until 1990s would be regarded as cases for non-intervention. The address by Secretary-General Kofi Annan to the UN General Assembly in 1999 triggered a debate on the question of "humanitarian intervention". Various crises in different parts of the world during 1990s drove home a point that force may be the only way to put an end to genocide, ethnic cleansing, and such other crimes against humanity. Kofi Annan captured the problem when he said, "If humanitarian intervention is, indeed, an unacceptable assault on sovereignty, how should we respond to a Rwanda, to a Srebrenica–to gross and systematic violations of human rights that offend every percept of our common humanity?...... surely, no legal principle–not even sovereignty–can ever shield crimes against humanity."[7] As fallout of the debate over humanitarian intervention, an independent International Commission on Intervention and State Sovereignty (ICISS) was formed.[8] It proposed six criteria for carrying out military intervention for a humanitarian cause: right authority, just cause, right intention, last resort, proportional means and reasonable prospects.

End of Cold War and super power rivalry too, has facilitated changed attitudes of the international community towards these problems. Most, if not all, of these are cases in the post-colonial states of the Third World. First among these are the cases of human rights violations. It is relatively easier to think of human rights as a part of the international domain because the UN Charter commits the member-states to respect human rights. Civil conflicts, ethnic clashes and genocide within states have also aroused the concern of international community in recent times. Failing state institutions is another accepted cause for international intervention in the post-Cold War period. Changing perception of intervention has, in turn, led to changes in the nature of UN peacekeeping operations.[9] The post-Cold War "second generation" peacekeeping has evolved much beyond the idea of passive presence in conflict-hit areas–from "peacekeeping" to "peace-building". They have taken over rather ambitious, multiple tasks of ending violence, especially civil strife; preventing renewed hostilities and rebuilding stable polities. The UN did such a job in Namibia. The UNTAG (UN Transition Assistance Group) was formed to supervise the transition of Namibia from South African rule to independence. It completed its task between 1989 and 1990. The UNTAG supervised the cease-fire and withdrawal of South African forces from Namibia. It managed the release of political prisoners as well as the return of exiles. It supervised the civil police of Namibia. Further, it oversaw the process of repealing of racially discriminatory laws and drafting of a new Constitution for Namibia. Another important task of the UNTAG was to create an atmosphere suitable for conducting free and fair elections. The other example is the UN role in Cambodia in 1992-95. The UNTAC (UN Transition Authority in Cambodia) supervised cease-fire and the disarming of all four conflicting factions in Cambodia. Further, it controlled the foreign affairs, defence and finance of Cambodia and oversaw the rehabilitation of the basic infrastructure of that country. It monitored the role of Cambodia's civil police. The UNTAC managed the return of thousands of refugees from the neighbouring Thailand. It also promoted general respect for human rights in Cambodia and conducted elections in 1993. The UN operation in Namibia was a success. The one in Cambodia was not so, as the situation in that country deteriorated once the UN left. Some more recent operations–the "third generation" peacekeeping–have been carried out even without the consent of all parties involved, and have required deployment of much larger forces.[10] One example is former Yugoslavia. This state with complex ethnic composition, held together with the force of Communism, began to disintegrate in 1991. Slovenia and Croatia declared their independence in 1991, followed by Bosnia-Herzegovina and Macedonia in 1992. Yugoslavia was, thus, reduced only to include Serbia and Montenegro. Soon a bitter ethnic conflict erupted in Bosnia-Herzegovina. "Nationalist" militias of Muslims, Croats and Serbs began ethnic cleansing in the areas under their respective control. The UN Protection Force for Yugoslavia (UNPROFOR) was deployed in 1992 in Croatia. Its mandate included maintaining cease-fire, ensure protection of basic human rights and assist humanitarian agencies in the return of refugees. Later, the UN peacekeepers were dispatched to Sarajevo to reopen the airport and support humanitarian relief efforts. Further, Chapter VII was invoked, UN safe areas were created in six Bosnian cities, no-fly-zone over Bosnia was enforced, and economic sanctions were imposed on Serbia and Montenegro. This operation was conducted in co-operation with the NATO. The UN peacekeepers proved ineffective, however, as they were not able to put an end to the massacre of the Muslims at the hands of Bosnian Serbs, aided from Serbia.

While these operations reveal the extent to which international perspectives on intervention has changed, it does not mean that the UN actually intervened in every case that demanded its attention, for example, in Afghanistan. Following the withdrawal of Soviet forces, Afghanistan was thrown into a civil war. But the UN did not send peacekeeping forces to bring about truce. As is mentioned above, the UN role was limited to offering good offices to conflicting parties to negotiate settlement. Refugees leaving Afghanistan to take asylum in neighbouring countries indeed created a humanitarian crisis. The UN intervened to provide food and shelter to the refugees. As seen above, this UN effort continued for over eight years. The Taliban regime was responsible for gross violations of human rights in Afghanistan–another cause for inviting the attention of the UN. However, the UN has not taken any action in this respect. Afghanistan did not become a focus of attention of the international community until the bombing of US embassies in two African cities. Yet, intervention by international community with a sanction of the UN resolution was not considered. Indeed, the UN resolution demanded that the Taliban regime hand over bin-Laden to the US. Following the 9/11 terrorist attacks the US launched a war in Afghanistan. It was not considered necessary to seek UN mandate for this operation. Old UN resolution was used to legitimise US war. Though the international community in general supported US war in the immediate aftermath of 9/11, the US preferred unilateral action over multilateral UN operation.

In Lieu of Conclusion

There is a strong case for the liberal international agenda of promotion of democracy, respect for international law and strengthening international organisations like the UN. The post-Cold War concern for Human Security, and consequent merging of boundaries between internal "justice" and external "order," has added further strength to the neo-liberal argument. It may become increasingly difficult in future for the international community not to act in cases of civil conflicts, genocide or other forms of human rights violations, or even failing state institutions; even if it means erosion of territoriality and sovereignty of states–the cardinal principle of post-Cold War international order. However, the possibility of unilateral action by big powers, as in case of US war in Afghanistan, causes serious damage to the new-liberal case. The US war in Iraq in 2003 has further defeated the case. While there is no doubt that the argument in favour of humanitarian intervention is very strong; it is equally important–or perhaps more important–that particularly the major powers, including India, avoid the temptation of unilateral action and simultaneously prevent others from doing so. In this regard, the six criteria formulated by the ICISS, mentioned above, are very crucial.

The question "who decides when and where to intervene" is important. But from a Constructivist perspective, another question will also be important, viz., whose ideas of order, justice, democracy, human rights etc. will prevail or dominate? Indeed, much of the debate in future is likely to address this question.

Notes

1. There are many sources on Afghan history before and after the Soviet invasion. A useful summary of events in Afghanistan before Soviet invasion can be found in Cyriac Maprayil, "The Soviets and Afghanistan" (1986, New Delhi, Reliance Publishing House). For analysis of Soviet role, see Amin Saikal and William Maley eds. "The Soviet Withdrawal from Afghanistan" (1989, Cambridge University Press, Cambridge).
2. For analysis of the situation in Afghanistan, see Zalmay Khalilzad and Daniel Byman, "Afghanistan: the Consolidation of a Rogue State," *The Washington Quarterly*, Winter 2000. For an evaluation of US role, see Kimberly Zisk Marten, "Defending Against Anarchy: From War to Peacekeeping in Afghanistan," *The Washington Quarterly*, Winter 2002-02.
3. http://www.historyteacher.net/WarInAfghanistan-Weblinks.htm provides several useful links to sources on the war, including links to primary sources.

4. Mihai Carp–"Building Stability in Afghanistan" *NATO Review,* Spring 2006, (available on http://www.nato.int/docu/review/2006/issue1/english/main.htm,) details NATO role in Afghanistan.

5. This information is based on the official UN document, "Afghanistan and the United Nations" available on www.un.org/news/dh/latest/afghan/un-afghan-history.shtml

6. The Charter of the United Nations is available at http://www.un.org/aboutun/charter/

7. Quoted in Margaret Karns and Karen Mingst, "International Organizations: The Politics and Processes of Global Governance," (2005, Viva Books Pvt. Ltd., New Delhi, First Indian Edition), p. 286.

8. Karns & Mingst, note 7, p. 287.

9. Details of UN peacekeeping operations can be found on the official UN link http://www.un.org/Depts/dpko/dpko/

10. Karns & Mingst, note 6, pp. 311-321.

7

Role of Global Civil Society Organisations (CSOs) in Afghanistan: Need for Synergetic Partnership for Comprehensive Development and Functioning Democracy

Sudha Mohan

'How come history takes such a long, long time?' The lament of Canadian songwriter Bruce Cockburn is applicable for Afghanistan. To paraphrase another songwriter, Sam Cooke, 'it's a long time coming, but change is going to come.' is also appropriate now for Afghanistan. (International Development Magazine) http://www.developments.org.uk/data/issue26/editorial.htm

Afghanistan: Assertion of Independent Identity in a Changing World

Afghanistan is one country that has found itself embroiled in crisis, clashes and confrontation without really being responsible for it directly. It is engaged in a great struggle to determine its national identity in a more complex, evolving and very changed world. This landlocked country is a mountainous region bordered by China, Tajikistan, Uzbekistan, Turkmenistan, Iran and Pakistan. It is sandwiched between the former Soviet republics of Tajikistan, Uzbekistan, and Turkmenistan to the north, Iran to the west, and Pakistan to the south. The majority of the country's estimated population of 26 million is Sunni Muslims, although there is a sizeable Shia Muslim community. Afghanistan also has several ethnic groups, the largest being Pashtuns, Tajiks, Uzbeks, Hazaras and Turkmens. Throughout much of recent history it has been vulnerable to competing outside pressures. A quarter century of internal strife, external invasions and civil wars ended in November 2001. But after this period there have been the beginnings of another protracted problem–one of rebuilding the state and society of this land-locked country–after the United States headed assault removed the Taliban, a religiously-based political force, (that they initially supported to fight the soviets) from power. Afghanistan never a strong state was weakened to a point of government collapse and natural fragmentation by the long war.[1]

The problems in Afghanistan are both complex and multifarious. It extends beyond the issues of internal strife and external security to other societal tribulations. These include political and institutional decline of state, problems of social and economic polarisation, and severe gender discrimination. Few other countries face such tremendous threats to their survival as national entities. Matters get still bleak when one looks at the statistical figures. For instance, Afghanistan is one of the poorest and most underdeveloped countries in the world. This makes the human development challenge for Afghanistan enormous. According to Afghanistan's National Human Development Report (NHDR) 2004, the Human Development Index ranks Afghanistan at 173 out of 178 countries worldwide and is also below the majority of Sub-Saharan African countries. For instance the percentage of Afghans with access to safe drinking water source is one of the lowest in the world–23 percent–while just 12 percent of the population has access to adequate sanitation.[2]

Widespread human rights violations, protracted and the worst drought in Afghan history resulted in four million refugees, 1.5 million internally displaced people, one million handicapped by landmines, and seven million—out of a population of an estimated 26 million—vulnerable to food shortages. Amid the chaos, war-affected women had no escape from a vicious cycle of violence. As a result, the status of Afghan women ranks among the worst in the world. Today, an Afghan woman dies in childbirth or complications of pregnancy every 30 minutes. Seventy percent of all tuberculosis (TB) cases occur in women, and the country suffers the highest TB rate in the world. An estimated 80 percent of Afghan women cannot read or write. Infant mortality rates are among the highest in the world and 300,000 children die each year from preventable diseases. Women and children are seriously undernourished. No statistics exist on mental health, but women are highly traumatized and suicide rates rapidly on the rise. The majority of the Afghan refugee and displaced population are women. And it is women who are charged with taking care of approximately one million orphaned children in addition to the elderly and handicapped while they themselves are heavily traumatized, malnourished, and under-supported. In December 2001, the UN and international parties meeting in Bonn brokered a political agreement among contending factions. The interim agreement promised provision of an international security force and a beginning of the process of nation building in Afghanistan.[3]

Thus, there can be little doubt about the profundity of Afghanistan's humanitarian crisis. The country holds Asia's or the world's worst records in a number of fields, including infant and maternal mortality, life expectancy, adult and female literacy, access to safe water, the estimated number of land mines, the proportion of mentally or physically disabled people, the number dependent upon food support, and the number of refuges and internally displaced people. It is estimated that well over a million people have been killed, and more than seven hundred thousand woman made widows in the fighting over the last two decades.[4]

This country besides suffering invasion and civil war since 1978 has also had natural disasters adding to its already vulnerable position. State and non-state actors have constantly violated human rights and most importantly the rights of women. The political, social and economic institutions in Afghanistan have disintegrated as a result of the ceaseless civil war that has torn apart the country for some twenty-five years. The war has resulted in deaths, displacement, and disability.[5]

With this brief thumbnail impression of Afghan society and polity, this paper purports to examine why financial assistance from outside becomes critical to alleviate the problems prevailing in the country. External help in the form of Global Civil Society Organisations (CSOs) in Afghanistan thereby becomes not only necessary but also inevitable with a weak state that is incapable of rendering even basic necessities of life. Given this scenario it becomes imperative to critically examine the role and motives of CSO–whether altruistic or ulterior–in their efforts. This paper will also attempt to address the need for a synergetic partnership between contending groups, namely, the government, CSOs and the people, for bringing about comprehensive development and functioning democracray in Afghanistan.

The political, economic, social and military chaos in Afghanistan is not an isolated or unique phenomenon. This is essentially due to the fact that such catastrophic experiences of the long suffering peoples of Afghanistan are part of a much wider suffering common to some post-colonial states and multinational societies, especially smaller and poorer ones, which are unfortunate enough to find themselves in a geo-strategic location that are inevitably pushed into long-drawn-out conflicts, that have long-term repercussions on every facet of life.

Multifarious Problems of the Long Suffering Peoples in Afghanistan

It is apparently clear from the brief thumb-nail description, of the multifarious problems in Afghanistan, which extend to all facets of life in Afghan society. The wide-spread nature of the problem in Afghanistan thus makes it both national and an international one. The conflict according to many scholars has become a transnational struggle which requires a synoptic and integrated solution.[6] The stakes are very high in the struggle for influence in Afghanistan. After the end of the Cold War, Afghanistan had lost strategic importance. But the break up of the Soviet Union, the emergence of Central Asian States, the discovery of large quantities of oil and gas in the Caspian area, the US policy of containment against Iran, Iran's determination to be an influential power in Central Asia, and the possibility that Afghanistan can be an alternative gateway to Central Asia, all have revived Afghanistan's strategic importance.[7]

Afghanistan's problems are larger and deeper than the character of any single internal actor, for the Afghanistan conflict has become a transnational struggle that requires a synoptic and integrated solution. It is necessary to find means of reconstructing the Afghan state along sustainable lines and this will require from the international community a long term commitment, in which moderate Afghans are partners, where a new Marshall Plan is devised for the region, and the Afghan people are identified not as sinners to be punished, but as victims to be rescued.[8]

Afghanistan embodied the consequences of international negligence in the post-Cold War era. But international inertia ceased on September 11. After September 11, the world suddenly discovered Afghanistan, which became the main focus of the global fight against terrorism. That leaving Afghanistan to the Taliban had been a huge mistake by the international community was now accepted wisdom, as it became clear that if the international community had stayed on to help rebuild Afghanistan at the end of the occupation by the Soviet Union in 1989 the country would not have become al Qaeda's base for global terror attacks. Five years on, peace still remains elusive in Afghanistan. The same destructive transnational forces that ripped Afghanistan apart in the 1990s continue to undermine its new democracy and threaten international security. A number of interdependent factors account for the resurgence of security threats to Afghanistan and the international community.

Second, despite being the world's main front in the war against terrorism, Afghanistan has received less per capita in reconstruction and security assistance than other recent post-conflict countries, including Iraq, Kosovo and Bosnia. Lack of resources has led to quick fixes to address basic needs at the cost of long-term development projects. A lack of internal security and economic development has left Afghanistan's war-torn society vulnerable to narcoterrorists, who draw in more than 2.3 million Afghan farmers in poppy cultivation. Peasants remain extremely poor, however, as most of the drug revenues go to drug lords and corrupt police officers.

Third, between 2001 and 2005 the basic institutions of centralized government were established in Afghanistan. But law enforcement institutions, which constitute the face of any government, have been neglected from the beginning. Judicial and police reforms—reforms that should have been the foundation on which other state institutions were built—were not implemented and were shelved indefinitely, due to a lack of resources. Consequently, a security vacuum has widened in areas where state institutions are either absent or too weak to protect people, particularly in the south and east—areas that have seen little or no assistance over the past five years.[9]

Thus, the conflict in Afghanistan is not simply an "Afghan" problem but a regional and even transnational and an international one. The problem at the heart of the crisis in Afghanistan lies in the collapse of political and administrative institutions that has resulting in the loss of personal security and the means of livelihood for the people of Afghanistan. With this kind of strategic, political, social and economic issues confronting Afghanistan, it becomes apparent as to how and why the civil society organizations began to fill in the gaps left by the inability and inefficiency of government institutions to tackle the multifarious issues confronting the trouble-torn nation.

Civil Society Organisation in Afghanistan

Civil Society has multiple meanings that are often ambiguous and amorphous. The term seems to have a particularly European historical experience that is applied to different contexts. Civil society gained public attention in the 1980s as an attempt to establish civility in society, was seen as the opposite of despotism, a 'space' in which groups can exist and something which would ensure better and more tolerable conditions of existence. From Hobbes to Gramsci there have been many variants on the notion of civil society. But the most important institutional component of civil society comprises voluntary groups of different hues and kinds including community groups, co-operatives, unions, associations, self help groups, foundations, social service agencies etc, as there is no such thing as 'the conception of civil society.[10]

Particularly in countries with weak or imperfect political mechanisms, civil society is often seen as an important means for self-determination and self-expression, providing citizens the opportunity to engage more fully in political and economic decision-making. In any country, the local context—religious, geographical, cultural, economic—influences how civil society expresses itself. It is sometimes not easy to draw a clear line around organizations that should be considered part of civil society. Because war has so decimated the institutions of state in Afghanistan, it is especially difficult to distinguish among types of CSOs and their functions. In addition, beginning in the 1990s and at an accelerated pace in the 2000s, international organizations have created local development committees or councils to serve as project implementers, further clouding distinctions among types and functions of organizations and their relationship to traditional institutional structures. Organisations and countries involved in conflict prevention and developmental aid have ignored Afghanistan for too long. The widespread human rights abuse and the economic, environmental, and regional security implications of the conflict are easily on a par with those of other conflicts that have received greater international attention. The post-Taliban reconstruction agenda likewise entails comprehensive social, economic and political change. The process was launched during the initial, four-year transition phase laid out in the Bonn Agreement of December 2001 (and known as "the Bonn period"), and followed by a five-year plan for economic, political and social development adopted at the 2006 London conference (known as the London Compact). It gives due recognition to conflict, tension and contradiction as an inherent part of the process of change. The main common feature is the effort to strengthen the central state and liberalize parts of society.[11]

But it must be mentioned here that assistance and more importantly an awareness and sensitivity towards the problems in the region has been low in the priority of most governments and most notably of the United States. It is mentioned by a noted scholar of Afghanistan Barnett R. Rubin,

(Rubin, who is director of studies and a senior fellow at the Center on International Cooperation at New York University, was the author of a Council Special Report on Afghanistan this year that overwhelming perception in the region is that the United States is not serious about trying to succeed in Afghanistan. "They see that we've spent perhaps seven times as much money in Iraq, that we put more troops into Iraq, and that we tolerate Pakistan's support for the Taliban, while we still treat General [Pervez] Musharraf, [Pakistan's president] as an ally. This is because everyone perceives that containing Iran, and trying to stop Iran's nuclear program, and perhaps destroying the Islamic regime in Iran, and perhaps changing the regime in Syria, and winning in Iraq are much higher priorities for the Bush administration than succeeding in Afghanistan."[12]

However, the situation seems to slightly more conducive with the new change in both the perception and as well as the need to assist in the development of the region with a focus on three areas. Among others there have been primarily three important reasons for an active civil society in Afghanistan.

International political imperatives: The 'war' against terror, the prevention of large movements of refugees to donor countries and the struggle against organized international crime, including drugs trade.

National political imperatives: The introduction of democracy in the recipient country, often implying the creation of a new political culture. The promotion of human rights, including gender equality.

Economic imperatives: The creation of an open market economy, and a lean and efficient state.

The military imperative: The need to mobilize armed forces in civilian activities; securing peace and delivering humanitarian and development aid.[13]

Rise of International Intervention in the form of Global Civil Society Assistance

In early 2002, the international community pledged USD 4.5 billion over a five-year period for the rehabilitation and development of Afghanistan. Funding has partly been channeled through internationally managed trust funds, such as the Afghanistan Reconstruction Trust Fund (ARTF), and partly through UN organizations and nongovernmental organizations (NGOs). There are some significant local NGOs that have been appreciated for their proactive role in the region. For instance the Afghanistan PEACE (Poverty Eradication and Community Empowerment) Initiative, which began in 1997, has developed a model for establishing community-based organizations. (CBOs). With this initiative, it attempts to demonstrate only with sustainable grassroots rehabilitation programme can there be an environment of peace. Another organisation, CARE, a U.S.-based NGO with programs in sixty countries, started work in Afghanistan in the 1960s. CARE's projects include running a food program for widows, building water systems, and getting food and medical supplies to remote areas. In other words there is emphasis upon social infrastructure development by this group.[14]

However, there has been a proliferation of NGOs since 2001.The sudden boom in the NGO sector in Afghanistan was a result of meeting growing demands of the population as well as the donor aid program. While in mid 2001 there were around 250 NGOs registered with four NGO coordination bodies, by November 2002 there were 1020 NGOs registered with the Ministry of Planning in Kabul. Of these, approximately 350 were international. The rise of the NGO sector is the "recognition that, in a country whose industrial productivity has collapsed and employment market evaporated, the aid industry is no longer peripheral; after agriculture, it is the second biggest sector of economy."[15]

The global assistance community is interested in addressing issues on the manner in which to operationalise UN human rights and gender equity principles, to reconcile these principles with the dictates of International Humanitarian Law, and to reorder the way in which the assistance actors work with each other in complex emergency situations, and how to re-energise and reform the UN, not least with a view to more muscular approaches to saving future generations from the scourges of war.[16]

However, it would be pertinent here to look at what the role of the UN has been in this war-torn and ravaged region. In one of the most interesting and insightful works on this subject, William Maley, an authority on the subject suggests that the crisis confronting Afghanistan runs deeper than the mere nature, structure and functions of the state. This issue has never been properly confronted by the UN, perhaps because its official, mindful of the terms of Article 2.7 of the United Nations Charter, see it as 'within the domestic jurisdiction' of the state, and the effect of this omission has been to adulterate the credibility of the UN effort as a whole. Intervention is fraught with difficulty but the post-intervention problems are far more daunting. These may include coping with new and fractious actors, managing complex processes of change, addressing fundamental questions of political philosophy, coping with 'spoilers' and low levels of trust, and avoiding inadvertent damage to the interventions beneficiaries-all in situations where resources may be scarce and intervening powers at odds with each other. Interveners should strive to absorb the lessons of past interventions and master the complexities of the territory on which they propose to act. (Third thesis talks about how 'Interventions will bring a range of new actors to the political landscape). He also discusses specialized and humanitarian UN agencies, the International Committee of the Red Cross and international advocacy and relief NGOs emerging in the scene.[17]

Complexities of Aid in Civil Society Assistance

Apparently Afghanistan seems deeply dependent on international aid, which makes up over 90 percent of the government budget.

The income from international aid was less than half that, $3.337 billion.[1] Whereas pledges of aid from the international community between January 2002—April 2006, amounted to $14.4 billion, only $9.1 billion were actually committed by February 2005, and of that only $3.9 billion disbursed (January 2002—February 2005) and $3.3 billion has been disbursed for ongoing projects. Of the total disbursements, *a mere $.9 billion worth of projects have been completed.* Such fine points escape many who point out that Afghanistan has been supported by an input of about $15 billion dollars from the international community since 2001. Ahmed Rashid reported that western donors *committed* on average $2.5 billion every year during 2002-5 for reconstruction, but less than half that money was *disbursed*. For its part, the US has spent $1.3 billion on reconstruction in Afghanistan over four years, "intending to win over Afghans with signs of progress. By way of contrast, the United States spends $10-$12 billion annually on military operations in Afghanistan.[18]

"The level of foreign assistance Afghanistan has received so far appears to be on the low side compared to other recent post-conflict cases." James Dobbins, President Bush's former special envoy for Afghanistan and an author of the RAND study, calls Afghanistan "the least resourced, large-scale American reconstruction program ever."[19]

International CSOs have been criticized for their "top-down" approach that often neglects to engage local populations and therefore fails to address the needs of these communities. In a very interesting but scathing account of the situation in Afghanistan the five-piece article 'Empty space' by Marc W. Herold. In the first article he identifies Afghanistan as the perfect *Neo-Colonial state of the 21st century*, followed in the second by looking skeptically on *Pseudo Development in Afghanistan*; in the third part he criticizes the American and its Western allies for *Selling Brand Karzai*, in the last part he paints a grave picture of *US Military Strategy to Maintain Afghanistan* as an empty space.[20]

Engaging local participation was deemed to be a particular concern in Afghanistan, where there is the collapse of social and political institutions and hence responsive feedback and inputs from people is the only way to gauge felt needs of the local population. Global CSOs also need to create conditions that would support the building of the indigenous civil society organisations that truly represent the needs and aspirations of the people and voice it in appropriate platforms to ensure both accountability and transparency. Engaging in reconstruction activities is a deeply political question. Currently, the focus of international donor policy is on emergency relief rather than long-term development. A long-term strategy for reconstruction would also have to focus upon issue of development, both physical and social. It is a process of expanding people's capabilities and entitlements which covers not just purely economic factors, but takes into account the political arrangements that affect people's lives. In fact, Amartya Sen goes further and looks at 'Development as Freedom.'[21]

This long term commitment towards development and also democracy will require the support of the United States and its allies as well as other regional powers. Unconditional aid is not a solution, but neither is non-engagement. The priority of the international community has to shift to include the needs, opinions, and values of the Afghan people, who continue to live in a country in crisis.[22] It must however be reiterated here that the challenges posed by Afghan development cannot be met by CSOs. Assistance in the form of NGO help can only supplement but cannot and should not supplant political effort, because in the long run it is the institutions that will eventually determine the pace and policy of development. The foremost task in Afghanistan is state-building, which must begin at the district or village level. If this foundation is not stable, there can be no secure structure above it. However, the Afghan government has not received the support it deserves in this endeavour-towards building more stable political institutions of governance and comprehensive development.[23] While there has been a lot of debate and controversy surrounding the problems of aid disbursal and inadequate funding and the reluctant role of the UN, there are other contested issues that have cropped up. For instance, there are concerns that have cropped up. These among others relate to booming trade in opium, the future of the U.S.-Afghan strategic relationship, Bush administration's plans to turn over greater control of Afghanistan to NATO next year and reduce U.S. troop levels, are durable state institutions really being created in Kabul, or is the rule of the Karzai government more illusory than real? In fact, these were some of the critical questions that were discussed at an October 19 American Enterprise Institute panel discussion.[24] There is increasing awareness amongst government officials and CSOs involved in the Afghan crisis that a synergetic relationship needs to be formed between diverse groups. In fact, active governments and mobilized communities along with the assistance of both local and global civil society organizations can together enhance developmental efforts.

New Paradigm of Peace, Development and Nation-Building in Afghanistan Conclusion or a Continuum

Attempts at building peace and rebuilding society in Afghanistan require that the international community-both political and civil society-rethink the terms in which the conflict is understood. This necessitates a more nuanced understanding of the background to the conflict that will allow real responses to be found. The problem at the heart of the crisis in Afghanistan lies in the collapse of institutions and the resulting loss of personal security and the means of livelihood for the Afghan population. Opportunities do exist for international engagement. This engagement should involve the leaders of Afghanistan's community organisation, across ethnicities and religions, including NGOs and local activists, in fact all those actors who have an interest in reconstruction and long-term peace. Engaging local community leaders would help to regenerate associational life and civic commitments. The goal should be to change the terms and conditions under which ordinary Afghans live, creating opportunities for communities to establish alternative economic activity in the country. In some parts of the country where traditional mechanisms of local government exist, such as the elected shura councils in South and East Afghanistan, these institutions could be targeted for a range of community-level strategies and interventions.

There is a growing awareness among the Afghan population of the need to focus aid on specific areas of concern including health care, education, de-mining, and agriculture. Projects in these areas would help to generate economic development of the entire country and shift assistance from arms and emergency aid to long-term development for Afghan communities. (As was pointed out earlier in this article) The Afghan Diaspora represents an untapped resource of young, educated professionals who can be engaged in providing skills and resources in rebuilding society.[25]

It has to also be understood clearly by the international community that the removal of a non-democratic regime does not automatically produce democracy. Democratic assistance needs to focus on determining outcomes, and more importantly on nurturing democratic culture, practices and institutions. Democracy promotion also means strengthening independent media; promoting the rule of law and an independent judiciary;

defending human rights and the fundamental freedoms of expression, conscience, and association; and supporting civil society, including woman's organisation, labour and business associations and non-governmental groups that educate citizens about democracy and empower them to participate in the political process and monitor government performance.[26] Towards this endeavour of establishing lasting peace, sustainable development and nurturing democracy, the Government in Afghanistan seems to have a strategy for reform and envisions an affordable and sustainable justice system that is accessible by all Afghans. The Government justice strategy addresses the need for reform specifically highlighting the following four areas. One, it emphasizes on the fact that the Government must lead on justice reform. Two, the international community is a vital partner in justice reform. Three, justice reform must be appropriate to Afghanistan. And four, justice reform should address state institutions and their capacity to deliver justice. Traditional institutions and their capacity to function within state and international norms.[27]

What is needed is a change in the nation-building approach that has been employed since the fall of the Taliban in November 2001; reconstruction and democratization should be pursued from the bottom up rather than the top down, community-based approaches to reconstruction and peace-building to foster local initiative, a prerequisite for sustainable development.[28]

Afghanistan has made remarkable progress in the six years that have elapsed since the fall of the Taliban. The September 18, 2005 parliamentary elections represented another important signpost on the country's path to democracy. Although down significantly from the 2004 presidential elections, voter turnout still compared favourably with other transition countries, and the polling proceeded with few violent incidents. This success provides further evidence of the steady maturation of a nascent democratic political culture in Afghanistan. While this milestone should be celebrated, we must be mindful that Afghanistan's political transition is far from complete, and the gains achieved could easily be reversed. As President Karzai stated in a speech in Herat in the days leading up to the election: "There's so much more work to be done ... Afghanistan is still not able to stand on its own feet." The Afghan government is dependent on international military and economic assistance and will remain so for a decade or more. It is critical that the international community not view the conclusion of the Bonn political process as a time to disengage from Afghanistan. State-building is intrinsically a long-term process, especially in a country emerging from a protracted civil war. In such a context, commitments should be measured in decades not years. It is vital that the international community recognize this fact and commit to maintaining current troop and aid levels.[29]

This country can without getting feeble stand firmly on its feet only on foundations of development that is comprehensive and democracy that is vibrant. But the path leading to sustainable development, functioning democracy and lasting peace requires an interface between state, non-state and international agencies. This would effectively and realistically mean working together in a synergetic relationship that can certainly help this region regain its political stability, social order, and economic strength in an ever-changing world.

Notes

1. Taqiq Ali, "Afghanistan: Between Hammer and Anvil," *New Left Review*, 2, March-April 2000.
2. For a statistical account of the socio-economic conditions in Afghanistan, see online information http://www.undp.org.af/nhdr_04/NHDR04.htm
3. Sima Wali, "Violence, Terror, and Accountability in Afghanistan," *Peace Review* Vol. 16, No. 1, March 2004, p. 2, and pp. 75–78.

4. Michael Keating, "Dilemmas of Humanitarian Assistance in Afghanistan," in William Maley (ed), "Afghanistan and the Taliban: The Rebirth of Fndamentalism?" Penguin Books, New Delhi, 2001, pp. 135-144.

5. "Building peace and Civil Society in Afghanistan: Challenges and opportunities," Report of Asia Society and the Carnegie Council, May 2001. This Report draws on a two-day symposium held in New York and Washington, D.C and is made available on the net at http://www.asiasource.org/asip/afghanistan_report.pdf

6. Barnett R Rubin, Ashraf Ghani, William Maley, Ahmed Rashid and Olivier Roy, "Afghanistan: Reconstruction and Peace building in a Regional Framework," Bern:KOFF Peace building Reports no 1/2001. *Swiss Peace Foundation,* 2001. Also see Barnett R. Rubin, "Afghans Can Be Our Allies," *The New York Times,* 22 September, 2001.

7. Anwar-ul-Haq Ahady, "Saudi Arabia, Iran and the Conflict in Afghanistan," in William Maley (ed), *Afghanistan and the Taliban: The Rebirth of Fundamentalism?* Penguin Books, New Delhi, 2001, pp. 117-134.

8. William Maley (ed), *"Afghanistan and the Taliban: The Rebirth of Fundamentalism?* Penguin Books, New Delhi, 2001, Preface xiii.

9. Ashraf Haider, "Afgan Democracy," *The New York Times,* 21 July 2006.

10. Sudha Mohan, "Civil Society Activism in the Age of Globalisation" in Rajen Harshe, (Ed), *Interpreting Globalisation: Perspectives in International Relations,* Indian Council of Social Science Research (ICSSR), Delhi and Rawat, Jaipur, 2004.

11. http://www.afghangovernment.com/AfghanAgreement Bonn.htm

12. Barnett R. Rubin, "Afghanistan at Dangerous 'Tipping Point'" 6 October 2006, Council on Foreign Relations. http://www.cfr.org/publication/11620/rubin.html

13. CMI Brief Vol. 4, No. 3, November 2005, available on www.cmi.no

14. *Poverty Eradication and Community Empowerment: Afghanistan PEACE Initiative 1997,* Islamabad: United Nations Development Program, 1997. Copy of the report on the project is available on the UNDP Afghanistan Web site at www.pcpafg.org/Organizations/undp/
15. Michael Keating, "Dilemmas of Humanitarian Assistance in Afghanistan," in William Maley (ed), *Afghanistan and the Taliban: The Rebirth of Fndamentalism?* Penguin Books, New Delhi, 2001, p. 136.
16. Ibid.
17. William Maley, "Twelve Theses on the Impact of Humanitarian Intervention," *Security Dialogue,* Vol. 33, No. 3, 2002, pp. 265-278. Also see William Maley "The UN and Afghanistan: 'Doing its Best' or 'Failure of a Mission'?" in Maley (ed) op. cit. pp. 182-198.
18. Data from Barnett R. Rubin, Humayun Hamidzada and Abby Stoddard, Afghanistan 2005 and Beyond. "Prospects for Improved Stability Reference Document," The Hague: Conflict Research Unit, Netherlands Institute of International Relations, Clinendael, April 2005, p. 63.
19. Barnett R. Rubin, Abbay, Stoddard Humayun Hamidzada, Abid Farhadi, "Building a New Afghanistan: The Value of Success, the Cost of Failure," Center on International Cooperation, New York University In cooperation with CARE March 2004.
20. Marc W. Herold, Departments of Economics and Women's Studies Whittemore School of Business & Economics Afghanistan as an empty space, posted on 26 February 2006. Available at http://www.fpif.org/
21. Sen A.K, *Development as Freedom,* New York, Oxford University Press, 1999.
22. Anderson, Mary B., *Do No Harm: How Aid Can Support Peace-Or War* Lynne Rienner Publishers, Boulder, Colo, 1999, http://www.afghannews.net/
23. For an interesting account of both the discussion and critical appraisal of Civil Society, see Anika Ayrapetyants

and Eric S Johnson, "Afghanistan Civil Society Assessment," *Counterpart International*, 1 June, 2005, www.counterpart.org

24. "Winning Afghanistan," *American Enterprise Institute for Public Policy Research*, October 2005 entitled http://www.aei.org/

25. *Building peace and Civil Society in Afghanistan: Challenges and opportunities*, Report of Asia Society and the Carnegie Council, May 2001. This Report draws on a two-day symposium held in New York and Washington, D.C and is made available on the net at http://www.asiasource.org/asip/afghanistan_report.pdf

26. For a critical discussion on the main oppositions to democracy see Cark Gershman and Michael Allen, "New Threats to Freedom: The Assault on Democracy Assistance," *Journal of Democracy*, Vol. 17, No. 2, April 2006, pp. 37-51.

27. *Justice for All A Comprehensive Needs Analysis for Justice in Afghanistan*, Government of the Islamic Republic of Afghanistan, Ministry of Justice, May 2005.

28. Mark Sedra "Afghanistan: It Is Time for a Change in the Nation-Building Strategy," *Foreign Policy in Focus*, 15 November 2002.

29. "Foreign Policy In Focus: Revisioning the International Compact for Afghanistan." htm http://www.fpif.org.

8

Afghan Undercurrents in the Underbelly of Central Asia

P.L. Dash

Introduction

A single factor that differentiates Afghanistan from rest of the countries of the region is the direct Soviet and American military and political involvement in that country for successive long years. An asymmetrical political configuration emerges when a big power engages a small and weak state in its pursuits of international relations with not so well defined regional objectives. The social and political upheaval in contemporary Afghanistan in the last two and half decades is therefore the involvement saga of these two militarily potential powers and the lingering impact they continue to exert on Afghanistan and its neighbours. The central locale of Afghanistan at the confluence of South, West and Central Asias has been the subject matter of analysis in many academic exercises. Among the several implications of big power involvement in Afghanistan is the resultant political volatility that keeps the country territorially divided. All regions are not equal, but all regions are politically unstable and economically backward. The writ of Karzai from Kabul does not work in the periphery. Local war lords, who rule the countryside, are loathe in accepting diktat from the capital and are reluctant to part with the power they have enjoyed so far and booty they continue to collect from the regions. The Pushtoon dominated border areas along the Durand line from Waziristan to Kandahar supplanted by dethroned Talibans and supported by Al Qaeda, the areas surrounding Herat and the bordering regions with Iran and the northern Tajik dominated areas, extending support to Kabul continue to look red at each other. The political problem has been compounded manifold by the presence of American troops to patronize a regime that is detested by the people. The pervasive feeling is that the Karzai government is one of non-resident Afghans loyal to the US. Despite elections, participatory democracy in true sense has been eluding the country.

And what dominates politics and the region are the American presence in Afghanistan and Central Asia to fight the Taliban and terror and, the colossal regional implications of the world's mightiest military power in a politically volatile region, and, in reaction to this, the realigned, re-emergent Jeehadi culture by religious fundamentalists headed by hounded Al Qaeda and deposed Taliban, the menace of their dealing with narcotic trafficking as the financial backbone of extremism and terrorism that continues to spew venom across the region. Based on various empirical surveys widely publicized since 9/11, this article begins with an argument about the sinister regional strategic design by the US, through Pakistan or otherwise, to further elucidate on these three aspects of contemporary Afghanistan.

US Designs

The most striking development in the recent decade in Central Asia in general and Afghanistan in particular has been the direct US military involvement. Soon after the Soviet disintegration and long before 9/11 happened, the USA had begun recognizing the importance of this region in strategic scheme of things. As a result, Central Asia in general and Afghanistan in particular formed the core of a region that catapulted itself from anonymity to limelight in US strategic planning. A host of agreements that the US had concluded with Central Asian states was demonstrative of the new importance attached to these countries by the Bush administration. In 1994, the US signed an agreement with Kazakhstan on defence cooperation the scope of which was further expanded by another agreement of 1997.[1] In the middle of 1994, all post-Soviet Central Asian states save Tajikistan joined NATO's "Partnership for Peace" programme. This eastward expansion of US led NATO in a region dominated by fifty plus millions of Turkish peoples not only attested implied US military presence in that part of the world, but threatened to do away with Russia's traditional sphere of influence. In further pursuit of their strategic goals, in December, 1995, the US made a Central Asian peace battalion with Kazakhstan, Uzbekistan and Kirgyzstan as members to ensure peace in Central Asia. In 1997, the then Assistant Secretary of State, Strobe Talbot, conceptualized American strategic perception of Central Asia, clearly defined US interests in the region and summed up the results of all efforts undertaken in that direction. Thus, the region that was ignored from the US policy radar for years was highlighted as a potential sphere of US influence.

In April, 2000, the US along with Kazakhstan, Kirgyzstan and Uzbekistan formed Central Asian Border Security Initiative. The objective was to fight possible outbreak of terror in that part of the world. Thus, on the eve of 9/11, the US had already made considerable headways in establishing military and strategic relationship with all countries of Central Asia, apparently to foil the Taliban design of exporting Islamic fundamentalism to the Central Asian neighbourhood. Aware of Al Qaeda activities and anti-US Taliban intentions, the US was almost prepared to encounter possible eventuality at the regional level in Central Asia. But the US had never imagined that such an eventuality would occur home, and that too with so many casualties at the twin towers, the roots of which would be directly traced to Afghanistan.

What had driven the US to Afghanistan for direct military intervention against the Taliban was the 9/11 that had shattered American economic pride and military might. The call of terror was as final as the US decision to entangle itself militarily in Afghanistan. Support of Russia as the only country that had enough grassroots experience with ground realities in Afghanistan became as essential as gaining a military foothold in neighbouring Central Asia. The US assiduously pursued negotiations for leasing out military bases in Kirgyzstan and Uzbekistan and quickly strengthened its potential presence in Manas and Karshi Khanabad military bases. It was from there the US poured in its support to the Northern Alliance to fight the Taliban. The encirclement of Afghanistan was thus complete with tacit understanding of all neighbouring countries including Russia and India who threw their support to the US anti-Taliban campaign.

The importance of Central Asia as a strategic foothold for US in the region has not evaporated even after the overthrow of the Taliban. The intensity of terrorist activities stemming from the clandestine presence of the Taliban in their hideouts in specific pockets along the Durand line, their trans-border export of terror to India, Russia and Central Asian states and their involvement in illegal narcotic trade worldwide are some of the worries that necessitate American military presence although nation wide debates about US withdrawal has more vociferously emerged in recent months. Despite simmering opposition to American military presence in Central Asian bases within each Central Asian country, a cost-benefit analysis of regional implications of Afghan instability draws a balance sheet as much in US favour as in favour of Central Asia in the ongoing fight against terror. Therefore, the visits of Donald Rumsfeld to Uzbekistan and Condoleezza Rice to Kirgyzstan at varying times through 2005 have convinced the Uzbek and Kirgyz leaders about the obvious efficacy of American military presence in the vicinity of Afghanistan where Al Qaeda and Taliban forces are down, but not entirely out; vanquished, but their fear continues to haunt the region.[2] From capital Kabul these nefarious elements have shifted their power base to the volatile border areas in the neighbourhood of both Pakistan and Iran. They continue their terrorist activities with overt backing of the likeminded Islamists and covert patronage of the Musharaff regime. The irony of the fact that it was Pakistan that had fostered and nurtured the Taliban and Al Qaeda in their anti-Soviet pursuits in Afghanistan. It is Pakistan once again now that has become a close American ally in the fight against the terror unleashed by the very same Taliban and Al Qaeda. The dilemma facing Pakistan is the inherent duality of its foreign policy overtures, disliked by Islamist forces within the country, detested by her neighbours and hotly debated within the US the issue of Pakistan as a long term viable ally in view of her nuclear proliferation records.

While analyzing the role of Afghanistan in regional scheme of things and factoring out the regional implications of US military presence in that country, two more recent aspects crop up prominently. First is the issue of Iran going nuclear and its past record of relations with Pakistan; and the second is the Indo-American nuclear Bonhomie. Both Iran and Pakistan in the west and east of Afghanistan are potentially capable of unleashing an Islamic war in the region. Both these states are Islamic states and their adherence to Shariaa Islam locates them nowhere closer to a moderate democracy. The nuclear proliferation history of both these countries in the past has been nothing but abominable. One is a clandestine supplier of P-2 centrifuge through A.Q. Khan, while the other has been a recipient of it.[3] Both countries insist on building modern weapons systems against the grain of international community and continue to make much ado about their national security. Both of them are what the US is not: undemocratic, Islamic, lacking freedom and civil society and tense with emotional Islamic fervour. Both countries behave adamant: Pakistan continues to shield A.Q. Khan and refuses US or IAEC access to question him. And Iran stubbornly goes ahead with her own nuclear designs, refusing access to international inspection. Much as the US may wish to turn them democratic, in foreseeable future, by all indications, they are unlikely to emulate any non-Islamic diktat.

While development of events has posited these countries with plenty of anti-US dispositions, ironically Pakistan remains a US ally and Iran a US foe. What binds Iran and Pakistan together is their Islamic credential and nuclear ambitions. These two factors are coincidentally the two sole reasons that starkly display them on the opposite camp of Indo-US nuclear deal. While Pakistan lobbies hard with the US to gain an equal status with India, Iran argues differently. It openly criticizes the US for its bullying tactics and says that as a sovereign nation it has every right to develop nuclear weapons. It suspects a probable Indo-US design and argues that all round Iran there are countries with nuclear weapons, which the US has failed to desist from developing nuclear capability. These countries in the east of Iran are Pakistan and India, in the north the Russian Federation, in the west Israel and in the immediate neighbourhood in Afghanistan and Iraq, the US itself is present as a nuclear power. Iran argues that all this endangers her national security, and all this obviates the need for Iran to go nuclear. That it can no longer live in nuclear isolation sounds logical! A light year of communication gap and plethora of disinformation since 1979, when the Khomeini revolution swept Iran, have made US-Iranian bilateral relations a regional roadblock to conflict resolution in the Central Asian periphery. Sensitive Iran as a cradle of Persian civilization, as an oil and gas rich country, as a Persian Gulf and Caspian Sea power and as central landmass connecting east, west, north and south– a virtual bridge between civilizations and cultures ought not be ignored by the US.

The Indo-US nuclear deal signed in the first week of March, 2006 coupled with India's vote against Iran's nuclear programme has generated fearful apprehensions in Tehran. The Ahmedinejad government in Tehran fears an encirclement of his country by the US-by Turkey through NATO, by pro-American regimes in Afghanistan and Pakistan, by leasing military bases in Central Asian countries, by befriending Azerbaijan where it has constructed the Baku-Ceyhan oil and Baku Irzhurum gas pipelines and by hooking India to a mutual nuclear deal. Iran has already worked out penalty for India by hinting at possible price revision of the trilateral $ 7 billion gas pipeline deal.[4] While all these developments in and around Afghanistan generate considerable apprehensions about lingering regional instability, the outcome of US entanglement in countries it has ignored thus far is a potential factor to bear with for many years to come.

Spill Over Extremism

The strand of Islam that overwhelmed post-Soviet Central Asia and generated awesome feeling the world over was primarily considered as the spillover effects of Afghan developments. The revival of Islam in Central Asia was swift and pervasive right through the period of Gorbachev's perestroika and glasnost in the second half of 1980s. The Soviet break-up had only accelerated the process of this revival. Countries from Saudi Arabia to Jordan to Pakistan to Iran to Turkey all vied to gain a foothold on the basis of their confessional affinity on the profaned soil of Soviet atheism.

They distributed the Holy Koran free, and even financed the Haj trip for believers. Afghanistan at that point in time was in the backdrop, building the base for a Taliban takeover. Once they saddled themselves in power in Kabul, Islam of the Koran was Talibanized to suit the objectives of the ruling elite. In practice, it was all un-Islamic. They banned formal schooling for Afghan girls, prohibited doctors and nurses from medical practice, punished lady teachers for their enlightening mission of educating youngsters, forced them to teach religious edicts edited by Taliban Imams, and virtually proscribed female education. The day they flogged a lady in full public view in the presence of television crews at the premises of a stadium as punishment for her misdeeds, the world opened up its eyes to the reign of Taliban terror, but it was just the tip of a larger iceberg of a colossal Islamic machine built jointly by the Taliban and Al Qaeda with overt support of neighbour Pakistan, and of course then encouraged by the United States.

After the 9/11, all US diplomatic efforts failed to yield any worthwhile results in bridling the Taliban. The adamant refusal of Taliban leader Mulla Omar to hand over Osama bin Laden to the US and continuing television diatribe of Taliban Ambassador to Pakistan once again proved that Pakistan was the central country in reshaping the regional power equation. When direct pressure on the Taliban proved unsuccessful, the matter of how to turn Pakistan from a close ally of the Taliban to an instrument of fighting the Taliban was hotly debated in policy making circle of the US.[5] Pressuring Musharraf to rope in truant Taliban was a Herculean task for the US administration. The US diplomatic overtures to Pakistan continued through the tenure of Bill Clinton despite the sanctioned imposed on Pakistan for its nuclear adventure, both test and proliferation activities. However, all these efforts proved as much futile then as it continues to be so even now. Pakistan's role in nabbing Osama has remained evasive. President Bush's announcement of "catching Osama dead or alive" has not materialized. Those hundreds and hundreds of Al Qaeda functionaries handed over by Pakistan to the US did not touch any of the upper echelon of its leadership. Since September, 2001, Pakistan has remained the façade of an US ally in the fight against terror, while its real role is disliked by the US officials and public alike. The whole development has compelled the US not to put all their eggs in the Pakistani basket; rather diversify the regional priorities of relations with other countries in South and Central Asia including India, Russia, Uzbekistan and Kirgyzstan as contingent plan for the future.

Meanwhile, despite elections that have legitimized a pro-US regime in Kabul headed by Hamid Karzai, Afghanistan remains a country divided along regional loyalty to ethnic warlords. An overall analysis of Afghan political development vis-a vis the Taliban Al Qaeda combine suggests that a broadly triangular fight is on in that unstable country involving three major political forces: The Karzai government in Kabul, Pro-Taliban forces in Kandahar and Waziristan and US and Pakistani forces present in both countries. Thus it is a waging battle between Kabul, Kandahar and Islamabad where the US too is involved. What the US desires to protect is democracy and human rights in Afghanistan. And what the Taliban want to preserve is terror through primitive rule in the guise of Islam. And both these objectives clash. Even in the new parliament that Afghanistan has elected for the first time in three decades, the representatives have been juggling along the lines of "former Mujahideens and Taliban commanders, communists, tribal dictators and urban professionals."[6] As efforts at reconstruction of war-torn Afghanistan continues to receive more limelight and millions of dollars pour in that direction, the radical elements feel apparently threatened and desperately take recourse to barbaric methods of brutal killing of innocent civilians including foreigners. The situation is far too unstable to build democracy and a civil society on the ruins of a war ravaged country, where religious radicals endeavour to horde the people to primitive style of governance under the banner of Islam. It is a different clash of civilization where the mules confront modernity and Mullahs democracy. Ever since the Taliban regrouping began in 2003, the Taliban have killed 53 people who they have suspected as American spies or local informers. All these cases are not as sensational as the brutal assassination of journalist Daniel Pearl or beheading of the Indian Engineer Suryanarayan. But the fact that the killings are on is indicative of a deeper malaise wrecking Afghanistan. It also vindicates Pakistani connivance in a sense that Taliban freely roam between Quetta and Kandahar in motorbikes and choose their soft targets. In just three months, the Taliban had bought their favourite machine of the killers-1150 motorbikes of Honda 125cc–900 from Quetta and another 250 in Loralai north of Quetta in Pakistan.[7] These motorbikes are likely to be used in upcoming months anywhere in Afghanistan, Pakistan and elsewhere in Central Asia by the killers. Thus from the vantage point of an outside observer one could impartially conclude that Pakistani patronage to Taliban and Al Qaeda functionaries is a foregone conclusion and a potential threat to regional stability.

Lingering Shadow of Islam

A cursory look at another theatre in the northern regions of Afghanistan provides us with a fuzzy picture of porous borders of Afghanistan along three Central Asian countries: Tajikistan, Uzbekistan and Turkmenistan. The lingering shadow of Islam is what combines the region into a single geo-cultural and geo-religious space. However, for fifteen years now political fluidity in Central Asia and regime instability in Afghanistan are what combine the region into a single, unstable political space where Islam is misinterpreted and misused. The fact that post-Soviet Central Asian countries fundamentally differ from their southern neighbours in terms of their high literacy level, keeps them away from the pernicious influence of Islamic fundamentalism. This literacy level has precisely enabled them to understand the finer tenets of Islam vis-à-vis the impact of Talibanized fundamentalism. Yet it is in these last fifteen years that Islam in public life has remained debatable as an influential force to reckon with.

Three factors come to interplay in the Central Asian situation: the indigenous Islamic movements in Tajikistan and Uzbekistan, the Njuma Namangani phenomenon of terror and Hijb-Ut-Tahrir movement for making Central Asia a Caliphate. Tajikistan is the only country in Central Asia where the communists, democrats and the Islamists have been sharing power after their sordid experience of a bloody civil war. Divided only by the Pyandz River from Afghanistan, Tajikistan experienced the grueling years of Islamic renaissance after protracted years of atheism. A glaring instance was the rapid proliferation of mosques: from just 17 around the time of Soviet collapse in 1991 to over 3000 in 1993.[8] Thus the Central Asian religious fervour was boiling much before the advent of the Taliban in Afghanistan. At that inceptive stage, the indigenous religious awakening was a clash between official Islam patronized by the state and the emergent Islam professed by the Islamic renaissance Party having branches all across Central Asia. The divide was unclear, but the increasing influence of Islam was widely felt. Apprehensions of the authorities about emergent Islam in an environment of post-communist political instability were gradually peppered with another apprehension; this time that of spreading Islam from Afghanistan.

The terror tone of the Islamic movement in Central Asia became loud and clear only after the Taliban settled in Afghanistan and only after Njuma Namangani spread terror and began preaching radical Islam as an alternative to existing, political governance almost in a similar fashion as did the

Taliban. The political divide between the Slavic and Orthodox oriented communist presidents and Islamic oriented fundamentalists thus widened on the ground of a power struggle that swept Tajikistan into a civil war for five years and threatened to spread across the region. Although, Namangani could not spread religious contagion like wild fire as he wished, that was no solace for the rulers of Central Asia. What it spread was enough to frighten the rulers and the ruled alike.

Two instances of terror spread across two neighbouring countries and linked to Namangani were singled out to inspire awe. When four Americans suddenly vanished in the mountainous region of Kirgyzstan for six days, the Americans and the Central Asians felt the heat of a wider nexus the Taliban had already established with the Islamic Movement of Uzbekistan working together with 2000 odd Namangani guerrillas. The Americans were kidnapped from Kirgyzstan as were the Japanese geologists from Tajikistan. They were holed up in inaccessible mountains from where flowed the demand for ransom. While $5 million ransom freed the Japanese, the Amrican hostages managed to escape to freedom on the seventh day of their capture. Systematic counter measures jointly undertaken by the Uzbek and Kirgyz and Tajik forces could not flush out these guerrillas from their hideouts. The Americans declared Namangani a terrorist and the IMU in Uzbekistan among 27 terrorist organizations. But that did not help improve the situation or emancipate the hostages. The maiden blow from Namangani and the IMU was meted out to Karimov when the IMU killed 16 innocent civilians in Tashkent in a car bomb blast.[9] Namangani's name became synonymous with terror in the Ferghana valley. Yet no body had the courage to challenge the Namangani guerrillas. They roamed free on the wasteland of Central Asian mountains and carried out their mission of abduction. They even organized assassination attempts at president Karimov.

The danger that underlines Islam in the periphery of Afghanistan is the increasing application of coercion on innocent people. The region has been passing through a critical phase of political transition, where incumbent presidents in all Central Asian countries do not desire to part with power, yet they talk loud of participatory democracy. What fuels antipathy to such reign are the efforts of the presidents to perpetuate their reign, some through orchestrated elections as in Kazakhstan and Uzbekistan, and others through a resolution to declare them president for life as in Turkmenistan. The case of Kirgyzstan is much the same even after the tulip revolution, and in Tajikistan Imomali Rakhmanov has been a face far too long in power. While change is desirable, the presidents think it is not inevitable. This generates a schismatic feeling among the deprived sections of the society to crave for an alternative power structure which is unavailable. And the religious elements are there to feel the gap and help instigate a politically tumultuous situation. It may not etch out an identity in the short run, but it creates a quagmire from which there is no easy escape.

Assessing the Central Asian situation in the light of post 9/11, Charles Maynes, the Editor of Foreign Policy from 1980 to 1997 wrote: "the principal Islamist movements in the region advocate policies that seem either otherworldly, unacceptable, or troubling: otherworldly, when the Islamic Movement of Uzbekistan and the Hizb-ut-Tahrir call for the unification of the entire Islamic world community under a restored Caliphate; unacceptable, when the IMU seeks the violent overthrow of the current government in Tashkent; and troubling, because the HT, although it advocates the peaceful seizure of power, holds extremely conservative views about the role of women in society, is virulently anti-Israel and has no real programme to solve social or other governmental problems"[10] Maynes further asserts that the "core issue in Central Asia today is how the political order can accommodate the rise of Islam."[11]

While weak states of Central Asia and failed states in the periphery have become a breeding ground for terrorists to actively participate in unwarranted ventures of regime change or regime perpetuation, the Al Qaeda, Hizb-Ut-Tahrir, Islamic Movements of Uzbekistan and their ilk are organizations that advocate Islam not as a religion, but an Islamic state as an alternative framework of governance. Their replacement agenda is incoherent, their goals unclear, their motive conservatively religious and their desire devoutly Islamic. But their methods of governance are piously against the prescription of Islam. When weak and failed states seek to transform their status through the strength of religion and seek the help of fanatics like Osama Bin Laden, as it did happen in case of Afghanistan, there arises a need for mutual cooperation. "The Taliban needed Al Qaeda to supply motivated troops in the absence of a real Taliban army, to give money in the absence of a state apparatus that could raise or manage money and to supply ignorant village mullahs with ideological guidance."[12] All this had happened in Afghanistan, because a state was largely absent there; all this is not happening in Central Asia because the state there is primarily dictatorial. However, the impact of Islam on public life in Central Asia is too dangerous to ignore.

Too dangerous to ignore, but too difficult to handle is Islam's cyber connectivity. The terrorists' organizations are officially soliciting financial support on the internet from likeminded devotees of Islam from across the world. The Al Qaeda has done so after it moved its base from Sudan to Afghanistan; the Chechen fighters in Russia's breakaway republic have done so and the LTTE in Sri Lanka have done it too. Internet has brought the world closer for all, including for the terrorists and they freely use the cyber path for money transfer, training instructions, propaganda, cadre recruitment, planning and execution of terror acts, coordination and many other activities.[13] From the commanding height to the cadre management at the grassroots level, internet transmits instant message across regions irrespective of the distance involved and Islamic terrorists are active on a swathe of land spanning from Chechnya to Indonesia via Afghanistan and Central Asia.

Narcotic Menace

In one of the most recent post-summit press conferences in Uzbek capital Tashkent, in the presence of the Indian Prime Minister Manmohan Singh, the Uzbek President Islam Karimov singled out Afghanistan as the narcotic hub of Asia. Criticizing the heroin boom in recent years, Karimov pointed out that no other country in the world can perhaps match the role of Afghanistan in production of opium and consequent narcotic trade of refined drugs. Year after year, poppy cultivation in Afghanistan has maintained a steady upswing, no matter whether the country is under the Taliban or post-Taliban rule. The presence of the International Stabilization Force in Afghanistan has not helped curb heroin production and Afghanistan currently "accounts for 80 percent of the global opium production."[14] All interdiction measures of recent years have failed to swoon Afghanistan off the drug track, and in fact, it continues to thrive on that. The reasons are simple. Poppy cultivation in arid Afghanistan is the most profitable crop for poor farmers. With little input it gives a bumper crop, where as wheat or fruits or melon requires considerable investments which the farmers cannot afford. Thus poppy comes as a natural choice when crop consideration arise. Secondly, poppy requires virtually no rain and no irrigation, while any other crop would require it the most. Thirdly, poppy has ready marketability and established transport links that brings assured profits as much for the growers as for the traders, agents, middlemen, drug makers and peddlers. The chain is well established from the farmland to the cities and beyond to international markets. For instance, within the post-Soviet space the mafia network for narcotic market is too efficient to make quick bucks töo swiftly. Close to Afghanistan is Gorno-Badakhshan on the Afghan Tajik borders where a kilogram of heroin costs $ 4-8 thousand depending on its purity. Marching ahead to capital Dushanbe it fetches $ 12-17 thousand. In Tashkent, the capital of neighbouring Uzbekistan, the same kilogram of drug costs $30-40 thousand. In farther Moscow, it could fetch a staggering price of $ 150-200 thousand, while in far away Europe the price tag for the same quantity of heroin is $ 250-300 thousand. This is long saga-a route that enhances the street price of drugs from Afghanistan to Europe.[15]

A survey of illegal drugs conducted by the UN agencies and published in the Economist in 2001 revealed further escalation of drug prices in the American market. Added to Afghanistan, it provided data on Pakistan. The wholesale price of a kilogram of heroin in Pakistan is $ 3000, but the farmer is paid just $ 90 as its value at the procurement level; while the American wholesale price, where the drug is exported, is $80,000. After shuffling hands of various peddlers, the retail US street price for drugs with 40 percent purity is $290,000.[16] The involvement of such big money in narcotic trafficking dwarfs all government efforts and throttles all interdiction measures because money greases the palms of all involved along the journey.

The undercurrents of narcotic trafficking from the underbelly of Central Asia, particularly originating from the Pakistan-Afghan and Afghan-Tajik borders pose a mortal danger to the governments in all Central Asian countries. The borders are porous, long and almost unguarded. Three Central Asian countries have 2300 kilometers of extremely porous border with Afghanistan: Tajikistan has 1309, Uzbekistan 137 and Turkmenistan 854 kilometers. Political volatility in the region in general and each individual country in particular has made it well nigh impossible to provide for effective and efficient border security. As a result, Afghanistan and its adjoining regions with all Central Asian countries and Pakistan is a safe and profitable haven for drug lords. Drugs and narcotic trafficking remains one of the three major worries along with Islamic fundamentalism and international terrorism-all these stem from Pakistan-Afghan soil and their tentacles spread not only across Central Asia; but also far beyond to Europe and America. Despite concerted efforts at identifying the ills plaguing the region and coordinated endeavour to fight international terrorism, Afghanistan remains the most worrisome legacy of yesteryears. Neither the Soviets then; nor the Americans now would be able to stem the rot in foreseeable future. Given their precarious political position in their respective countries, Central Asian presidents are more so unlikely to arrest the influence of drug lords and war lords and encourage them to step in to building a civil society.

Notes

1. Winsten de Kitspotter, "The Great Game in Central Asia," *Nuclear Control,* No. 1, 2005, pp. 81-93.
2. Joel Brinkley, "US can maintain its Central Asian Base: Rice Reaches Agreement with Kirgyzstan," *The Times of India,* Mumbai, 13 October 2005.
3. K.Subrahmanyam, "A Case of Sour Grapes," *The Times of India,* Mumbai, 3 May 2006, p. 14.
4. *The Hindu Business Line,* 4 May 2006, p. 10.
5. "The 9/11 Commission Report, Final Report of the National Commission on Terrorist Attacks upon the United States," Authorized Edition, WW Norton and Company, New York-London, 2005, pp. 182-183.
6. "Afghanistan: A place for warlords to meet," *The Economist,* 7-13 January 2006, p. 32.
7. Ranjan Roy, "Forgotten War, Taliban is alive and well in Afghanistan," *The Times of India,* Mumbai, 5 May 2006, p. 16.
8. *The Hindustan Times,* 8 August 1993. For a detailed discussion see P.L.Dash, "The Tajik Cauldron," in Mustaq

A.Kaw (Ed.) *Central Asia: Continuity and Change,* University of Kashmir, Srinagar, 1999, pp. 152-157.

9. P.L.Dash, "The Heroin Highway to Hell," in Mahavir Singh and Victor Krassilchtchikov (Ed.) *Eurasian Vision,* Felicitation Volume on the 70th Birthday of Prof. Devendra Kaushik, Anamika Publishers, New Delhi, 2003, pp. 310-311.
10. Charles William Maynes, "America Discovers Central Asia," *Foreign Affairs,* Vol. 82, No. 2, March-April 2003, p. 130.
11. *Ibid,* p. 124.
12. Charles Fairbanks, "Base Debate: America in Central Asia," *The National Interest,* Summer, 2002, p. 46.
13. Thomas L. Friedman, "The World is Flat: The Globalized World in the Twenty-first Century," Penguin Publishers, 2006, pp. 534-535.
14. *The Times of India,* Mumbai, 27 April 2006, p. 12.
15. Irina Komissina and Azhar Kurtov, Narkotiki Tsentral'noi Azii: Novaya Ugroza Tsivilizatsii, Rossiya I Musulmanskii Mir, No. 1, 2001, p. 59.
16. *The Economist,* London, 28 July 2001, p. 6.

9

Context and Consequences of American Intervention in Afghanistan in the Post-9/11 Strategic Environment

Anand P. Mavalankar

American intervention in Afghanistan after 11 September, 2001 terrorist attacks in the United States needs to be understood and interpreted with the broader framework of the internal balance of forces within Afghanistan as well as evolution of the wider international environment since 9/11. Given the complex internal social and political conditions within Afghanistan as well as experience of its statehood, we need to examine the American intervention in Afghanistan in view of the wider historical context of the evolution of the political society of the country.

Context

Afghanistan is roughly the size of Texas (a southern state of the United States of America) which has quarter-million square miles of barren, mostly dry terrain. It is inhabited by a large majority of Pashtu-speaking Afghans, and Orthodox Muslim Pathans[1]. Being land-locked between Russia, Iran, and

Pakistan, with a narrow mountainous fuse of land pointed east to China, Afghanistan had no independent identity until mid-18th Century. The British Governor-General, Richard Colley Wellesley (1760–1842) was the first representative of an imperial power to send envoy to Afghanistan's Amir to ward off any possible threat to British India posed by French machinations at that time[2]. It marked the beginning of the "Great Game" that dominated European diplomacy in its dealings with Asia during the 19th century.

As far as Russia was concerned, Russia's push to the South occurred first during the reign of Peter the Great (1682–1725), who considered Russia's expansion into Asia as his country's destiny and the absorption of Turkish and Persian Khanates on his border as Russia's "civilizing mission."

For Britishers, the "Eastern Question" had become a primary concern when then foreign minister of Britain, Lord Palmerston (1784-1865) insisted in 1837, "we have long declined to meddle with the Afghans and have purposely left them independent but if the Russians try to make them Russian, we must take care they become British."[3]

Subsequently, the demarcation of Durand Line in 1893 was crucial to Britain for two reasons. It served to legitimise British India's additions to its Baluchistan and North-West Frontier tribal zones since the Second Afghan War. Secondly, it solved the international dispute with Russia's imperial force for Afghanistan which was then considered finally as a geographically defined national entity for the first time.

The Anglo-Russian Convention divided Persia into northern and southeastern "spheres of influences." Russians retained the northern sphere, while the Britishers retained the southeastern sphere. At the time, Britain had full control over Afghanistan's foreign policy. However, the Bolshevik Revolution of 1917 effectively ended the Anglo-Russian convention.

On February 2, 1919, King Habibullah wrote to India's new viceroy, Lord Chelmsford, and demanded "absolute liberty, freedom of action, and perpetual independence" for Afghanistan. After the murder of Habibullah, Amanullah Khan, youngest son of Amir, effectively asserted for Afghanistan's national independence from British Suzerainty. The Third Afghan War began on May 6, 1919 and Amanullah appealed for an armistice on May 28, 1919. In August 1919, both Britain and Afghanistan worked out a treaty that declared Afghanistan as a "fully sovereign state."

During the Second World War, Germany offered the government of King Zahir Shah military as well as economic support. Although Afghanistan reaffirmed strict neutrality during the war, Kabul was keen to take advantage of the impending British withdrawl from India by reabsorbing the tribal areas that were under Britain's control since the Second Afghan War. At the time, Kabul strongly sponsored a separate Pashtunistan ("Land of the Pashtus" or Pathans) movement, calling for the creation of a pathan nation that would integrate the Pashtu-speaking tribes of the North-West Frontier. This movement was considered as a serious territorial threat by the Muslim League. After Pakistan's emergence as a sovereign independent state, trade with Afghanistan was cut off. Due to the hostility between these two states, Afghanistan was the only nation-state that voted against admitting Pakistan as a member-state of the United Nations in 1948.

As far as Russia's relations with modern Afghanistan were concerned, the first major milestone was the first Russo-Afghan Treaty of Trade and Friendship signed in Kabul in 1920. As regards the United States of America, Washington had extended formal diplomatic recognition to Kabul in 1934, but no permanent U.S. mission was established there until 1943. Under Shah Mahmud's aegis, America's early Afghan initiative came in the form of the Helmund River Valley project. In 1956, Washington did not oblige Kabul in regard to her requests for arms and ammunition. At the time, Kabul appealed to Moscow for its military hardware. The Soviet Union responded positively without attaching any conditions.

In 1964, a new constitution was approved by the Grand Tribal Assembly (Loya Jirga), proclaiming Afghanistan a constitutional monarchy, whose "sacred religion" was Islam, an "independent, unitary and indivisible" state. American-educated Dr. Abdul Zahir was "elected" (he was actually chosen by King Zahir and later confirmed by popular mandate) President of the lower house of the People (Wolesi Jirga). His most articulate opposition came from the Marxists of the far Left, led by Babrak Karmal.

Afghanistan's modernization and economic development was greatly assisted by the Soviet Union, due to its geographic proximity. The coup on April 27, 1978, was masterminded by Taraki, who preclaimed Afghanistan as a "Democratic Republic," and himself its President-Prime Minister. Throughout early 1979, opposition to Taraki's government increasingly became violent in all parts of Afghanistan. Thousands of Russian advisers were based in Kabul to help Taraki run his government and army. In December 1979, Soviet Union moved its armed forces directly into Afghanistan.

The Soviet invasion of Afghanistan in 1979 and the Soviet occupation of Afghanistan from 1980 to 1989 were perceived in terms of the rivalry between the two superpowers in the cold war era. Similarly, the local actors and their strategies were interpreted largely in terms of the global security issues that had linkage with the prevailing Soviet-American rivalry at that time. The Soviet invasion was viewed as domination of Soviets over warm-water seas, which was considered as a reaffirmation of the objectives of the pre-1917 Russian empire. It was also perceived as the 'Great Game' that involved the confrontation between the British and Russian empires in the 19th century. The Soviet invasion of Afghanistan in 1979 was meant to secure a route to the Indian Ocean. Even the emergence of Taliban was viewed as a tool of Pakistan's anti-Indian strategy and pursuit of influence in Central Asia[4]

Such geopolitical interpretations however, exclude proper assessment of certain specific factors that are responsible for political violence in Afghanistan since 1979. American invasion of Afghanistan in 2001 and the past-2001 Afghanistan political landscape need to be linked to internal sources relating to political society of Afghanistan in the post–9/11 strategic environments.

At the outset, it is necessary to outline these contending interpretations for the purposes of drawing a conceptual linkage between the nature of different factors and the political violence that erupted in the political society of Afghanistan. Mainly, these factors include tribalism, ethnicity and Islam.

Tribalism

In a tribe-based segmented society of Afghanistan, a recurrent process of fission and fusion occurs time and again. In the 18th Century, as a result of the disintegration of the Persian and Mughal empires, the Ghilzai and later the Durrani Pushtun tribal confederation were able to exploit in order to impose their own will on neighbouring population. It is pertinent to note here that the Pushtun tribes overthrew King Amanullah in 1929.[5]

Ethnicity

Another major cause of political violence in Afghanistan relates to the question of ethnicity. One notices hierarchy among the principal ethnicities in Afghanistan. They include the Pushtuns, the Tajiks, the Uzbecks and the Hazaras. Up to the 1950s in the tradition of colonial ethnographic literature, an 'essentialist' idea of ethnicity was prominent. Here the concept of 'ethno-genesis' involved objective criteria such as language, history, religion etc. The new approach to ethnicity, however, focuses on a social relationship. This is clearly a departure from the illusory supposition that communities are natural objects. As per the new approach, identity is posed in its relation with other groups. Here the concept of an ethnic 'frontier' implying an altogether more subjective and relational idea of ethnicity is employed.[6]

In Afghanistan, the identity of each individual is defined by a series of affiliations, from the most general—to the *umma* (The Muslim community as a whole)-to the narrowest, the close family. In the tribal context, the idea of a *qowm* specifies precisely these identities when they are mobilized within a solidarity network. This Arabic term refers to a patrilineal group, which is used in a more generalized way for any solidarity group by the Afghans. In other words, macro-ethnicities were posited as collective actors. As Dorronsoro observes: ".....it was not 'ethnicities' that made war, but political organizations with ideological objectives and particular institutional practices."[7]

This ethnisation of politics remains a crucial element of the political landscape of Afghanistan after the American invasion of the country, in the wake of the new American policy relating to the "war on terror". The prospect of winning this war and reconstructing the political society of Afghanistan hinges on the form such ethnicisation of politics takes in the long run within it.

Islam

The role of Islam in Afghanistan must be examined in terms of response of its religious establishment to the changing circumstances in the country. The relations between the state and the *ulema* need to be examined within the broader question of the legitimacy of political power. After the Soviet withdrawal from Afghanistan, the ulema were instrumental in legitimating the political order in a highly segmented society.

Having reviewed these three broad interpretations, we must examine the preceding conditions relating to the Afghan resistance to the Soviet occupation of Afghanistan for most of the 1980s. Clearly, there were two groups–(i) the *ulema* and (ii) the educated individuals that came from the towns to provide the dynamic leadership in the resistance. During the war against the Soviets, there was a polarization between the educated Islamists and the fundamentalist *ulema*. The supremacy of the Taliban in the late 1990s was a 'clerical revolution' which gave rise to a regime that was unconventional in the Muslim world.

In the 1990s, the organizations run the *ulema* or by the educated Afghans successfully mobilized resources at their disposal. For these two groups, control of the state, by capturing Kabul was the major objective. The Taliban was successful during the 1990s in establishing their monopoly of power in Kabul till the American intervention in 2001.

The American Intervention

The American intervention reestablished the regional authorities as one of the key players in the domestic politics of Afghanistan. At the same time, the rivalry between the two groups was temporarily suspended, when Kabul was occupied by the American intervention and the presence of international forces, including those coming from the NATO. Although it was meant to reconstruct Afghanistan in a full-fledged manner, the central authority in Kabul could not ensure that its will prevail in the rest of Afghanistan. So the civil war has continued to hamper the reconstruction of central political authority in Afghanistan. Secondly, it has led to ethnicisation of the war. And thirdly, aims of the fundamentalist *ulema* in giving pronounced Islamist character to the Afghanistan polity have continued to influence the thinking of the influential elites, the *ulemas*.

The larger question after the American invasion of Afghanistan relates to the legitimacy of the Afghan State. With the collapse of the Taliban regime, the Americans and its NATO allies have made efforts on the basis of Pushtun nationalism. However, this is challenged by tribes and *ulemas* in Afghanistan.

After the American invasion, there is growing tension between the neo-patrimonial state dominated by the Pushtuns and those who are opposed to them. The neo-patrimonial state is defined by the appropriation of the partially institutionalized political culture by a group essentially oriented towards the maintenance of its own power.[8] The reconstruction of the political society under Hamid Karzai's Presidentship has involved development of specific state-run institutions that is marked by the predominance of a restricted group, which is able to perpetuate its hold on power. And yet the use of Islam as a fountainhead of legitimacy was noticed during the Afghan constitutions of 1923, 1931, 1964, 1977 and 1987, where is recognition of Islam as the official religion was clearly visible.

Dilemma of the Karzai Government

At present, the central government of President Hamid Karzai is faced with a dilemma as to what shape the Afghan polity should take in the post-2001 period. If Karzai scrupulously allows other ethnic groups in Afghanistan to have their legitimate and proportionate share of power in the government and the wider political process, other ethnic groups and tribes would challenge the legitimacy of the Karzai dispensation. That may well provide space to the *ulemas* as well as other tribes. But it may lead to political fragmentation of Afghanistan. This may militate against the liberal model launched by the Americans which were instrumental in bringing the collapse of the Taliban regime that was distinctive by virtue of its fundamentalist Islamic practices during its reign in the 1990s.

On the other hand, if the Karzai government insists and works toward the Afghan national identity based on the Pushtun ethnicity, and in particular the Pushtu language, it would be characterized as a deliberate effort to construct a Pushtun nation-state. This would generate severe criticism from the conservative political force of the *Ulema*. In other words, insistence on Pushtun nationalism could lead to serious tension between the Pushtuns and the Islamic fundamentalists for an indefinite period in future.

There is no doubt that the quest for legitimising the state of Afghanistan after the American intervention and the US-led war has led to rapid politicisation of the political society in Post-Taliban Afghanistan, especially among the groups of educated Islamists and the ulema. The resistance offered by the fundamentalist Pro-Taliban forces continues to undermine the liberal model of governance provided by the Karzai government, with assistance from the United States and its other allies. Further, a huge number of radical militants have taken refuge in the region on the Afghanistan-Pakistan border.

Clearly, the American and other NATO-led troops have faced, at times, fierce armed conflict with small groups of fighters in Afghanistan. The crisis in Afghanistan after the American war in the post–9/11 strategic environment has to be viewed in relation to the role of Al-Queda network in constantly undermining the 'liberal' roadmap of reestablishing the state authority of Afghanistan.

Al-Qaeda, Radical Islamic Revivalism and Post-9/11 strategic environment

The Al-Qaeda movement is a good illustration of radical Islamic revivalism, which has, in recent decades, used their doctrines of violence toward outsiders, particularly the United States. *Salafi* writings have portrayed the United States as an instrument of Satan, oppressing Muslims and threatening Islamic civilization with its secular culture and power. The

U.S. is considered the leader of a "Zionist-Crusader" alliance dedicated to destroying Islam. Apart from a pact between the United States and Israel, the alliance is perceived to have oppressed Muslims in Bosnia, Chechnya, Lebanon and Iraq. Bin Laden and other radical revivalists have characterized the United States as a sworn enemy of Islam that must be resisted with force. Further, Laden has often considered the American regime as equivalent to the Mongol barbarians who invaded the Islamic world during the Middle Ages.[9]

Osama bin Laden was converted to theological radicalism in the early 1970s. in the war against Afghanistan, he honed his skills as a military leader. It turned out to be a rallying point for radical Islamic revivalists to resist the Soviet invasion of Afghanistan. At the time, bin Laden worked closely with Abdullah Azzam, a Palestinian member of the Muslim Brotherhood, helping him to recruit young Muslims for the Afghan front and to prevent outbursts of factional violence between Sunni and Shiite volunteers. Toward the end of the war, both leaders differed over the proper strategy for bringing about Islamic revival. Azzam was keen to concentrate on constructing an Islamic state in Afghanistan. Osama bin Laden was, however, determined to carry out a war against several Kafir (infidel) countries, including apostate Muslim countries and the Western countries such as the United States.

In the late 1980s, Osama bin Laden established the Al-Qaeda network to train Sunni Arab Muslims who had fought against the Soviet troops in Afghanistan. Since then they were given a broader mandate to fight against the larger war with the United States. Al-Qaeda's goal of establishing a Pan-Islamic caliphate throughout the world has posed a huge challenge to the Westphalian sovereign nation state-system. Its course of action includes working with allied Islamic extremist groups to overthrow the allegedly "non-Islamic" regimes and expelling Westerners and non-Muslims from Muslim Countries. In February 1998, it issued a statement under the banner of

"The World Islamic Front for Jihad against the Jew and Crusaders," proclaiming it the duty of all Muslims to kill U.S. citizens-including civilians–and their allies. Such ambitious and violent notion of Jihad constitutes extreme form of radical Islamic revivalism. Keeping this in view, Al-Qaeda has operated in Sudan, Egypt, Saudi Arabia, Yemen, Somalia, Afghanistan, Indonesia, Malaysia, Singapore, Bangladesh, Pakistan, Bosnia, Croatia, Albania, Algeria, Tunisia, Lebanon,the Philippines, Tajikistan, Azerbaijan, Kenya, Tanzania, Chechnya, and Kashmir in India.[10]

Given the above-stated position of Al-Qaeda, the terrorist attacks on World Trade Centre and Pentagon on September 11, 2001, produced a qualitatively different post-9/11 strategic environment. In a fundamental sense, the 9/11 phenomenon reveals the impact of radical Islamic revivalism in the form of a distinct radical political theology. It challenged the Westphalian authority structure of the international order.

Actions of Osama bin Laden and other such radical revivalists are motivated by religious beliefs about the ultimate ground of existence. This has far-reaching consequences for the emerging political landscape of Afghanistan in the post-9/11 strategic environment. Apart from the various factors alluded to above relating to the changing nature of the domestic politics of Afghanistan, Al-Qaeda's critique of the Westphalian international order sharply questions the 'liberal' model of reconstituting political society of Afghanistan.

Conclusion

In this essay, we have endeavored to show that a complex historical context of the Afghanistan political society must be properly appreciated to comprehend the full significance of American intervention in that country. As regards post-9/11 strategic environment, careful attention must be given to factors internal to domestic politics in Afghanistan, with a view to assessing the consequences of the American intervention. Lastly, the distinct religious character of Al-Qaeda network has to be understood for the purposes of determining the prospects of 'liberal' model in reconstituting the political authority in contemporary Afghanistan.

Notes

1. Olof Caroe, *The Pathans, 550 B.C.-A.D. 1957,* Oxford University Press, Karachi, 1976.
2. Stanley Wolpert, *Roots of Confrontation in South Asia : Afghanistan, Pakistan, India and the superpowers,* Oxford University Press, New York, 1982, p. 53.
3. W. Baring Pemberton, *Lord Palmerton,* Batchworth Press, London 1954, p. 95.
4. Ahmed Rashid, *Taliban, Islam, Oil and the New Great Game in Central Asia,* I.B. Tauris, London, 2000.
5. Leon Poullada, *Reform and Rebellion in Afghanistan, 1919-1929 : King Amanullah's failure to transform a tribal society,* Cornell University Press, Ithaca, 1973.
6. Fredrik Barth, Ed., *Ethnic Group and Boundaries: The Social Organisation of Culture Difference,* Geo. Allen & Unwin, London, 1969.
7. See Gilles Dorronsoro, *Revolution Unending Afghanistan: 1979 to the Present,* Translatated from the French by John King, Hurst and Co., London, 2000, p. 15.
8. *Ibid.,* pp. 25-33.
9. Roy "Afghanistan: An Islamic war of Resistance," in Martin Marty and Scott Appleby, eds., *Fundamentalism and the State,* No. 3, University of Chicago Press, Chicago, 1993.
10. Peter L. Bergen, *Holy War, Inc: Inside the Secret World of Osama bin Laden* Free Press, New York, 2001, p. 196.

10

U.S. Policy in Afghanistan: The Challenges and Critical Dilemmas

Vaishali Singh

This paper will focus on the impact of the American War on Terrorism on Afghanistan; through the U.S. attack on Afghanistan in October 2001 till subsequent developments there. As a post-conflict society, Afghanistan faces numerous difficulties. Attempts to simultaneously reconstruct the country and build the capacity of people to provide for their basic needs are crucial, despite the complexity of the situation, involving the continued local authority of militias controlled by regional leaders and growing narcotics trafficking. In terms of U.S. policy, a situation such as the Taliban's support for Al Qaeda in Afghanistan suggests the potential for future similar scenarios that could require a significant military response from the US. However, for Afghanistan the crucial question remains whether the U.S. will prioritize the long-term commitment to stabilization in Afghanistan over the hunt for Bin Laden, and engage in nation-building.

Brief Narrative of Past US Involvement in Afghanistan:

The first extensive American contact with Afghanistan was made by Josiah Harlan, who was variously a soldier, a Quaker, a Freemason and an adventurer from Pennsylvania and was later an adviser in Afghan politics in the 1830s. US involvement in Afghanistan in the nineteenth century had been minimal. However in the post Second World War phase US involvement in Afghanistan increased significantly. While in the 1950s, the US declined Afghanistan's request for defense cooperation, in the period between 1950s and 1979 the US extended an economic assistance program focused on the development of Afghanistan's physical infrastructure. The US Peace Corps was active in Afghanistan between 1962 and 1979. Following the April 1978 coup launched by the People's Democratic Party of Afghanistan relations between the US and Afghanistan deteriorated. In February 1979, U.S. Ambassador Adolph "Spike" Dubs was kidnapped and later murdered in Kabul. Subsequently, after the December 1979 Soviet invasion the US terminated all bilateral assistance to Afghanistan. President Jimmy Carter immediately declared that the invasion jeopardized vital U.S. interests, because the Persian Gulf area was "now threatened by Soviet troops in Afghanistan."[1]

The US then launched covert operations in Afghanistan through the CIA, which began to supply all sorts of financial and especially arms supplies to the Afghan rebels. However the particulars regarding the actual commencement of aid to the rebels in Afghanistan is a matter of debate because according to the memoirs of the former CIA director Robert Gates aid to the rebels began nearly six months before the Soviet invasion i.e., in June 1979.[2] During the period of Soviet occupation of Afghanistan, the U.S. provided about $3 billion in military and economic assistance to *mujahideen* resistance movements to achieve a Soviet withdrawal

In fact the involvement of the CIA in the evolution of the Taliban and Al Qaeda in the years before the September 11 attacks has become a matter of infamy and condemnation for the US government.

After the fall of the Soviet-backed Democratic Republic of Afghanistan in 1992, Afghanistan was thrown into civil war between competing *mujahideen* warlords. The Taliban meaning "students" or the Islamist and Pashtun nationalist resistance movement emerged victorious after the civil war and ruled most of Afghanistan from 1996 until 2001.

When the Taliban came to power, Osama bin Laden was able to forge an alliance between the Taliban and his Al-Qaeda organization. It is understood that Al Qaeda-trained fighters known as the 055 Brigade were integrated with the Taliban army between 1997 and 2001 and so a close connection was forged between the Taliban and bin Laden.

9/11 and US Reaction

The September 11, 2001 attacks were a series of coordinated attacks carried out in the United States, by nineteen men affiliated with Al-Qaeda, who hijacked four American airliners. Two of these airlines were crashed into the World Trade Center in New York City; the third aircraft crashed into the U.S. Department of Defense headquarters, the Pentagon, in Virginia; the fourth plane crashed into a rural field in Somerset County, Pennsylvania. Following this in October 2001 the United States invaded Afghanistan in an operation codenamed Operation Enduring Freedom marking the beginning of the US "War on Terrorism" campaign. The stated intent was to remove the Taliban from power because of the Taliban's refusal to hand over Osama bin Laden for his involvement in the September 11 attacks. The US military action led to the partial disintegration of the Taliban. As Afghanistan had become Al Qaeda's main base and the land from which further attacks on the US were likely to be launched unless it was attacked and the regime was destroyed, the Bush Administration took the War against Terrorism to Afghanistan, Al Qaeda and the Taliban. On September 21, 2001 the Taliban formally rejected the demand that Osama be turned over to the US. By late September more than three hundred aircraft, two dozen warships and 28000 military personnel had been concentrated in the Indian Ocean and Red Sea within striking range of Afghanistan. President Bush was keen on naming the mission Operation Infinite Justice, but several Muslim governments objected stating that only 'Allah' could provide infinite justice, and hence the mission was named Operation Enduring Freedom.

However since the 2001 invasion of the country, the US is interested in the emergence of a broad-based government, and a national reconstruction process within Afghanistan. The U.S. is actively assisting the Afghan people as they rebuild their country and establish a representative government that contributes to regional stability, is market friendly, and respects human rights.

Background to the Current Politico-Security Challenges in Afghanistan

In late 2001, major leaders from the Afghan opposition groups and diaspora met in Bonn and agreed on a plan for the formulation of a new government structure that resulted in the inauguration of Hamid Karzai as Chairman of the Afghan Interim Authority (AIA). The Afghan Government, with the support of the international community, has made significant progress in implementing the Agreement on Provisional Arrangements in Afghanistan pending the Re-establishment of Permanent Government Institutions (Bonn Agreement). The UN Security Council reiterated, "its endorsement of the Agreement on provisional arrangements in Afghanistan pending the re-establishment of permanent government institutions, signed in Bonn on 5 December 2001 (S/2001/1154) (the Bonn Agreement)."[3] The Bonn Agreement provided for interim governance of the country. It charted out a process whereby provisional governing institutions would gradually increase in legitimacy, culminating in a fully representative Government after the holding of free and fair elections. The Bonn Agreement set out a framework for establishing a new government in Afghanistan. In addition, multilateral, bilateral, and nongovernmental organizations providing humanitarian assistance and longer-term development assistance have each developed independent strategies, which have resulted in a highly fragmented reconstruction effort. To bring coherence to the effort, the Afghan government developed a National Development Framework and Budget. The legitimacy of the Government would be rooted in the new Constitution. The widely detested Taliban regime was thus replaced with a somewhat fragile pro-Western government under the leadership of Hamid Karzai.

In July 2002 a nationwide Loya Jirga was organised by the interim administration, with about 2000 delegates, either selected through elections in the various regions of the country or allocated to various political, cultural and religious groups. The word Loya Jirga is from the Pashto language—*loya* meaning "grand" and *jirga* meaning "council". The Loya Jirga is an assembly unique to Afghanistan in which, traditionally, tribal elders-Pashtuns, Tajiks, Hazaras and Uzbeks-have come together to settle affairs of the nation. The July 2002 Loya Jirga formed a new Transitional Administration, with Hamid Karzai elected as Interim President.

The process of drafting the new Constitution began in November 2002 and continued through most of 2003. The Constitutional Loya Jirga was convened in Kabul on 10

December 2003 to finalize and ratify the draft Constitution. A total of 502 delegates attended, of whom 20 per cent were women and on 4 January 2004, the delegates approved the new Constitution. The Constitution became the official law of Afghanistan when the 2003 Loya jirga approved it by the consensus on January 4, 2004. It evolved out of the Afghan Constitution Commission mandated by the Bonn Agreement. The Constitution provides for an elected President and National Assembly.

The constitution of Afghanistan provides for a pure presidential system, but one that places a great emphasis on parliamentary control of the executive, vesting most of the power in the central Government. It also calls for an independent judiciary, headed by a Supreme Court, and a legal framework that is consistent with the tenets of Islam. It is significant that the new Afghan Constitution provides equal rights to men and women and guarantees that women will make up at least 25 per cent of the representatives in the lower house of parliament.

Afghanistan has passed seven major milestones in the road to implementation of a constitutional democracy:

1. The Bonn Agreement of December 2001 agreed upon a framework for political reconstruction in Afghanistan.

2. The Emergency Loya Jirga of June 2002 saw the implementation of a representative government and installed Hamid Karzai as the interim President.

3. The Constitutional Loya Jirga of January 4-16, 2004, approved Afghanistan's nationally mandated constitution in 40 years.

4. Afghans went to the polls on Oct. 9, 2004 and Hamid Karzai became the first democratically elected

president of Afghanistan. Karzai got 55.4% of the votes cast in the elections and he has been elected for two terms ending in 2009.

5. Elections to the Afghan national assembly were held on September 18, 2005 and on December 19, 2005 the new Assembly was inaugurated.

The former King Zahir Shah holds the honorific, "Father of the Country," and presides symbolically over certain occasions, but lacks any governing authority; the honorific is not hereditary.

The 18 September 2005 polls represented the final step of the plans laid out in the December 2001 Bonn agreement, which ushered in a post-Taliban government in Afghanistan. With the completion of the elections, Afghanistan has now, at least on paper, put in place all of the necessary institutions needed to become a democratic state. Assembly and Provincial elections held in September 2005 marked a new beginning for a truly democratic Afghanistan and greater government influence throughout the countryside. Understanding this, Al Qaeda and the Taliban in fact attempted to increase the level and frequency of attacks leading up to September to disrupt elections and to discredit Afghanistan's legitimate government. Al Qaeda, Taliban, and other anti-coalition militias continue to attack coalition, International Security Assistance Force (ISAF) and Afghan security forces, and aid workers and other non-combatants. Afghanistan is still very unstable, which hinders the difficult process of democratisation. In this context, parliamentary and provincial elections were undeniably an important step forwards to reinforce the State and give direct political representation to the people. A deluge of candidates-5800 for the 249 seat lower House of Parliament and 34 Provincial Councils–saw voters grappling with some of the largest ballot papers in the world. Voters in Kabul waded through 14 broadsheet pages containing photographs and symbols of more than 700 candidates choosing just two.

Just about a month later on October 9, 2005 an estimated 8.4 million Afghans turned out to cast ballots in Afghanistan's historic presidential election, which had eighteen candidates, including one female candidate running for the Presidential post. On December 7, 2005 Hamid Karzai was sworn in as Afghanistan's first democratically elected head of state. Subsequently on December 19, 351 men and women representing Afghanistan's different provinces, tribes and ethnic groups were inaugurated in a ceremony at the National Assembly in Kabul.

The Government of Afghanistan prepared a *National Development Framework* (NDF) in April 2002 and the *Securing Afghanistan's Future* report (with its international partners) in March 2004. In addition, the National Budget *Public Investment Programmes* provide strategy for some sectors.

The Afghan Government has articulated its overarching goals for the well-being of its people in the *Afghanistan Millennium Development Goals Country Report 2005–Vision 2020.*

The US Presence in Afghanistan

Almost six years ago, the US initiated military action in Afghanistan, with two aims: firstly, to defeat Al-Qaeda and their Taliban allies, and secondly, in concert with the Afghan people and the international community, to facilitate the creation of democratic conditions which would thwart the terrorist sanctuaries within Afghanistan.

The overarching U.S. Government strategy for winning the war on terrorism and rebuilding the state of Afghanistan is predicated on six lines of operation that include improving governance; defeating the terrorist threat and improving security; improving rule of law and justice; enhancing economic and social development; implementing regional and donor strategies; and integrating and synchronizing United States Government actions.[4] In Afghanistan, the United States is one of many bilateral and multilateral donors of aid helping to implement the Bonn Agreement.

After the attack the US administration realized that it was important to protect the interim government in Afghanistan. To that end in December 2001 the US convinced the United Nations to assemble the International Security Assistance Force (ISAF) to stabilize Kabul. The US led coalition in Afghanistan is strong with forty nations involved in Operation Enduring Freedom and NATO's International Security Assistance Force (ISAF). The U.S. military has nearly 20,000 troops under Enduring Freedom, and about 1,700 coalition troops from 18 nations, the total is over 20,000. 36 nations are providing forces to ISAF, which today numbers over 9,000 troops. Coalition and NATO forces surged additional battalions during the assembly election period as was done during the Presidential elections.

Beginning as mainly a protection force for Kabul in 2002, ISAF expanded stabilization and security operations into the North in June 2004, fulfilling stage 1 of ISAF's expansion plan. On 31 May 2005, NATO implemented the 2nd stage of ISAF expansion, taking responsibility for the western portion of Afghanistan, and resulting in ISAF being responsible for half of the country. As part of the stage 3 expansion, NATO/ISAF has agreed to expand its areas of operation further from northern and western Afghanistan to southern Afghanistan. NATO completed its 3rd stage of expansion in summer 2006, which transferred responsibility for stabilization and security operations in southern Afghanistan, including Kandahar, the traditional home of the Taliban. The expansion of ISAF promises to increase international participation in Afghanistan. Nonetheless, the US will continue to remain the single largest contributor of troops and capability even as the NATO/ISAF mission expands.

Security Problems

In Afghanistan today insecurity rooted in terrorist activities, factional fights and drug-related crime remains the major concern of the country. Therefore the major challenge for the US and the Afghan government is to ensure that the peace process become irreversible and security in Afghanistan realized. The continuing scenario of insecurity, involving attacks against non-governmental organizations (NGOs), has been a major cause for the protracted advance of reconstruction process. "In too many areas, individuals and communities suffer from abuses of their basic rights by local commanders and factional leaders....Judicial institutions remain weak, and the narcotic economy is largely unchecked. Insecurity from factional armies and extremist activities continue to destabilize many areas."[5]

Despite the fact that over six years have elapsed since the US attacks on the Taliban and Al-Qaeda operatives in Afghanistan, concerns remain about the continuing security and political and economic challenges of reconstruction in Afghanistan. The reconstruction and stabilization of Afghanistan is a vital national security imperative for the United States. The US is apprehensive that without the necessary reconstruction of Afghanistan, the country will once again become a haven for terrorists. The reconstruction of Afghanistan requires a very significant investment of American capital, both financial and diplomatic. Furthermore, this reconstruction is proving to be difficult to implement unless the security situation in Afghanistan is dramatically improved; security implying the need to establish stability and basic order throughout the country. Within Afghanistan the problem of security broadly arises from the fact that vast areas of country are still disputed territory, with the resurgent Taliban launching attacks throughout the south and southeast.

The US administration comprehends that the lack of security is the most significant factor that might ensure a return of a stateless society in Afghanistan. Though routed out of their strongholds and camps after 9/11, replenished and reorganized elements of Al Qaeda and the Taliban remain at large and constitute a threat, both real and symbolic, to the overall reconstruction effort, gaining financial support from drug interests. Terrorists, drug lords, and warlords, are holdovers, protagonists, and allies from the period of protracted civil war in Afghanistan. In fact, the drug trade and consequent drug finance generated, risks turning Afghanistan into an unrestricted narcotics backed state.

The number of American deaths in the Afghan operation dubbed Enduring Freedom is now 295.[6] Fighting in the country has persisted, particularly along and near the Afghan-Pakistani border, where remnants of the Taliban have endured over the years.

The U.N. Security Council has repeatedly expressed its concern over the increased number of attacks against humanitarian personnel, coalition forces, ISAF, and the Afghan government officials, targeted by Taliban and other rebel elements. These incidents have disrupted humanitarian assistance and the overall recovery effort. The year 2005 had been the most violent since the US invasion of Afghanistan in October 2001. Nearly 1,000 people were killed in 2005 compared with 850 in 2004. A sustained offensive by Taliban and counter attacks by the coalition forces caused about 4,000 violent deaths in 2006. The year 2007 is witnessing more lethal attacks and counter-attacks between Taliban and international forces.

The Refugee Situation

Following the end of the Communist backed regime in 1992, and the installation of the interim *mujahidin* government, almost 2 million Afghan refugee populations repatriated. However, the subsequent political instability and worsening economic circumstances in Afghanistan prevented national recovery and reconstruction and also unfortunately stalled repatriation generating a situation in which there was renewed population displacement inside and outside the country.

According to a report by the UNHCR in Afghanistan, the primary challenges for the refugees trying to return, "are security and political instability, the perceived weakness and partiality of the administration in Kabul, absence of functioning legal and judicial systems to ensure basic human rights, vulnerability to local commanders, slow economic and social progress especially in rural areas, limited employment opportunities, insufficient access to land and water, conservative customs and attitudes, opportunities for former civil servants and professionals, limited reach and impact of reconstruction programmes."[7]

The ongoing insecurity, exacerbated in the run-up to the 2005 legislative elections, remains a problem, for refugees trying to return. The security situation is a key concern for Afghan refugees in Iran and Pakistan. Nonetheless, the fact remains that millions of Afghan families are returning to their native land they face the daunting prospect of having to rebuild not just their lives, but also their country's future. A serious housing shortage affects most parts of Afghanistan, especially the cities. Therefore despite the return of almost 3 million Afghans to their homes since the Bonn Agreement, significant numbers still remain displaced. Their return and rehabilitation will largely depend on improved political and security conditions therefore ensuring their economic and social recovery.

Warlords

Although in this post election period the central government has the constitutional authority over the provinces, in reality factional chiefs are in control of local government. During the conduct of Operation Enduring Freedom US relied on these warlord led factional militia to defeat the Taliban; eventually these militia commanders or warlords empowered themselves while contributing to the fragmentation of power and frustrating the reform process.

The ISAF had deployed Provincial Reconstruction Teams (PRTs) to help extend the authority of the central government and facilitate stability. However, the PRTs have been "hamstrung by the policy constraints of troop-contributing nations, resource limitations, and "national caveats" to act decisively against local thugs, drugs, and official mugs."[8] After the elections the demobilized militia leaders and former warlords have been integrated into the government, and some are currently members of the National Assembly, but they continue to undermine the rule of law.

Today, the warlords are in command of much of the country and are instrumental in promoting an illegitimate economy fueled by the smuggling of arms, drugs, and other goods. They also refuse to give hundreds of millions of dollars in customs duties collected at border points in the regions they control, depriving the central government of precious revenue to finance the reconstruction process in Afghanistan. These warlords wield local power and have set up patronage networks through access to foreign aid, weapons, tax revenue, natural resources, and the illicit narcotics trade.

Narcotics Driven State

The United Nations Office on Drugs and Crime (UNODC) estimates that Afghanistan accounts for eighty-seven percent of global opium production. According to the UN, the value of the illegal narcotics trade in Afghanistan in 2005 is estimated at two-billion-seven-hundred-million dollars, the equivalent of more than fifty percent of Afghanistan's gross national product. According to the UN, eighty percent of this money goes to drug trafficking networks rather than to the two million Afghan farmers and labourers believed to be involved in opium poppy cultivation. Within Afghanistan too the use of illicit drugs is ubiquitous; there are a total of 1.25 million drug users.[9]

Since world demand for opium and its derivatives is strong, narcotics production is much more profitable than the production of legitimate crops opium cultivation continues actively and nearly 87% of the world's opium supply is provided by Afghanistan. In 2004, opium cultivation increased by two-thirds, reaching an unprecedented 131,000 hectares resulting in output of 4,200 tons, representing a 17% increase in opium cultivation. This happened despite the fact that a bumper harvest was lost to bad weather and disease which resultantly lowered the opium yield per hectare. Moreover, opium cultivation has spread to all 32 provinces in Afghanistan making narcotics the main engine of economic growth. The licit economic activity in Afghanistan contributes about $4.6 billion to the 2003-04 GDP; however the society is so intertwined with the opium production process that the illicit opium economy is now equivalent to about 60% of Afghanistan's economy. Recently, describing the plight and desperation of the poor Afghan farmers who resort to poppy cultivation, T. Jawad the Afghan Ambassador to the US said, "In an environment of total insecurity—social, political and economic—people have leveled their pomegranate orchards, their vineyards, and turned them into poppy fields, because it takes only three months to harvest poppy."[10]

Afghanistan's economy continues to rely heavily on illicit drug trade. Lawlessness and a weak central authority are the most prominent reasons for the revival of the heroin trade in Afghanistan. At the 'London Conference on Afghanistan'[11] the Government of Afghanistan launched an updated National Drug Control Strategy (NDCS). It is a counter narcotics strategy based on a four pronged approach i.e., targeting of traffickers and trade; strengthening and diversifying legal livelihoods; developing effective counter-narcotic institutions; and demand reduction.[12]

In any case, sustainable progress in reducing opium production will depend on long-drawn-out efforts by the authorities. The authorities should pursue vigorously the implementation of the multi-pronged anti-narcotics strategy, built upon eradication, interdiction, alternative livelihoods, and education. Only a successful implementation of this strategy could have substantial macroeconomic consequences, as the growing importance of opium in the economy is straining the country's internal security and political stability.

Economy

Afghanistan is one of the world's poorest countries. Gross Domestic Product (real) for fiscal year 2004/5 grew by an estimated 8.0% and 13.8% was projected for 2005/6.[13] According to the World Bank, Afghanistan's non-opium GDP in 2004 was $5.8 billion. The UNODC opium survey for 2005 shows that the total export value of Afghan opium is $2.7 billion and the total licit and illicit GDP of Afghanistan amounts to $8.5 billion.

The country is rebuilding after almost three decades of conflict and is in the process of transitioning from a state-based model to a free market economy. For a healthy economy it is important that an open market economy and a democratic political system take root in Afghanistan. While the will to promote democratic values and an open-market economy is strong within the business community, the tools for achieving these goals are limited inside Afghanistan. It is imperative that the Afghan government implement programs that will create a unified national approach to improving the investment climate and strengthen business associations. Some of the most visible barriers to a sound business climate in Afghanistan today are corruption, accountability on behalf of government officials and lack of access to resources. Additionally, Afghanistan's economy remains heavily reliant on agriculture, making it vulnerable to climate.

The Afghan government faces many challenges in terms of improving the investment climate in Afghanistan. Although currency reform was completed in early 2003 and in April 2004, President Hamid Karzai declared Afghanistan "open for Business," the country still lacks an investment climate. A lot of work remains at the practical level of reforming the legal and regulatory framework. There is a need to build trust between the Afghan government and the private sector both inside and outside Afghanistan, to establish and improve trade routes both inside and outside the country and simultaneously strengthen the linkages between the Afghan private sector and international private sectors. The government has started working towards improving the country's physical infrastructure, which was largely destroyed, while at the same time struggling to provide basic services and humanitarian assistance to a growing population.

Afghanistan faces major challenges in developing a sustainable fiscal position, for example salary costs currently represent about 75 percent of operating expenditures. Foreign aid pays most of the cost of the security forces, the long-term sustainability of the army and police is a major challenge. Even if the country's non-drug taxable economy grows by ten percent a year above the current rate, the cost of maintaining the security forces is not going to be sustainable from the country's own resources for many years.[14] Only an intensive and sustained effort to improve revenue collection will lead to a sustainable fiscal balance. Additional effort is needed towards allowing for a further monetization of the economy. Although the enactment of new central bank and commercial banking laws has paved the way for modernization of Da Afghanistan Bank (DAB) and the entry of new commercial banks.[15] There still exist several administrative impediments to the development of the banking sector, including the absence of comprehensive laws supporting financial market development. The Government of Afghanistan needs to take seriously its reforms in the fiscal sector with primary focus on improving budgetary management, enacting some important tax policy measures, introducing a program of customs reform, and gaining control over national revenue. Many of the provinces have been acting as semi-independent states, remitting only a part of their revenues. The government needs to come up with a reliable mechanism to verify the total amount of provincial revenues and expenditures.

The economic reconstruction of Afghanistan has to go hand-in-hand with its political reconstruction. Since after the US attack on Afghanistan a multi-billion dollar international effort to help reconstruct Afghanistan is underway; but the important thing is to link the these reconstruction efforts to viable business opportunities. While the signs of donor fatigue have not yet fully emerged, yet with each passing year, funding is likely to decrease. For the Afghan government erecting strong partnerships with the international community and laying the basis for private investment have become top priorities.

US Reconstruction Strategy in Afghanistan

With the rapid collapse of the Taliban regime, American policymakers and commentators have been vigorously debating what a post Taliban Afghanistan should look like. In fact the policy debate concerning Afghanistan is switching from issues of military options to the nature of US policy in post Taliban Afghanistan.

US reconstruction assistance following armed conflict in Afghanistan is part of broader, long-term assistance effort comprising humanitarian, military, economic, governance, and democracy-building measures. The post-conflict situation in Afghanistan is notable for the volatile and highly politicized environment in which assistance operations are taking place. A secure environment, a strategic vision, and strong leadership are the key components needed for effective implementation of assistance efforts. However, there are a number of challenges to these efforts, including the need for sustained political commitment, adequate human and financial resources to carry out operations, coordinated assistance, and the support of the local people and civil society within Afghanistan. In addition to the constant political jockeying which is occasionally violent and the ongoing military action to root out remaining Al-Qaida and Taliban elements, Afghanistan suffers from enormous poverty, extensive warlordism, a crumbling infrastructure, and an extensive illegal narcotics trade. Therefore, the post conflict period in Afghanistan has been ridden with continuing security problems caused by terrorist incidents, political jockeying among the warlords, and the Karzai government's lack of control over the majority of the country.

Complex issues of ethnicity and regionalism continue to shape the reconstruction effort in Afghanistan today, as the United States and other international donors analyze the impact of their programs. The reconstruction effort in Afghanistan is part of a two-front struggle, one front against radical fundamentalists; and the other against the centrifugal forces pulling the country apart. As has been noted by many observers of Afghanistan's recent history, there are two primary internal threats to Afghanistan's economic and political viability. The first of these threats is a resurgence of the Taliban or another radical fundamentalist group that would undercut the nation's steps toward democratic capitalism. The second is that tribal elders, regional commanders and regional forces would remain strong, slowing the drive toward national cohesion. US reconstruction efforts–especially, although not solely, those in the security arena, including efforts to rebuild the national army, police, and intelligence services–must balance these competing threats. Reconstruction programs must be designed to create a viable nation state in Afghanistan, and to overcome irregular authorities in the countryside. But, simultaneously, local ethnic/tribal leaders, which often provide a measure of regional stability, must not be dismantled before Afghan national institutions are fully functioning, thereby opening the door for a fundamentalist resurgence. The permanent stability of Afghanistan will depend on the establishment of what is often called "good governance" which includes building democratic institutions, upholding the rule of law, and insuring a participatory role in government for all Afghan citizens.

U.S. military forces, with coalition allies, continue to be engaged in active combat operations in Afghanistan, in order to ensure that those Taliban and Al-Qaeda forces that planned the World Trade Center and Pentagon bombings are not in a position to launch similar attacks in the future.

On May 23, 2005 President Bush and Afghan President Hamid Karzai signed a joint declaration concerning the strategic partnership between the United States and Afghanistan to help Afghanistan meet the challenges it faces in developing better security, more democratic government, respect for human rights, and a market economy. According to the joint declaration, in order to address Afghanistan's post-Taliban challenges, the two countries are establishing closer cooperation, including "regular, high-level exchanges on the political, security, and economic issues" with the primary goal of strengthening U.S.-Afghan ties "to help ensure Afghanistan's long-term security, democracy, and prosperity."[16] In fact the declaration stipulated that "[T]he Afghan Government, over time, will move to assume Afghan security force sustenance costs; and the Afghan Government intends to maintain capabilities for the detention, as appropriate, of persons apprehended in the War on Terror."[17]

US and Afghan delegations met again from March 20–22, 2006 in Washington to begin a dialogue on governance and economic and security issues within the framework of a U.S.-Afghan Strategic Partnership initiative, launched in 2005. The US reaffirmed the importance of its long-term commitment to Afghanistan. Additionally, the US committed to launching the Afghan Building Capacity program to bolster the capabilities of institutions in Afghanistan, including those at both the national and provincial level and indigenous NGOs. The U.S. also committed itself for the establishment in Afghanistan of Reconstruction Opportunity Zones along the Pakistan-Afghanistan border, for the purpose of granting duty-free treatment to selected goods produced jointly in designated areas of Afghanistan. The Joint Declarations further said that the US would support Afghanistan's participation in the Central Asian Trade and Investment Framework Agreement.[18]

The US has endorsed the next steps for the Businesses Building Bridges initiative for strengthening the private sector in Afghanistan, by enlisting U.S. business leaders who will provide strategic guidance on how to activate private sector development, as well as build partnership with Afghan entrepreneurs[19]

In the context of the reconstruction strategy in Afghanistan the emergence of the Afghan National Army is of critical importance. Afghanistan has a long tradition of guerrilla and paramilitary warfare and has many individual factions. Afghanistan does not have a traditional military in the Western sense. The Afghan National Army, currently being trained by the United States with the assistance of the international community. The Bonn Agreement called for all militia forces to come under the authority of the central government, but regional leaders have continued to retain their militias and the formation of a national army remains a gradual process.

Given that the US has a major presence in Iraq and only a secondary presence in Afghanistan, critical dilemmas remain. These dilemmas are mostly security related like disarmament, factionalism, warlordism, and the illicit drug trade. Although the Afghan army now numbers over 26,000 trained and equipped troops, the challenges that the country faces are so complex that they are certainly beyond the capability of the ANA. Nonetheless, US hope is that as ANA capability grows, it can transition greater responsibility to the Afghan Government and reevaluate the U.S. force posture. America's investment in the ANA over the next several years is key to building a lasting peace in Afghanistan, and subsequently, will prevent terrorist threats with global reach from reemerging in the region. The relative success of the ANA is not duplicated by the Afghan National Police (ANP). The ANP is inclusive of the National Police, Border Police, Highway Police, and Counter-narcotics Police. ANP was supposed to have a combined force of 65,000, but that target has not been reached. ANP personnel being mostly illiterate and poorly paid are susceptible to bribes and there are many instances of desertions.

Therefore, while the nascent Afghan national army is gaining experience in terms of operational effectiveness in partnering with allied forces, it is doubtful whether it is capable of operating independently. For the US the biggest challenge will be the eventual transition of full security operations to the Afghan army and police. If the ANA along with the ANP are to assume real responsibility for maintaining internal security in Afghanistan then there needs to be increased funding along with a realistic timetable for training the armed forces that can effectively become the backbone of the country's internal law and order, not just a task to be checked off by the US.

Role of the United Nations and the International Community

Right from the start the UN had decided that it would follow a minimalist approach in terms of involvement in Afghanistan and in that sense keep it different from its missions in other places like in Kosovo and East Timor. It was the UN Special Representative of the Secretary General Lakhdar Brahimi who had advocated a "Light Footprint" to typify the minimalist approach that the UN was planning to adopt in Afghanistan. The UN mission in Afghanistan is called the 'United Nations Assistance Mission in Afghanistan' (UNAMA). The UN has not taken up responsibilities in the maintenance of law and order within Afghanistan. It has only assumed limited responsibilities in terms of economic reconstruction. The UN's role is actually been hindered because of lack of funds. While there had been a lot of rhetorical commitment on the part of the international community to assist in reconstruction, actual donations have not been forthcoming.

The recently agreed upon Afghan Compact represents a framework for international co-operation in Afghanistan for the next five years.[20] The Afghan Compact noted that although the Bonn Agreement had been fully implemented, "Afghanistan's transition to peace and stability is not yet assured, and that strong international engagement will continue to be required to address remaining challenges."[21] Some of the benchmarks laid out in the Afghanistan Compact are the urgent need for stamping out corruption, bolstering good governance and upholding international human rights standards. The Afghan Compact is in essence a development plan for Afghanistan, akin to an agreement between the Afghan government and its international donor partners, assuring continued global support for Afghanistan until 2010. The "Afghanistan Compact" acknowledges that the country's "transition to peace and security is not yet assured" and requires "strong international engagement." Further the Compact recognized the security problem arising from the hundreds of militia and it states that "all illegal armed groups will be disbanded by end-2007 in all provinces." Kabul estimates that there are some 10,000 "illegal" militias and has launched a new plan with Japan as the lead country to disarm these people.

Indian Perspective

Relations between India and Afghanistan have been steadily growing, especially after the installation of a democratically-elected Government headed by Hamid Karzai. It is interesting that many top functionaries of the Karzai Government, including Karzai himself, have either studied or have been trained in India.

The Indian Prime Minister Manmohan Singh visited Afghanistan in August 28-29, 2005. The visit was the first to Afghanistan by an Indian head of Government in nearly three decades. The last Indian Prime Minister to visit Kabul was Indira Gandhi in 1976. The visit of the Prime Minister had been preceded by the visit of then External Affairs Minister K Natwar Singh to Kabul and after that by the visit of the Afghan President Hamid Karzai to India in February 2005. President Karzai visited New Delhi again in April 2006.

India is helping Afghanistan in areas as diverse as infrastructure, education, healthcare and social welfare. The reason for New Delhi's tremendous interest in the reconstruction process and in strengthening democratic institutions in Afghanistan is to prevent it from becoming a failed state and help the Afghan government avert the resurgence of the Taliban and Islamic fundamentalists. India is currently involved in 25 different projects in Afghanistan, including construction of power transmission projects, arterial roads, parliament building, rebuilding of mosques and schools. During Karzai's visit in April 2006, India again announced an assistance of 50 million US dollars (approx Rs 225 crore) to Afghanistan, taking the total aid to the war-torn country to 650 million US dollars (approx Rs 2700 crore). New Delhi also offered another 50 million US dollars as Line of Credit.[22] India and Afghanistan have also signed Memoranda of Understanding for promoting cooperation in Rural Development, Education Exchange Programme and on Standardisation.

An estimated 2,000 Indians are working on India-aided projects. For their protection, 500 Indo-Tibetan Border Police (ITBP) personnel have been deployed after killing of M. Ramankutty in November 2005. This has so far prevented attack on any of the project sites. However, the recent killing of Indian telecom engineer K. Suryanarayana is a sad commentary on the ineffectiveness of the United Nations that supervises a 20,000 International Security Assistance Force (ISAF), officered by NATO member-nations. Suryanarayana was working for a Bahrain firm and not on an Indian-aided project, was, unfortunately, not guarded by the ITBP. India operating four consulates in Afghanistan, two of which, at Jelalabad and Kandahar, are located near the Pakistan-Afghanistan border.[23] The other two consulates are at Herat and Mazaar-e-Sharief. It is likely that more ITBP personnel will be sent to protect the Indian mission in Kabul and the consulates in Jalalabad and Kandahar and they would join the 200 commandos already present in the country.

One of the main problems that India faces in terms of providing assistance to Afghanistan is that Pakistan continues to deny transit facility to Indian goods. During President Karzai's visit to India in April 2006, India and Afghanistan also decided to set up a joint committee of Commerce Ministers to review implementation of bilateral Preferential Trade Agreement and promote bilateral trade and signed three MoUs, including those covering education and rural development. The fact remains that much of the terrorism and armed opposition directed against the Kabul government has supporters, access to resources, and bases of operation in Pakistan.

Historically during the period of the civil war in Afghanistan, India had always supported the Tajiks and elements of the former Northern Alliance. India's support to the Northern Alliance grew further after 9/11 and the subsequent US-led war against terror in Afghanistan. Pakistan has succeeded in alienating large sections of the Pashtun tribe from the Indian government; India should concentrate on cultivating the emergence of a multiethnic coalition in Afghanistan that encourages the participation of the Pashtuns.

Conclusion

While the Afghan government is struggling to ensure a democratic election and the coalition forces are working to establish a secure situation on the ground, the narcotics question still remains as a serious security concern. The need now is to build the administration necessary to effectively tackle opium cultivation. If the narcotics problem in Afghanistan is allowed unabated it will become ever more serious undoing the political and military successes of the last few years. For the newly installed Afghan government and the US ensuring that a variable security environment is established along with the instruments of democracy, the rule of law and developmental infrastructure in Afghanistan is the most severe dilemma. The challenges from the opium economy and terrorist threat from the Taliban and Al Qaeda remnants, remain.

For the U.S. Department of State and the U.S. Agency for International Development (USAID), Afghanistan provides unique challenges and post-9/11 high-level recognition of the direct links between what happened at the World Trade Center and the Pentagon with events in rural Afghanistan elevated humanitarian and reconstruction programs to the stature of geo-politics, and drove national security down to the level of building schools in isolated villages.[24] Understanding the interplay between humanitarian and anti-terrorist programs is likely to be critical to effective U.S. foreign policy in the war against terrorism.

It is significant that after years of being a stateless nation, a system of governance is being rebuilt. In a series of efforts beginning with the Bonn process in December 2001, Afghans have taken several steps towards reconstituting a national government. The constitution approved in January 2004 is regarded by many observers as among the most progressive and enlightened in the Muslim world. It mandates a strong central government and presidency, with a two-house national assembly, and an independent judiciary. Astride the arteries of the old Silk and Spice Roads, Afghanistan is already profiting as a transit sector for commercial traffic between its neighbours in South and Central Asia. Should a natural gas pipeline be built from Turkmenistan to Pakistan, it will likely travel a route above the Herat-Qandahar sector of the Ring Road. In essence, Afghanistan has begun the process of rejoining the world economy.[25]

The US should go after Osama bin Laden, Aiman Zawahiri, Mullah Muhammad Umar, and Gulbudeen Hikmatyar with severe intensity. They remain the real and symbolic leaders of the terrorist networks and organizations whose activities are the cause of the periodic alerts in the US and around the world, not those adversaries in Iraq. The fact that they remain at-large undermines the confidence in US policy among Afghans, reduces the credibility of the Afghan government and international reconstruction efforts, and sends the wrong message to Afghan and Pakistani tribes in their respective border areas.

However, most parts of Afghanistan remain extremely poor. Growing political stability and continued international commitment to Afghan reconstruction are needed to create an optimistic outlook for maintaining improvements in the Afghan economy in 2006. Expanding poppy cultivation and a growing opium trade may account for one-third of GDP and looms as one of Kabul's most serious policy challenges. Afghanistan reconstruction therefore must be undertaken in the context of the multiple transitions entailed by the process of post-conflict reconstruction: a security transition (from war to peace), a political transition (to the formation of a legitimate and effective state) and a socioeconomic transition (from a "conflict" economy to sustainable growth). The uppermost significance must be given to the protection of basic human rights and to ensure a lasting peace, security, and the establishment of law and order. There can be no reasonable prospect of the stable conditions that the reconstruction process requires, or for repatriation to progress, if entire regions of Afghanistan remain unsafe and resultantly unviable. Afghan women have the lowest levels in the world with regards to health. Issues including illiteracy and widespread poverty need to be addressed. According to Unicef, 90% of women give birth by themselves and 1,600 women die in child-birth for every 100,000 babies born. From a political point of view, there must be an effort to create strong institutions, helping the ruling Afghan classes to have a positive future vision of their own country.

While the political targets in terms of adopting an enlightened constitution (January 2004), holding a successful presidential election (October 2004) and parliamentary elections (September 2005), have been met, the real aim of ending the conflict and establishing peace and stability is yet to be fulfilled.

The U.S. government reconstruction program in Afghanistan–in its humanitarian, security, political, and economic aspects–is both appropriate to the needs of the Afghan people and the complex realities of their long-suffering country, and an effective weapon against terrorism. About 20,000 U.S. soldiers remain on the ground in the country, providing security while Afghan police and army forces continue to build. American and NATO forces will need to be there for some time, notably Special Forces who can pursue Taliban fighters who use terrorist tactics. But a legitimate new legislature will make it that much harder for the Taliban and its foreign recruits to find popular sympathy or sanctuary.

In any approach that the US follows it has to keep in mind that Afghanistan is an extremely patriarchal, tribal and maybe even misogynist society, that derives from the Taliban regime. This is one of the main reasons for the clear political, social and economic backwardness of the country. The clash isn't between civilizations, or even between religions, but, between "closed" societies and those that are more or less "open," be they already democratic or on the road to democracy. Finally, the US must ensure the end of all deleterious interferences from border countries–from Pakistan in particular. The US should ensure that the pace and financial support for the creation of adequate Afghan security forces is increased. The US government should intensify pressure on Afghanistan's neighbours and Persian Gulf nations not to aid and support forces connected to the security threats to Afghanistan. Many challenges still remain to the Afghan reconstruction. The pace of the physical reconstruction of institutions in Afghanistan is slow and security threats continue to impede the development of institutions.

An unstable Afghanistan has led to a pattern of armed border clashes, illegal narcotics trafficking, terrorism, and the rekindling of ethnic and sectarian tensions throughout the region. Afghanistan poses an enormous challenge to an international community which is in fact lacking effective policy options for containing the dangerous spillover of Afghanistan's political, military, and social upheaval into neighbouring states. Even though the war is over in Afghanistan it continues to engage U.S. interest in such areas as containing terrorism, curbing illegal drug trafficking, and checking human rights violations. In trying to pursue U.S. interests, policymakers face a stark set of policy options, each carrying considerable risks and limited prospects for success. Thus, U.S. policymakers and other international actors face the difficult challenge of balancing the constraints posed by political will with the sobering task of managing the myriad tensions sparked in the post-Taliban Afghanistan.

Security in a post-conflict society finds its meaning in the notion of "human security," which assures the sustainability of the peaceful environment. Along with security the leading concern for the Afghan government is the establishment of good governance. War and internal strife have devastated virtually all institutions in Afghanistan. The Afghan government and the international community are faced with the daunting task of rebuilding the country. In order to bring stability, security, and prosperity in Afghanistan, new systems of government and governance must be developed. Therefore, good governance through a strong central government is needed for providing essential services and to ensure an end to violence which still continues in large parts of Afghanistan.

Afghanistan as a legitimate state is merely emerging; it still has a long way to go before it is accepted as a responsible and lawful nation. The international community has the responsibility of being patient and maintaining an uncompromising commitment to Afghanistan's success. Afghan government has to realize that the country's long-term security depends on building an integrated strategy against terrorism in partnership with the international community.

Notes

1. Jimmy Carter, *State of the Union Address;* 23 January 1980.
2. Robert Gates, '*US Intelligence and the End of the Cold War*', Texas A&M University, 19 November 1999.
3. Resolution 1386 (2001), Adopted by the Security Council at its 4443rd meeting, on 20 December 2001; S/RES/1386 (2001); p. 1.
4. "Situation in Afghanistan," Nancy J. Powell, Acting Assistant Secretary for International Narcotics and Law Enforcement Affairs; Testimony Before the House Armed Services Committee, Washington, DC, June 22, 2005.
5. Report of the Security Council mission to Afghanistan, 31 October to 7 November 2003; United Nations S/2003/ 1074; p 2.
6. Figure has been taken from the US Department of Defense website http://www.defenselink.mil/releases/
7. "Afghanistan-Challenges to return," UNHCR (United Nations High Commissioner for Refugees); Geneva, March 2004; p 2.
8. Ali A. Jalali, "The Future of Afghanistan," *Parameters*, Spring 2006, pp. 4-19.

9. "Afghanistan: Drug Use Survey 2005" Ministry of Counter Narcotics (Government of Afghanistan) and UNODC; November 2005.
10. Leo Shane III, "Afghan Ambassador: Economic growth, Security key to Stopping Drug Trade," *Stars and Stripes* (Mideast edition) 14 May 2006; Available at http://www.estripes.com/article.asp?section=104&article=36284&archive=true
11. From 31 January to 1 February 2006 the UK hosted a major international conference on Afghanistan, co-chaired by Afghanistan and the UN. The conference had three aims: to launch the "Afghanistan Compact," the successor to the Bonn Agreement; to provide an opportunity for the Government of Afghanistan to present its Interim National Development Strategy to the international community; and to ensure that the Government of Afghanistan has adequate resources to meet its domestic ambitions and international commitments.
12. "National Drug Control Strategy: An Updated Five Year Strategy for Tackling the Illicit Drug Problem," Kabul, January 2006; Available at http://www.fco.gov.uk/Files/kfile/NDCS%20-%20Final%20PDF%20version.pdf
13. The figures are from the International Monetary Fund's Country Report on Afghanistan, published in March 2006, and its April 2006 World Economic Database. All figures are for the legal economy only.
14 Afghan government, "Afghanistan's Millennium Development Goals Report 2005, Vision 2020, Summary Report," http://216.239.51.104/search?q=cache:30h0VO73K3cJ:www.ands.gov.af/src/src/MDGs_Reps/1.summary%2520report%2520english.pdf+afghanistan%27s+%22vision+2020%22&hl=en.
15. Five commercial banks were licensed in 2003/04. Standard Chartered, National Bank of Pakistan, Afghan International Bank, First Microfinance Bank, and Habib Bank.

16. "Joint Declaration of the United States-Afghanistan Strategic Partnership," The White House, Office of the Press Secretary, 23 May 2005.
17. *Ibid.*
18. "Joint Statement: United States-Afghanistan Strategic Partnership" U.S. Department Of State, Office of the Spokesman, 21 March, 2006.
19. "Joint Statement: United States-Afghanistan Strategic Partnership," U.S. Department Of State, Office of the Spokesman, 21 March 2006.
20. "Building on Success, The London Conference on Afghanistan," 31 January–1 February 2006 "The Afghan Compact," Available at http://www.ands.gov.af/admin/ands/ands_docs/upload/UploadFolder/The%20Afghnistan%20Compact%20-%20Final%20English.pdf
21. *Ibid.*
22. "PM Manmohan Singh's Opening Remarks at the Joint Press Interaction with President Hamid Karzai," New Delhi, 10 April 2006.
23. Mahendra Ved, "Indian presence in Afghanistan worries Pakistan," 1 May 2006; Available at http://www.india-defence.com/reports/1857
24. "U.S. Strategy in Afghanistan on the Eve of National Elections," Andrew Natsios, USAID Administrator; Statement before the House International Relations Committee, Washington, D.C., 29 September 2004.
25. Testimony of Thomas E. Gouttierre, Dean of International Studies and Programs and Director of the Center for Afghanistan Studies University of Nebraska at Omaha, Omaha, Nebraska, "Afghanistan Continuing Challenges," Hearing before the Committee on Foreign Relations United States Senate, One Hundred Eighth Congress, Second Session, 12 May 2004, Washington DC.

11

India, Russia and Afghanistan: The Strategic Stakes

Jagmohan Meher

The September 11 terrorist attacks on the United States and its response since then changed the strategic calculations of many countries towards Afghanistan and the region to a great extent and brought to the surface a number of trends that were less visible earlier. The threat perception and the sense of national and personal insecurity were heightened. The rise of Islamic fundamentalism vindicated and reinforced the strategic stakes involved as far as the US was concerned. The sense of "clear and present danger" in Jammu and Kashmir, and Central Aṣia and Chechnya respectively made India and Russia feel like they are on the front lines of the America's anti-Taliban war. They shared a degree of commonality in their assessment of the threat of the Taliban regime and their supporters. Both the countries openly supported the US policy and accepted the necessity of the American military operation as well as the importance of the bases in Pakistan, Afghanistan and Central Asia. But as the war in Afghanistan winds down, resentment and apprehension about the continued and protracted American military presence in the region came to the fore in India and Russia (and in other countries). While the Russians consider Afghanistan as their traditional "sphere of influence," the country has considerable strategic significance and geopolitical implications for India as well. Both the countries feel disconcerted over the prolonged American presence in their own backyard. Thus, the US-backed Afghanistan is seen by the two countries as empowering, as well as constraining at the same time.

The massive American engagement against the Taliban/Al Qaeda has indirectly downgraded the latter's involvement in Kashmir and Central Asia (and Chechnya). Now that the US would practically be doing "the dirty work" for them, New Delhi and Moscow feel empowered in their protracted struggle against international terrorism. The US military presence in their own neighbourhood is also a limiting factor because it would let Washington define the strategic issues for New Delhi and Moscow in regions hitherto out of bounds to the Americans.

The role and reach of the American involvement in Afghanistan over the last five years shows that the sole superpower is unlikely to leave the country any time soon, a development that would clash with the long-term Indian and Russian interests. Moscow and New Delhi might be interested to maintain cordial ties with Washington for their own strategic reasons and compulsions, but a permanent American presence in their own neighbourhood is unlikely to be accepted by them. At the same time, neither country has the resources or favourable political conditions to intervene in Afghanistan in a big way. Only an Indo-Russian joint effort to maintain a visible and credible presence aimed at diluting the significance of the US military presence would serve their common strategic and geopolitical interests in the long run.

Even though there are anxieties about the US' strategic role in Afghanistan, the American war against the Taliban and Islamic terrorism is leading to a rare kind of Indo-Russian military, strategic and intelligence cooperation. Such continued cooperation between the two great powers of Asia will go a long way in enhancing their strategic partnership for the promotion of peace in Afghanistan and the region. This is also important for reasons that go well beyond the war against terrorism and Afghanistan. It is imperative that the two sides seize the opportunity to solidify their relationship. As India's Defense Minister George Fernandes declared in 2002: "Afghanistan is the sphere where the Russian and Indian approaches are identical."[1]

This article aims at exploring how Afghanistan looked from the perspective of New Delhi and Moscow in the pre as well as post 9/11 scenarios and peeps into the strategic dissonance between Indian and Russian interests vis-à-vis the US with a view to envisage the future trends. It suggests that India and Russia should work together in close collabouration with the regional actors to contain and neutralise the US presence in Afghanistan and the Southwest Asia in the larger interests of peace and security in the region.

THE INDIAN ASSESSMENT

Before the American invasion of Afghanistan, India envisaged that the country's Taliban regime and Al Qaeda's access to Central Asia, as well as to the Indian state of Jammu and Kashmir (backed by Pakistan), as a clear threat to her security. It was nervous about the fall out of a Taliban success on the internal security situation in Jammu and Kashmir where the number of Afghan war veterans from different parts of the world had increased dramatically.[2] These mercenaries, many of whom settled in Pakistan Occupied Kashmir (POK), had joined several Kashmiri militant outfits and created havoc in the valley as a part of carefully crafted Pakistani strategy of "death by a thousand cuts."[3] The testing time for India came in 1999 when Pakistan, backed by the Taliban/Al Qaeda regime, intruded into the Kargil region of Jammu and Kashmir with a view to internationalise the issue.[4] The 2001 terrorists' attack on the Indian Parliament was also considered to be the handiwork of the Afghan mercenaries having links with Pakistani Intelligence agencies and Afghan extremists.

Secondly, the traditional Indo-Afghan friendship and the people-to-people empathy between the two countries influenced Pakistan's policy towards Afghanistan. Islamabad's aim is to negate Indian influence in the country. Pakistan's quest for strategic depth and its desire to deny India an entry point into Central Asia (via Afghanistan) were major concerns in India's strategic thinking. Pakistan's anxiety over the Afghan situation doubled with the opening up of the Central Asian Republics in the aftermath of the demise of the Soviet Union. Kabul now had greater leeway and more options to get around the Pakistani embargo. Consequently, Indo-Pak rivalry and competition for influence in Afghanistan gained greater salience.

Thirdly, India was concerned about the spread of Kalashnikov culture, a fallout of the civil war in Afghanistan, which afflicted the Pakistani society. Sophisticated weapons like the dreaded AK-47, light machine guns, rocket propelled grenades, plastic bombs, rocket launchers, anti-tank grenades etc. were easily available (and on the cheap) even in small Pakistani towns and parts of Jammu and Kashmir. Cross-border links between arms smugglers in India and Pakistan also cause a serious law and order problems in adjoining provinces in this country.

Fourthly, the clandestine ISI activities in promoting terrorism and other forces of instability across the borders (especially in Indo-Bangladesh and Indo-Nepal borders) are disturbing challenges to India's foreign policy and the national security apparatus. The ISI, by all accounts, was also involved in supplying arms to the terrorist organizations and colluding in the drug trade. But what was most alarming was the nexus among the Pakistani military/ISI and Afghanistan's Taliban regime and its Al Qaeda mentors in sponsoring terrorism in not merely Jammu and Kashmir but also all over India.

India had time and again raised these issues and expressed its concern in various international forums to put pressure on Pakistan and Afghanistan. In a high level conference on security policy held in Munich in February 1999, leading personalities like German Chancellor Gerhard Schroeder, the then US Secretary of Defense William Cohen, and defense ministers and representatives of Britain, France and other European countries along with the diplomats from China, Japan and India participated. Brajesh Mishra, the then national security adviser to the Prime Minister of India, said on behalf of the Indian government: "We are witnessing the erosion of the strategic frontier on the Amu Darya that for the last 150 years had preserved strategic stability in a vital part of the Eurasian landmass. In its place, fundamentalism and extremism are taking root and fuelling terrorism. This is matter of extreme concern to my country." The other significant portion of Mishra's speech was that India sees Russia's diminished influence in Central Asia and the partial withdrawal of Russian border guards from Tajikistan as a serious threat to her security.

In order to check these destabilizing forces of Islamic extremism and international terrorism emanating from Pakistan and Afghanistan, India joined hands with Russia and the Central Asian states and continued its support to the Northern Alliance.[5] This was a part of India's clandestine efforts to counter the terrorist threat. The British based *Jane's International Security* reported on 15 March 2001 that India was supplying the Northern Alliance with military equipment, advisers and helicopter technicians, and both India and Russia were using military bases in Tajikistan and Uzbekistan for their operations. In fact, India played no small part in sustaining the efforts of the Alliance, which, succeeded in denying the Taliban total control over Afghanistan. There was also speculation about some kind of military action well before September 11, 2001. "India and Iran will facilitate U.S. and Russian plans for 'limited military action' against the Taliban if the contemplated tough new economic sanctions don't bend Afghanistan's fundamentalist regime," the magazine said.

The Post 9/11 Indian Perspective

The post 9/11 American invasion of Afghanistan had remarkable "empowering" effects at the domestic, regional and international domain in addition to its geo-political and strategic ramifications favourable to India as stated earlier. At the domestic level, the extremists elements from among the 150 million Muslim population of India–who had hitherto considered the Taliban/Al Qaeda as their ideological inspiration and Pakistan's ISI links as supply line–got a severe jolt. For the first time, their unlawful activities came under heavy scanner of the State and their religious extremism questioned everywhere. Such enhanced vigil and pervasive popular resentment naturally had a restraining effect at the regional level. India attained an upper hand in Afghanistan vis-à-vis its arch rival Pakistan, thereby gaining a lot of strategic mileage. The so-called Pakistani "strategic depth" in Afghanistan was virtually lost with the American invasion and India's support to the anti-Taliban forces. In addition, Indian geo-political and strategic leverage also was enhanced in the whole region including Central Asia and Iran. At the international level, the changing security perceptions of India and the US led to a marked improvement in their bilateral relations. It was the Afghanistan issue and the war against terrorism that brought both the countries to a new level of cooperation. For the first time in their history, the US administration indicated that the world's largest democracy, situated next to China, next to Pakistan-Afghanistan, West Asia and Central Asia, is needed as a stabilizer in the region.[6]

It also marked a new qualitative beginning in the India-China relations facilitating unprecedented opportunities in bilateral trade and commerce and more significantly, in moving away from the hostile legacy of the border war of 1962.

After the events of September 11, India asserted that her stand against the Taliban regime, Pakistan, and Al Qaeda as the key promoters of international terrorism was vindicated. Accordingly, New Delhi redoubled its diplomatic campaign to pursuade the US to put pressure on Pakistan to stop its cross-border terrorism in Kashmir. Washington considered it equally imperative to achieve the elimination of terrorists and their infrastructure in the POK because they also served as reservoirs for the anti-U.S. jihadis. In view of these strategic apprehensions, Indians openly supported to America's global war against terrorism and opted for closer military and strategic cooperation with Washington.

To Pakistan's annoyance, India's post 9/11 policy seems to have paid some dividends and helped New Delhi regain a bit of lost ground. Almost all top leaders of Afghanistan including the Indian educated Hamid Karzai[7] have visited India over the last five years and helped reestablish New Delhi's traditional link with Kabul. India has reactivated its cultural ties with Afghanistan and helped strengthen its economic and political relationship so as to further its strategic interests in that country and beyond. The Indian objective of establishing strategic ties with Central Asian Republics has also witnessed a new beginning with a relatively stable Afghanistan.

India is also mindful of restoring Afghanistan's linkage to its historic Silk Route ties with Central Asia, which is now possible with the ouster of the Taliban regime. Today, the Caspian Sea, bordered by Iran in the south and Turkmenistan and Kazakhstan in the east, is recognized as the world's third richest oil and gas reservoir after the West Asia and Russia. It is common knowledge that as our economy grows around 7/8% each year, our thirst for energy will also increase. Already Indian oil company, ONGC Videsh Ltd. has a 15% holding in Kazakhstan's Alibekmola oilfields and 10% holding in the country's Kurmangazi oilfields. It has also shown interest to put down a minimum 20% stake in Uzbekistan's oil and gas fields as well.[8] To transport Caspian energy, India needs a land route through Afghanistan which is now being explored. This kind of strategic opportunity would not have been possible if a Pakistan-backed Taliban regime were in power in Afghanistan and had its sway over neighbouring Central Asian states.

Under these circumstances, for obvious reasons, India is not unhappy over the presence of international military forces led by the US in Afghanistan and Pakistan. New Delhi perceived that it would counter the Taliban, which once again is fighting against the Kabul regime with the help of Pakistan. In the India view, it would be reasonable to depend on the capability of the US-backed Hamid Karzai government. Taking such stakes into consideration, India reestablished diplomatic ties with Afghanistan and set up an embassy in Kabul. Subsequently consulates were opened in Mazar-e-Sharif in the north, Herat in the west, and Kandahar and Jalalabad close to the Pakistan border in the south. To enhance its strategic presence, New Delhi is also helping develop a new export route for landlocked Afghanistan through Iran (thereby circumventing Pakistan).

India is also purportedly involved in some aspects internal politics in Afghanistan. In late 2002, it offered to train 60 Kandahar police personnel disloyal to the then Kandahar governor Gul Agha Shirzai, who was allegedly close to Pakistan's Inter Services Intelligence (ISI). The governor, tried to counter the Indian move by disarming some police stations, which led to fighting and the death of two policemen culminating an open India-Pakistan antagonism in the country.

Pakistani Army and intelligence community involved in that country's Afghan policy became apprehensive of the Indian moves. A leading Pakistani journalist reported in early 2003 that the rivalry between India and Pakistan over Afghanistan was "hard to control." He quoted a European ambassador in Kabul as saying: "India sees Afghanistan as a means to undermine Pakistan's western border and Pakistan is retaliating."[9]

At the bilateral level, New Delhi promised to deliver military vehicles and train the new Afghan National Army (ANA) officers.[10] In fact, Indians developed a huge presence quickly by providing civilian aircrafts (including several used Boeing and Airbus passenger jets), buses and hospital equipments to the impoverished country. In August 2005, Indian Prime Minister Manmohan Singh made a historic visit to Afghanistan[11] and assured Karzai of New Delhi's continued cooperation and assistance in stabilizing that country's security and democracy. In April 2006, Karzai made his fourth visit to India since he became the Afghan leader in late 2001. This time, he led a 110-strong delegation made up of cabinet ministers, members of the Afghan National Assembly, and business people. During the four-day mission, he signed several bilateral agreements. New Delhi also pledged an additional $50 mn in assistance to Afghanistan, bringing the total Indian support commitment to $650 mn.[12]

Like Pakistanis, many Indians view Afghanistan and Central Asia as an extension of their regional geopolitical competition with Islamabad. For many policy makers in New Delhi, close cooperation with Afghanistan is a cost-effective policy to keep Pakistan under check. Now that India is emerging as a global player, New Delhi is unlikely to allow Afghanistan to once again become a pawn of Pakistani. One significant area of Indo-Afghan cooperation is the construction of Afghan roads by India's state-owned Border Roads Organization (BRO), a modern construction organization committed to meeting the strategic needs of the Indian armed forces. In a significant strategic development, when the neo-Taliban killed a BRO employee in November 2005, Indian authorities decided to deploy approximately 200 Indo-Tibetan Border Police commandos in Afghanistan to provide security to the Indians working in various construction projects in that country.[13] Since the partition of the sub-continent in 1947, this is for the first time that the Indian security forces have been stationed in Afghanistan, which demonstrates India's determination to have a strong foothold there.

It is a well known fact that the gaining of "strategic depth" in Afghanistan has been a major objective of Pakistan's regional policy. Such a policy is influenced by basically two factors. The "success" of the anti-Soviet guerrilla war of the 1980s triggered the belief in Islamabad that with no apparent cost to itself, it could play a major role in the geo-politics of Central Asia. And that only Afghanistan could provide the strategic leverage vis-a-vis the energy-rich Muslim states of Central Asia and the energy-seeking multi-nationals backed by the US. Since Afghanistan is seen as a shorter energy route, Pakistan is keen on gaining political control over the country.[14] Unable to keep its own house in order, the Pakistani military regime has, since 2003, accused India of setting of camps in Afghanistan to train Afghans and Pakistanis as terrorists with a view to destabilize Pakistan. With the current instability in Baluchistan and the intractable turmoil in the Pak-Afghan border areas, the suspicion of Indian involvement in the troubled country has grown. Islamabad charges that with its presence in Afghanistan, India is encircling Pakistan with consulates and commandos and is financing anti-Pakistan militant organizations within that country.[15] Consequently, Islamabad wants to see major share of power to remain in the hands of the Pashtun tribal leaders who have close links with the government establishments in Pakistan. This would also restrict the Northern Alliance's sphere of influence to the extreme north of the country, away from Pakistan's borders.

Since India maintains close links with the leaders of the erstwhile Northern Alliance, the strategic concerns of Pakistan have become more acute. America's anti-Taliban war thus, has the effect of empowering India and down-grading its rival Pakistan at all levels and also compelling Islamabad to come to the negotiating table "renouncing" her long-standing policy of state-sponsored terrorism against India.

The Constraints on New Delhi

But at the same time, Indian policy makers and military planners are "disturbed" by the massive American military presence in close proximity to our borders. New Delhi is not certain about what ought to be done with the US' extraordinary military activities in Pakistan, Afghanistan and Central Asia. Among the other strategic anxieties over the massive American presence is that it could complicate India's relationship with Moscow, especially if the Russians become more apprehensive on this score. A negative response from Moscow, although aimed at the US, could pose new and powerful challenges to Indian strategic interests in Afghanistan and for that matter, in Central Asia. Similarly, if the US departs from Afghanistan and Central Asia after containing the Taliban/Al Qaeda terrorists to a considerable extent, India could revive its traditional strategic interests in the region on its own.

Another "limiting" factor is that the presence of American military forces in Afghanistan is unlikely to eliminate the threat of Islamic extremism and terrorism from the region. In fact, it is proving to be the other way round. The presence of foreign troops has always led to mass movements and rebellion in the country and such a risk is ever present. The initial enthusiasm about the American led reconstruction of their country (genuinely felt by the Afghan people that peace and prosperity were returning) has clearly faded. Today, the dislike of foreigners working in their country is on the rise among the Afghans. Anti-American protests and demonstrations have been very common in the streets of Afghan cities. It is, therefore, most likely that some measure of opposition/insurgency will continue to exist in the country so long as foreign troops are stationed there. And in that circumstance, with its huge Muslim population and the militarily vulnerable Jammu and Kashmir state, India would not remain unaffected from the fallout.

Protracted American military presence in Pakistan, Afghanistan and Central Asia, will also come as an impediment on India's regional geo-political interests and diplomatic clout in the region. The US will have a say on every Indian move in the whole South-west Asian region–a region that includes both South Asia and the Persian Gulf and stretches into Central Asia. Whether it is gas pipelines through Turkmenistan-Afghanistan-Pakistan-India, or oil/gas "lifeline" from Iran-Pakistan-India,[16] America will be a factor in the pipeline politics so long as they have military presence in the region. And as energy has become a strategic determinant in New Delhi's external relations, some kind of strategic dissonance will continue to persist between New Delhi and Washington over the various geo-political issues in the region (which will be detrimental to the Indian interests).

There are also possibilities that the US may take "intrusive political and diplomatic steps" to bring about change of regimes in Syria, Iran or even Saudi Arabia. This has generated alarm among the regimes in the region.[17] The increasing display of American political and strategic interests in Nepal and Bangladesh is also a cause of concern for New Delhi, which has traditionally not accepted outside interference in South Asia (also called "near abroad"). Another constraint on India's strategic interest vis-à-vis Pakistan is the entrenched and permanent nature of American military presence in Pakistan on the pretext of fighting the Taliban in Afghanistan. US presence restricts India's freedom of manoeuvre against Pakistan. However, there is also the hope that peace in

Afghanistan would lead to an eventual US withdrawal from Pakistan as well. Hence, a peaceful Afghanistan without foreign troops would bring in the fresh air of optimism in India's strategic calculations in the whole region.

THE RUSSIAN ASSESSMENT

After the disintegration of the Soviet Union and the rise of Islamic fundamentalism and terrorism subsequently, Russia found itself surrounded by tough neighbours in an unstable geo-strategic environment. Its main objective in Afghanistan was to prevent the further strengthening of the Taliban type Islamic or nationalist movements in the Central Asian Republics, especially in Tajikistan and Uzbekistan or even in some Islamic enclaves in Russia itself (including Chechnya). The deteriorating security scenario was compounded by the flow of drugs and weapons and in a worst case scenario, a possible flood of refugees culminating in an eventual defeat of the then Northern Alliance.

Trouble for Russia and Central Asian states began with the Taliban takeover of Kabul in 1996. The fundamentalist regime institutionalized state sponsored terrorism in the name of religion and provided militants with bases, training facilities, weapons and money. It also provided sanctuary to a host of militant groups from the Arab world. Moscow believed that Pakistan and its intelligence agencies contributed significantly to the emergence and success of the Taliban. Some Russian sources also pointed fingers at the intelligence services of the US of having supported the Taliban, which Moscow regard as a massive threat to its interests in Central Asia and elsewhere.[18] The spillover effects of the growth of extremism and fundamentalism soon spread to the "softer belly" of Russia, a traditional cause of serious concern for Moscow. Russians became fearful about the Islamic guerrillas from neighbouring Chechnya with links to Al Qaeda following an August 1999 incursion into Russia's Dagestan region and subsequent explosions in Moscow and two other cities in September that year killing over 300 people.[19] Russian concern became more acute in January 2000, when the Taliban became the only government in the world to recognize Chechnya's independence. In fact, in May 2000, there were reports of Russia considering the possible air strikes against some terrorist camps based in Afghanistan, which were providing training to Chechens and other militants fighting against Russian forces.[20] Russia was also unhappy about the Pakistani role in supporting and financing the Islamic terrorist organizations.[21] The Russian Foreign Ministry was of the view that Pakistan welcomed certain Chechen rebels, such as former President Zelimkhan Yandarbiyev "with open arms." He was expelled only after the Russian embassy in Pakistan intervened.[22] It is also believed that ISI of Pakistan was training Chechen fighters in camps located in Afghanistan and Pakistan along the same lines as they trained the Afghans against the Soviet Union in 1980s. But, Moscow never launched open military attacks against Taliban/Al Qaeda training camps in Afghanistan.

The geo-politics of the Afghan civil war throughout 1990s was deeply rooted in cross border ethnic relationships. For a decade, Russia supported the Northern Alliance along with all the newly independent states of Central Asia, only because Moscow wanted to see a buffer against the spread of Pashtun extremism of the Taliban regime. That buffer had virtually been eliminated due to the Taliban control of Afghan territory bordering Uzbekistan, Turkmenistan, and Tajikistan.[23] Russians probably accepted that they did not have the capacity to address the potential and emerging security threats such as terrorism, Islamic extremism, and drug trafficking. The failed state of Afghanistan under the Taliban epitomized the worst-case scenario, but a number of other states in Central Asia had also suffered from some of the same pathologies. Moscow viewed Afghan instability less as an opportunity to exert influence and more as a danger to Russia's interest.[24] This marked a significant change in Russian foreign policy under Putin and in a sense, a kind of strategic retreat of Moscow from what it considered to be its sphere of influence for a long time. This policy was partly motivated by the increased importance that Putin gave to economic factors in prioritizing regional interest.

Post 9/11 Russian Policy

Within weeks after the September 11 attacks on the U.S., President Putin opted for closer relationship with Washington, and launched a massive supply operation for the Northern Alliance, mostly a Tajik force that was aligned with the pre-Taliban government of Afghanistan.[25] Russia and the US acted for a time as *de facto* allies in the anti-terror campaign. For quite some time, it appeared that the new US-Russian understanding over transnational terrorism had narrowed the strategic gulf between them on several other issues including even the missile defense. One reason for this sort of cooperation was that after the disintegration of the Soviet Empire in the early 1990s, Russia was unable to maintain stability in Central Asia. It helplessly watched the civil wars and instability in Afghanistan for almost a decade. Moscow had accepted the fact that despite its military and economic support, it was not possible for the Northern Alliance to topple the Taliban regime. Once the US military became involved, the Taliban crumbled and the Northern Alliance swept through the country in a few weeks. In this way, Russia tacitly recognized its own constraints as well as the key role of the US in combating terrorism. American military presence in Afghanistan culminating in a strategic foothold in Central Asia was not only gracefully accepted by President Putin as a *fait accompli*, but the way the Russian leadership handled the situation also revealed his political maturity and immense pragmatism. Putin's decision to support Bush included acceptance of the US forces and, then their military bases in Central Asia, sharing substantial intelligence, and offer of over flight rights, etc. In fact, it was for the first time since the World War II, intelligence cooperation between the US and Russia was in full swing. Moscow was also instrumental in securing the consent of Central Asian leaders to allow Americans to set up military bases and use them in the war against the Taliban regime. Russia also very generously extended necessary humanitarian relief during the first weeks of the war. The Russian President seems to have perceived that in order to fulfill his economic development agenda, security and stability on Russia's borders was essential. Hence, the US invasion of Afghanistan as well as closer cooperation with Washington became acceptable to Moscow.

Secondly, with the American military presence in Afghanistan and the region, Russia felt the need for some kind of geostrategic realignment and readjustment of its relations with the regional actors. This kind of change of perception was necessitated because of the shifting of the focus of the American security policy to the extremist Islamic terrorism in the whole Eurasian landmass. One conspicuous result of these changes was the weakening of international pressure on Russia on its hard line policy in Chechnya. Thirdly, Russians understand that Afghanistan is intrinsically important to Russia's Eurasian security and that it is central to the many threats to and opportunities for Russian goals in the region. If the US does succeed in defeating terrorist networks in Afghanistan, that would be immensely beneficial to Moscow. At the same time, Russians will be happy only if the United States withdrew from the region after completing the task quickly. In such a scenario, Russia would probably have an opportunity to re-establish its strategic presence in the region. But if the American presence results in greater instability, terror and insecurity, things would become difficult for Putin back home. But the Russian President seemed optimistic and probably he will travel this road at least in the foreseeable future.

Fourth, Russians seemed to be confident of adequate leverage in Afghanistan through the leaders of the former Northern Alliance, which received support from Moscow for long years. With the onset of the anti-Taliban war, Moscow considerably increased its level of support. Twelve military transport aircrafts were sent to Bagram airport (about 40 miles from Kabul) to assist the Northern Alliance forces. In 2002, Russia donated $ 100 million in military equipment to the Afghan army of the Tajik leader and country's former Defence Minister General Mohammed Qasim Fahim. It also supplied some vintage weapons from Russian inventories free of charge.[26] But it did not send any contingents of soldiers to the International Security Assistance Force (ISAF), which had been established by a resolution of the Security Council on 20 December 2001. During Karzai's visit to Moscow in March 2002, Putin expressed his willingness to help build up the new Afghan armed forces. Many people in the Kremlin tacitly accepted that the political environment in Afghanistan was relatively favourable to them now than when the Taliban was in power.

The "Limiting Factors" for Moscow

But, this perception did not last long and the Russians began to grow apprehensive about the long-term American military presence in Afghanistan and Central Asia. The fear of possible "encirclement" by the US seems to be widespread. In the four and half years since 9/11, the US and Russia behaved more like rivals competing vigorously to influence regional leaders. The US interest in expanding the existing infrastructure in the region to meet future strategic contingencies made the Russians uneasy. Moscow's future strategic role in Afghanistan and Central Asia seemed to be undermined. Russians felt that the US was establishing itself permanently in their own sphere of influence and that could spark a series of geopolitical contests.[27]

- While the US went to Central Asia only to "solve the Afghan problem," Russia has more immediate regional interests that compel Moscow to maintain a long-term presence. Russians fear that the US might seek control of Central Asia's oil and gas reserves and that Moscow could end up having NATO on its borders. America's unilateral moves based solely on its own self-interest have led to unsettling strategic dynamics,[28] according to Moscow.

- Initially the American forces were to stay only as long as the regional terrorism threat remained. But after the successful Afghan military operation, American officials have quietly voiced the possibility of making permanent what were supposed to be temporary military bases.[29] In fact, by the time combat operations in Afghanistan ended officially on 1 May 2003, the US had established forward bases housing a combined total of close to 3000 troops in Uzbekistan and Kyrgyzstan and had begun close cooperation on tactical and intelligence matters with the Central Asian states. A permanent American military presence in Afghanistan and the region has certainly far-reaching repercussions on the strategic thinking in Moscow.[30]

- Russian nationalists are incensed that the US had entrenched itself in the only region in which Moscow could claim hegemony. "Moscow will accept US bases in Central Asia only for the duration of the Afghan anti-terrorism operation and no longer,"[31] Russian Defence Minister Sergei Ivanov said in late 2003. Also, the Ivanov Doctrine,[32] named after him, identifies "the expansion of military blocs and alliances to the detriment of the military security of the Russian federation or its allies" as primary threats to Russian security. The doctrine embraces the use of preemptive military force in response to any military or economic threats, and represents a blueprint for the post-September 11 era to safeguard Russia's influence in its "near abroad."

- The starkest evidence of the US–Russian rivalry in Central Asia is to be found in Kyrgyzstan where both Washington and Moscow have established military bases outside Bishkek. American officials have extolled the value of their existing facilities for playing a key support role for the ongoing US anti-terrorist operation in Afghanistan. They contended that they want to expand their influence in Central Asia because of the "worsening situation in Afghanistan."[33] But with a relatively peaceful Afghanistan after the Presidential and Parliamentary elections, American case no longer sounds convincing to the Russians.

- In spite of relatively good relations with the US, Moscow's regional geo-political dynamics dictate that Russia cannot afford to be a bystander to the changing military and strategic balance of power in its backyard. For example, the US-Uzbekistan relation was moving in such a direction and many Russians fear that, "Uzbekistan will become a second Turkey," a strong ally of the US.[34] Following NATO's recent policy announcements of increased engagement in Afghanistan and Central Asia, leaders in Moscow grew more concerned and resolved to protect and preserve the country's strategic space in the area.

- One of the challenging jobs for the US-backed Karzai government is the disarmament of warlords which has direct linkage on Moscow's influence in Afghanistan. The long term relationship between the former Northern Alliance and Tajikistan, and Russia would be affected if Tajik warlords and commanders are forced to disarm. Resistance will increase if the intended moves from Kabul are seen as an attempt to restrict their power. One reason for Moscow's open support for the Tajik dominated Northern Alliance was that Russia and its allied governments in Tajikistan and Uzbekistan equate Pashtun domination with Islamic fanaticism. They are afraid that this contagion may spread if the Pashtun, even if many of them are anti-Taliban, come to dominate the ruling coalition in Kabul. American-sponsored Karzai also adds to their concern.[35] While the Northern Alliance was Russia's instrument on the ground, the US had provided the Alliance's air force. But it was not part of the American game plan for the Alliance to take Kabul since the former was egged on by Moscow, and also backed by New Delhi. Indeed, the Bush administration had promised Pakistan that it would keep the alliance out of Kabul. If Karzai goes too far against the Northern Alliance members, Moscow could certainly respond negatively.

- Russia's disagreement with the Karzai administration's policy of reconciliation with the Taliban militants has also created a rift between Moscow and Kabul. Russian Defence Minister Sergei Ivanov said that dividing the neo-Taliban into "good" or "bad" factions was unacceptable to Moscow. During a visit to New Delhi in December 2004, Ivanov remarked that Russia and India were "concerned about the attempts to Pastunize Afghanistan," referring to the Pashtun ethnic group to which most members of the neo-Taliban belonged. The policy of reconciliation with the neo-Taliban was tantamount to "starting a new war," the Defence

Minister warned.[36] These differences between Russia and Afghanistan may not be sorted out so long as the Karzai administration is backed by the American military might.

THE EMERGING TRENDS

From the preceding analyses, it is crystal clear that the impact of September 11 and the American anti-Taliban war in Afghanistan that followed have changed the entire strategic landscape in the whole region. It is a momentous event in the history of Afghanistan as it is the first arrival of Western armies since Alexander the Great conquered the region in 334 B.C. In this radically altered scenario, India and Russia share lots of global and regional strategic concerns because the stability of Afghanistan has a larger meaning for both of them. The US' military presence in this volatile landmass was bound to have a profound effect on the strategic thinking of both the countries as both of them have never had discarded the region as a sphere of US influence which now appears to be an unconcealed reality. Hence, Indo-Russian strategic future will partly be shaped by what happens in Afghanistan in the near future, including the nature and duration of the US presence. If the situation in Afghanistan deteriorates, then unalloyed security concerns will dominate. If Afghanistan stabilises and yet the US presence lingers on and becomes permanent, the emerging geo-political trends will be in a state of flux. However, from out of such a fluid situation, a few ongoing developments are worth examining as they will help indicate the emerging trends with far-reaching geo-political implications for India, Russia, and global politics in the years to come.

The first and foremost dimension of the emerging geo-political trends obviously emanates from the permanent nature of the US military presence in the country and the region. No Afghan, or for that matter, no American has an answer as to how long the US will fight its war against terrorism in Afghanistan.[37] From their ever expanding military infrastructure as well as official statements, it is clear that the US has no withdrawal strategy–how and when to leave Afghanistan. In a cold war "containment" mindset, the US created and expanded the remnant military bases and replaced its marine expeditionary forces with the army regulars for a "long haul." Both Army and Air Force units have established permanent bases.[38] In the context of nation-building in Afghanistan, just on the eve of the second anniversary of the September 11 terrorist attacks, President Bush declared that "America has done this kind of work before" in Germany and Japan after World War II.[39] It took four years to hold the first elections in Germany after the war ended in 1945, and 54 years to win the wider struggle against Communism, the President added. It was clear that the US would not cut and run.[40] After three and half years of the American military presence in the country, on 23 May 2005, President Bush and President Karzai signed a joint declaration concerning "strategic partnership" between the US and Afghanistan. The agreement stipulated that US military forces will continue to have access to Bagram Air Base and other mutually determined facilities, and that US and coalition forces "are to continue to have the freedom of action required to conduct appropriate military operations based on consultations and pre-agreed procedures." It was also declared that the US will "consult with respect to taking appropriate measures" if Afghanistan perceives that its "territorial integrity" or "independence is threatened."[41]

But the Afghan opposition to the agreement was clearly visible as anti-American demonstrations erupted in several cities following its signing. This shows that Afghans, though needing the US assistance to ensure security and root out Taliban/Al Qaeda elements, are not in favour of a permanent and prolonged American military presence.[42] Afghans have developed a sense of xenophobia about the Americans and a sense of resentment that foreigners are working in the country is intensifying.[43] Fearful about their own future, more and more people are switching gears back to neutral, stance or to supporting the Taliban or their local warlords (instead of US-backed Hamid Karzai).[44] If the Bush administration is boastful of the so called "success story" in Afghanistan and thinks that the war on terrorism is over, it is living in a fool's paradise. In fact, the trend is just the other way round. There has been a surge in violence across the country recently with increased insurgent activity in the mountains and border areas, bomb attacks in the cities and fatal attacks on aid agency workers and contractors working in rural areas.[45] Even the capital Kabul is no longer known as a "safe heaven" as it used to be.[46] *The New York Times* recently reported that coalition and Afghan forces now clash daily with large groups of Taliban fighters across five provinces of southern Afghanistan. The security situation has deteriorated so badly, that one international security official in Kandahar recently said members of American and Canadian Special Forces units had told him that they were "not winning against the Taliban."[47]

In a late February 2006 US Congressional hearing, the director of the Defense Intelligence Agency told the Congress that the insurgency in Afghanistan was growing and presenting a greater threat to the expansion of the central government's authority "than at any point since late 2001." In its annual hearing on national security threats, speaking before the Senate Armed Services Committee, Lt. Gen. Michael D. Maples said, "despite significant progress on the political front, the Taliban dominated insurgency remains capable and resilient threat. He said that the attacks in Afghanistan were up 20 percent between 2004 and 2005, suicide bombings increased "almost fourfold" and use of makeshift bombs, similar to those used in Iraq, had "more than doubled."[48] Clearly, the trend is toward more violence, more insurgency, more organized crime and strong resistance to the already fragile Karzai regime. The level of insurgency is heading to some kind of an "Iraqization" of Afghanistan as the Afghan insurgents are increasingly emulating the tactics of the Iraqi rebels–including the use of suicide bombers. The rising carnage in the country has still not reached Iraq-like levels, but the trend is running decidedly in that direction.

America's regional policy in the Southwest Asia has also some direct bearings on the emerging geo-political trends in Afghanistan. One of the main planks of the American neoconservative agenda is the use of military force against unfriendly regimes. The recent bellicose statement on Iran, notwithstanding the chaos in Iraq, sets the tone of Washington in coming days. President Bush has said that military action against Iran is a possibility. It shows that the US will continue to pursue an aggressive policy towards the region. An air campaign to destroy Iran's nuclear sites or a full-fledged military invasion would probably prompt Tehran to unleash a clandestine war on the US forces in Afghanistan (and also in Iraq). This kind of situation could be far more explosive and deadly for the Americans than it already is. Iranians have been known for their opposition to the Taliban, but they can influence the forces opposed to American presence and destabilize their already insecure neighbours. In the event of an US attack on Iran, new security concerns will crop up and the ongoing geo-political trends will take a new dimension.

Another track of the US policy that will have perpetual adverse repercussions in the Afghan situation is towards Pakistan. The US has made it clear that General Pervez Musharraf would continue to play a pivotal role in the US war on terror, even if his cooperation in tracking bin Laden and his colleagues over last four years is widely acknowledged to be inadequate. There is also every possibility that the Pakistani General would not allow capture of Laden (and others) just because he wants to further his own agenda, which is different from that of the US. A look at General Musharraf's record since he took over power in Pakistan shows that he is playing tricks.[49] It seems that General Musharraf finds it advantageous to permit Al Qaeda and the jihadist Taliban to function in his country since without that threat looming large, Washington will have no use for him. And yet, he will remain an indispensable card in the American strategic thinking.[50]

In Central Asia, especially in Uzbekistan, the worst Russian fears seem to be real. The US officials have confirmed that Washington is negotiating long-term use of a major military base in Uzbekistan to expand the global reach of American forces.[51] "Access to this airfield is undeniably critical in supporting our combat operations" said one official at the Pentagon, who also declared that the US has paid $15 mn to Uzbek authorities for use of the airfield since 2001. American military planners, US Special Operations Forces, intelligence and reconnaissance missions, and air logistics flights have to use the Karshi-Khanabad (K2) airfield in southeastern part of the country, which is strategically located and in fact, has been heavily relied by the military. As the Pentagon carries out the repositioning of US forces overseas, the Bush administration is appreciative of the strategic and geopolitical benefits of the Uzbekistan base.[52] Some Pentagon officials are thinking about the possibility of base facility and deployment of US forces in Turkmenistan as well. Such a deployment could exert pressure on Iran to comply with international demands for curbing its nuclear programme.[53] Turkmenistan has adhered to a policy of neutrality during the post-Soviet era, it must be added.

Despite such high-handedness on terrorism and religious extremism, there is still a feeling in India and Russia that the US was not responding fully to the terrorist threat because it was not affecting the US interests directly. Leaders of both the countries have pointed fingers at the US for its "selective approach" and "double standards." During his December 2002 visit to New Delhi, President Putin underlined his fundamental difference with the US on the war against terrorism. For the US, terrorism was a global phenomenon, while for Putin, the real danger was its becoming the tool of secessionist movements. For India and Russia, terrorists' threats in Jammu and Kashmir and Central Asian regions and Chechnya respectively clearly exist. Recurrent killings and explosion of suicide bombers in the volatile Indian state reminds the policy makers in New Delhi that Pakistan has not stopped its policy of cross border terrorism. Similarly, the Beslan school tragedy in Russia's North Ossetia republic in 2004 and hostage taking in a Moscow theatre earlier claiming hundreds of victims in both the incidents awakened the country to the dreadfulness of religious extremism and terrorism linked to Afghanistan.[54] There were also reports of Taliban hand in Andijon massacre of Uzbekistan in May 2005 where hundreds of innocent lives were lost.[55] While the enduring American military presence in Afghanistan and the region is not going to eliminate the specter of terrorism and Islamic fundamentalism, the menace provided a good pretext to the US entrench itself in a region so vital to India and Russia.

Conclusion

In the present scenario, India and Russia should play by the rules of realpolitik and cope with the ongoing geopolitical trends in the region. They should insist on a three-point formula to resolve the Afghan crisis. It involves respect for the territorial integrity of Afghanistan, with stable government, non-interference in its internal affairs, and a well-defined role for the United Nations to help establish permanent peace in the country. Such a policy would pressurise Washington to come up with some concrete proposals and eventually force them to look for an exit plan.

India and Russia must measure their strategic stakes in terms of the hurdles the Americans have to cross in Afghanistan. Americans also know that any permanent solution to the Afghanistan problem has to be in conformity with the strategic interests of countries like India, Pakistan, Russia, China, Central Asian republics and Iran. New Delhi and Moscow should work together closely to find out an amicable settlement through consensus among all these countries.

India and Russia could also cooperate with each other on the question of military base facilities in Central Asia which is vital to maintaining peace in Afghanistan. Russia can play a key role in providing a safety back up to Indian military in Tajikistan[56] by reinforcing the Moscow's 201st Division already in the country (guarding the Tajik-Afghan border).[57] Such cooperation between New Delhi and Moscow will help dilute the rationale for outside presence in the region.

Despite all these emerging trends, there is a strong suspicion both in New Delhi and Moscow against a permanent American presence in Afghanistan and the region, irrespective of Washington's good or bad intensions. One school of thought believes that acting in concert with the Americans does not take away Indo-Russian primacy in Afghanistan. In fact such an approach, it is believed, would reduce the risks inherent in the absence of US interventions and make the Indo-Russian regional policy less costly and controversial. The prolonged crisis in Iraq and the plan to attack Iran (if there is a plan) will also not allow Bush administration to devote much attention to Afghanistan and the Central Asian region. Russia's growing economic influence in Central Asia and that of India's in Afghanistan could help them both in achieving their strategic objectives in Afghanistan.

But at the same time, it is true that the US' permanent military presence in this part of Asia is in conflict with the strategic interests of the people of this region. For New Delhi and Moscow, the American presence has been both a boon as well as a bane. But the size, stature, geography, history, population and even military capability of India and Russia demands that they play a rightful role and apply their innovative diplomatic skill to fight the menace of terrorism as well as the undue outside interference in the region. The reinforcement of such a relationship is imperative in the interests of both countries and their peoples as well as for peace and security of Afghanistan and the whole region. In the long run, it may be difficult for the US to overlook a clear expression of Indo-Russian displeasure over its military engagement in Afghanistan and the region on a permanent basis.

Notes

1. As quoted in Martin Malek, "Russian Policy Toward South Asia," *Asian Survey,* Vol. 44, No. 3 (May/June 2004), pp. 296-397.
2. Ahmed Rashid, "The Taliban: Exporting Extremism," *Foreign Affairs,* Vol. 78, No. 6 (November/December 1999), pp. 22-23.
3. For an analytical study on the subject, see C. Raja Mohan, "Catharsis and Catalysis: Transforming the South Asian Subcontinent," in Ken Booth and Tim Dunne eds., *World in Collision: Terror and the Future of Global Order* (New York: Palgrave Macmillan, 2002), pp. 205-214.
4. Riyaz Punjabi, "Kargil Aggression: The Continuum of a Strategy," *Journal of Peace Studies,* Vol. 6, No. 3, 1999, pp. 3-8.
5. The anti-Taliban alliance led by the legendary Tajik commander Ahmed Shah Masud who was killed in September 2001.
6. See Chidanand Rajghatta, "India, US sign 10-year defence agreement," *The Times of India,* 30 June 2005. Among other things, the land mark agreement aims at defeating terrorism by strengthening the capabilities of the two militaries.

7. President Hamid Karzai did his masters degree in Political Science from Himachal Pradesh University, Shimla, India.
8. Ibragim Alibekov, "India set to Expand Presence in Central Asia," *eurasianet.org,* 3 December 2003.
9. As quoted in Ahmed Rashid, "Jockeying for influence, Neighbours Undermine Afghan Pact," *eurasianet.org,* 15 January 2003.
10. Ahmed Rashid, "Dangerous Neighbours," *Far Eastern Economic Review,* 9 January 2003, p. 19. Also see, Rashid, "Jockeying for influence, Neighbours Undermine Afghan Pact,"
11. It was the first visit by an Indian premier since Indira Gandhi's visit in 1976.
12. India will construct a new building to house the new Afghan Parliament, a project that promises to be a lasting legacy of India's commitment to Afghanistan's democracy and reconstruction. See Indrani Bagchi, "Afghan democracy gets Indian touch," *The Times of India,* 30 June 2005.
13. Amin Tarzi, "Islamabad Anxious as Kabul gets chummy with New Delhi," *eurasianet.org,* 16 April 2006.
14. For an in depth study on the subject, see V. D. Chopra, "Strategic Role of Afghanistan," in V.D. Chopra, ed., book *Global Challenge of Terrorism,* (New Delhi: Gyan Publishing House, 2002).
15. Tarzi, "Islamabad Anxious as Kabul Gets Chummy with New Delhi,"
16. Former Indian Petroleum Minister Mani Shankar Ayar talked about extending such pipeline to China and eventually to Myanmar.
17. J. N. Dixit, *India's Foreign Policy: 1947-2003,* (New Delhi: Picus Books, 2003), p. 508. Dixit, a former Indian Foreign Secretary, reveals that India's cooperation with the major powers to balance off USA's unipolar influence without confronting the US was an unarticulated objective. See, p. 509.

18. Malek, "Russian Policy Toward South Asia," p. 392.

19. Giles Whittell, "Bin Laden Link to Dagestan Rebel Fightback," *London Times,* 6 September 1999. The Chechnya-based militants who took over parts of Dagestan included in their ranks Arabs, Afghans, and Pakistanis, most of whom had fought in Afghanistan.

20. One estimate suggests that on occasion, the Russian air force bombed Taliban positions, and that the military advisors from the Russian 201st division worked for the Northern Alliance. See Malek, "Russian Policy Toward South Asia," p. 398. With the 201st Motorized Rifle Division (12,000 soldiers) and border troops of 7,800 guarding the 1,200 kilometer border with Afghanistan, Moscow maintains in Tajikistan its last extensive military presence in Central Asia.

21. There was a meeting in Pakistan at Peshawar, between various Chechen, Uzbek, Tajik and Uygur rebels in April 2001 to make joint plans and efforts to send fresh recruits to Chechnya.

22. Malek, "Russian Policy Toward South Asia," p. 393.

23. For the Central Asians, the war in Afghanistan was by now truly coming home.

24. Andrew C. Kuchins, "Is Russia rising?" *Demokratizatsiya,* 1 January 2003.

25. In fact, Russians were supplying money and weapons to the Northern Alliance for a long time, but in a small scale. See James Risen, "Russians Are Back in Afghanistan, Aiding Rebels," *The New York Times,* 27 July 1998.

26. Malek, "Russian Policy Toward South Asia," pp. 399-400. It may be mentioned that all armed formations in Afghanistan were overwhelmingly equipped with Soviet and Russian weapons and technology.

27. For a balanced view on the post 9/11 geopolitical scenario in terms of "the American Intrusion" and "Russian Responses," see Leszek Buszynski, "Russia's New Role in Central Asia," *Asian Survey,* Vol. 45, No. 4, (July/August 2005), pp. 546-565.

28. Ilan Berman, "The New Battleground: Central Asia and the Caucasus," *The Washington Quarterly*, Vol. 28, No. 1 (Winter 2004-05), pp. 59-69.
29. Stephen Blank, "US Strategic Priorities Shifting in Central Asia," *eurasianet.org*, 25 March 2004.
30. In late 2005, Russian defense ministry asked the US government to clarify how long the war in Afghanistan was going to last, expressing Moscow's displeasure with the presence of US forces in Afghanistan. See Nasreen Ghufran, "Afghanistan in 2005: The Challenges of Reconstruction," *Asian Survey*, Vol. 46, No. 1, (January/February 2006), p. 92.
31. As quoted in Stephen Blank, "US Strategic Priorities Shifting in Central Asia," *eurasianet.org*, 25 March 2004. Also see Thom Shanker, "Russian Official Cautions U.S. on Use of Central Asian Bases," *The New York Times*, 10 October 2003.
32. The doctrine was unveiled in October 2003. See Russian Ministry of Defense, "Urgent Tasks of the Development of the Russian Federation Armed Force," reprinted by the *Russian Information Agency* (RIA) Novosti News Service, 3 October 2003.
33. Todd Diamond, "US Unilateralism Fuels Great Power Rivalry in Central Asia," *eurasianet.org*, 10 January 2003.
34. As quoted in Gregory Feifer, "Uzbekistan's eternal realities: A report from Tashkent," *World Policy Journal*, Vol. 19, No. 1, (Spring 2002), pp. 81-89.
35. Mohammed Ayoob, "South-west Asia after the Taliban," *Survival*, Vol. 44, No. 1, (Spring 2002), p. 54.
36. Amin Tarzai, "Afghanistan: Was Taliban involved in Uzbek violence?" *eurasianet.org*, 19 May 2005.
37. For a critical assessment on the ongoing US involvement in Afghanistan, see Sean M. Maloney, "Afghanistan: From Here to Eternity?" *Parameters*, (Spring 2004), pp. 4-15. Also see, by the same author, "Afghanistan Four Years On: An Assessment," *Parameters*, (Autumn 2005), pp. 21-32.

38. In addition to their permanent military presence in Afghanistan, the US has laid down its long-term footprints with several Army and Air Force bases in Kyrgyzstan, Uzbekistan, and Pakistan which shows that the Americans are not going to go back any time soon.
39. Amy Waldman and Dexter Filkins, "2 U.S. Fronts: Quick Wars, but Bloody Peace," *The New York Times,* 19 September 2003.
40. Waldman and Filkins, "2 US Fronts."
41. Pamela Constable, "Karzai Dismisses Taliban Threat, Minimizes Differences with US," *The Washington Post,* 25 May 2005, p. A16. Also see the "Joint Declaration of the United States-Afghanistan Strategic Partnership," Office of the Press Secretary, The White House, Washington DC, 23 May 2005.
42. Ghufran, "Afghanistan in 2005: The Challenges of Reconstruction," p. 92. Regional actors such as Russia, China, and others also expressed their concern over the new US-Afghan strategic partnership.
43. See Editorial, "Afghanistan: Unraveling," *The New York Times,* 1 June 2006. The editorial writes: "Afghans have long been renowned for their hostility towards foreign troops on their territory, as the 20th century Russians and the 19th century British learned the hard way. Until now they have made a conspicuous exception for the 21st century Americans, who helped them shake off Taliban misrule and then promised their poor and war-shattered country an international rebuilding effort on the model of the post World War II Marshall Plan. More than four years later, Afghanistan's patience is running out."
44. N.C. Aizenman, "Afghan Crime Wave Breeds Nostalgia for Taliban," *The Washington Post,* 18 March 2005, p. A01.
45. Pamela Constable, "New Attacks Foment Fear in Afghanistan," *The Washington Post,* 13 April 2006, p. A16. Southern part of the country said to be in a very precarious

law and order situation. The Taliban appear to be moving their insurgency into a new phase, flooding the rural areas of southern Afghanistan with weapons and men. The scale of the militants' presence and their sheer brazenness has alarmed Afghans and foreign officials far more than in previous years. See Carlotta Gall, "Taliban Threat is Said to Grow in Afghan South," *The New York Times*, 3 May 2006.

46. Carlotta Gall, "Anti-US Rioting Erupts in Kabul; at least 14 Dead," *The New York Times*, 30 May 2006. Also see, Pamela Constable, "Shaken by Riots, Afghans Gripped by Uncertainty," *The Washington Post*, 31 May 2006, p. A10.

47. As quoted in Carlotta Gall, "Taliban Surges as U.S. Shifts Some Tasks to NATO," *The New York Times*, 11 June 2006.

48. As quoted in *The Washington Post*, 1 March 2006, p. A08.

49. For Pakistani involvement in Afghanistan after 9/11 incident, see Jagmohan Meher, "Bush on Afghanistan: Dozing at the Dossier of Musharraf," *Mainstream*, 27 December 2003, pp. 91-94.

50. K Subrahmanyam, "Asian Drama: After Iraq, US Targets Iran with Pak Support." *The Times of India*, 20 January 2005.

51. Ann Scott Tyson and Robin Wright, "Crackdown Muddies U.S.-Uzbek Relations: Washington in Talks on Long-Term Use of Base," *The Washington Post*, 4 June 2005.

52. However, the US regional position was drastically declined with Uzbekistan's decision in late July 2005 to evict US military forces from an airbase at Karshi-Khanabsd. Russia rushed to fill the geopolitical vacuum by rapidly strengthening bilateral ties with Uzbekistan. See Dmitry Shlapentokh, "Russia's Foreign Policy and Eurasianism," *eurasianet.org*, 2 September 2005.

53. Ariel Cohen, "Uzbekistan: A Policy Providing Ground for Washington," *eurasianet.org*, 31 May 2005.

54. Mark N. Katz, "Russia and America after Beslan," *eurasianet.org,* 13 October 2004.
55. Amin Tarzi, "Afghanistan: Was Taliban Involved in Uzbek Violence?" *eurasianet.org,* 19 May 2005.
56. India has upgraded an air base at Ayni, about six miles outside of the Tajik capital Dushanbe.
57. Kambiz Arman, "Russia and Tajikistan: Friends Again," *eurasianet.org* 28 October 2004.

12

Musharraf's Afghan Mischief

Jagmohan Meher

The devastating terrorist attacks on New York and Washington D.C. which ensued American military strikes against the Taliban regime in Afghanistan provided a great opportunity to Pakistan's military dictator General Pervez Musharraf to legitimize his rule and be a 'friend' of the Bush administration. He successfully portrayed himself and his government as an ally of the United States and extracted substantial economic aid and diplomatic backings as Washington's "courageous" and "visionary" leader in the anti-terrorist war. Just as the Soviet invasion of Afghanistan in 1979 'legitimized' General Zia-ul-Haq's rule and guaranteed his longevity, American invasion of the country rescued General Musharraf in 2001 and turned the probable "rogue state" into a "major non-NATO ally" of the United States.[1] With President George W. Bush Jr.'s "infinite" war on terrorism and indefinite search for Osama bin Laden, and Afghanistan remaining a priority area for Washington, General Musharraf has been handed a *carte blanche* with his uniform as Army Chief as well as "President" of Pakistan.

But a glimpse at the General's Afghan 'records' since his 1999 military coup shows that the Pakistani ruler has always been playing tricks under his sleeves, notwithstanding his joining the war against terrorism and the subsequent window-dressings to please Washington. In retrospect, it appears that Musharraf coercively joined the war not to bring about any structural transformation in his Afghan policy but to limit the losses his country would suffer as a result of collapse of the friendly Taliban regime in Kabul. Even after six years of the post 9/11 wars, Afghanistan continues as an area of the General's treacherousness where the Bush administration is still dwelling upon a fool's paradise.[2]

The Gimmicks of the General

First, among several reasons of the military coup, when he overthrew Nawaz Sharif, one was his apprehension that the democratically elected Prime Minister might buckle to American pressure and reverse Pakistan's policy toward the Taliban. As a result, one of the first priorities of the new ruler was to cancel a top-secret mission being planned with the United States to send commandos into Afghanistan to capture Osama bin Laden. Musharraf also resisted U.S. pressure to forcefully intercede with the Taliban leadership to achieve bin Laden's extradition.[3] Had the Al Qaeda leader been killed or captured through commando raids or extradited at that time, 9/11 would not have happened and thousands of innocent lives would have been saved. It was Musharraf who allowed Osama bin Laden and Mullah Omar to enjoy Pakistani support and hospitality to the maximum possible extent before the terrorist's attacks on the US,[4] and more reticently beyond that.

Second, in continuation of this policy, Musharraf, as he is, behaved like a die-hard patron of the Taliban and Al Qaeda during the American military operation in Afghanistan beginning October 7, 2001.

- The General floated a nightmare scenario before the Americans pretending that once the Taliban are defeated his hold on power would be in danger, implying threats of a potential "radical implosion" of Pakistan.

- He wanted the Americans to "engage" the Taliban regime in negotiations before taking military action against it.

- The General told his nation that he had to cooperate with Washington in order to "save Afghanistan and Taliban being harmed."[5]

- He pleaded to shorten the bombing campaign, and not to bomb the Taliban frontlines.

- He demanded suspension of military operations during the holy month of Ramazan.

- He desperately requested the Americans to prevent the Northern Alliance from entering Kabul and demanded that Kabul be declared "demilitarized."

- He advocated only weakening the Taliban regime and was anxious to figure out "moderate" Taliban (consisting of defectors from the movement) willing to join the new dispensation.[6]

  When thousands of Pakistani fighters and army officers fighting alongside the Taliban were trapped in Kunduz, Mazar i-Sharif, Kabul and Kandahar, the Pakistani "President" had to request the Americans for their smooth evacuation to Pakistan.

Alongside Pakistani personnel, hundreds of hard-core Al Qaeda and Taliban cadres were airlifted to Pakistani cities and despite several American requests; US agents were not allowed access to these evacuated personnel after their nighttime airlift. In other words, Musharraf tried his best to have the fundamentalist regime in place and so also the Al Qaeda network, its infrastructure, and terrorist training camps etc. All that cosmetic changes the Pakistani ruler wanted to bring about were just exploring the possibility of so called 'moderate' elements in the existing Taliban/Al Qaeda set up.

Third, at a time when Americans and the Northern Alliance soldiers were fighting both the Taliban/Al Qaeda cadres as well as thousands of Pakistani regulars in disguise, President Bush sought assistance from Musharraf to close off all possible escape routes for Osama bin Laden and associates from the Tora Bora mountainous region into Pakistan. The General did deploy 4, 000 Pakistani regular army along the border to satisfy his Big Boss, but he was equally confident of doing exactly the opposite of what the US President had asked for, i.e. he ensured free entrance of the Al Qaeda and Taliban forces into Pakistani territory and to disappear unnoticed.[7] During these crucial days, he was always trying to misguide and confuse the military operation putting the U.S. Special Forces off the scent by sometimes saying that Osama was died and sometime claiming he was hiding in the tribal areas of the Pak-Afghan borders. There are also reports of Pakistani officials having foiled American raids against Taliban and Al Qaeda through misinformation or by alerting suspects to the impending operations. CIA later confirmed that Bin Laden paid $15 million to Musharraf's army and "bought his way out" of Afghanistan during the US siege of Tora Bora which is less than 20 miles from the Pakistan border. While the army and ISI were helping the Al Qaeda and Taliban fighters' escape, the American forces were endeavoring to catch them. Decapitating the terror threat, therefore, depend on Musharraf being willing to root the fugitives out, or to let others do so inside Pakistan.

Fourth, cross-border terrorism from Pakistan into Afghanistan is continuing unabated, and the victims are innumerable innocent lives along with American troops deployed there to hunt down Al Qaeda/Taliban remnants, and the International Security Assistance Force (ISAF) to maintain law and order in the country. Under the secured cover of the Pakistani dictator, the Taliban/Al Qaeda has regrouped in Pakistan and allied itself with Gulbuddin Hekmatyar, the fundamentalist anti-US extremist. There are mounting evidences to suggest that under Musharraf's patronage, Pakistani army and intelligence personnel are fighting alongside the remnants of the Taliban and Al Qaeda to destabilize the U.S. backed Hamid Karzai government in Afghanistan.[8] If the "body bag" conscious Americans withdraw from the country, that will ensue a vacuum which will allow the Taliban and Al Qaeda to return with as usual Pakistani auspices. And so long as American presence is there, Musharraf's clandestine support to terrorists will continue which the Pakistani leader knows, would ensure an American long rope for his survival in the saddle with moderate doses of aid.

Fifth, General Musharraf–after being wined and dined at Camp David and granted aid worth billions of dollars by President Bush–appears to have strengthened perceptions within the Army and ISI that they can do anything since the United States, now militarily bogged down in Iraq, badly needs them in the war against terrorism. In fact, his success in pursuing such a policy in last six years gives him confidence that he can continue to permit jehadi extremists to function on his soil and turn it to his advantage by milking the US for weapons and economic aid. The direct result of this mindset is clearly visible in Pakistan's current policy towards Afghanistan, where the authorities in Islamabad do not bother, and openly allow the free movement of Taliban/Al Qaeda terrorists in Pakistan, especially in Baluchistan and North West Frontier Province. Even around the heart of Islamabad, the nation's capital, the so-called "banned" terrorist leaders do not hesitate to move and address public gatherings. For instance, as late as September 2003, Fazlur Rehman Khalil, the former head of Harkat-ul-Mujahiddin and presently Jamiat-ul-Ansar (who has openly supported Bin Laden's call for attacks on the United States) delivered a sermon to hundreds of worshippers at the Red Mosque and exhorted listeners to participate in jihad as police officers lounged outside.[9] How dare a prominent terrorist leader come to Musharraf's headquarters and give inflammatory speeches right in the backyard of the America's "partner" in the anti-terrorist campaign? Also, according to US officials thousands of Taliban are living in Quetta, the capital of Pakistan's Baluchistan Province, and being recruited to fight the US forces. Taliban leaders are openly giving press conferences and talking to reporters on mobile phones[10] and yet Islamabad is practically doing nothing to stop them despite repeated requests by the Afghan and the American leaderships to take action. One despairing American diplomat recently asked, "If journalists can find the Taliban and talk to them, how come the Pakistani government cannot round them up?"

Musharraf's Current Policy

Musharraf's Afghan policy and his handling of various terrorists groups fighting against the Karzai government show that the Pakistani dictator double-crosses his commitments before the international community. (1) He takes steps to break off "official links" with the Taliban and Al Qaeda only to provide clandestine support by his ISI. (2) He bans several terrorist organizations, merely to let them re-emerge under new names with the same leaders and their office shifted to a new location. (3) Bank accounts of terrorist outfits are frozen, but only after informing their leaders well in advance so that they have enough time to move the funds. (4) Large-scale arrests of terrorists and their sympathizers are made for wide media campaign and once the international camera and headlines capture the news, they are comfortably released.

(5) Offices of terrorist outfits are sealed, declared outlawed, but as per a report 7000 new cadres have been recruited during the last one year by some Jihadi groups in Pakistan. (6) Some senior army officials were fired on allegations that they were supporters of the Taliban / Al Qaeda, but there are mounting reports and evidence of hundreds of middle-level officials having direct links with the terrorist networks. (7) Politicians, retired army officers, and other high-profile people who have openly rendered support (even through public platforms) to *jihadis* are never accounted for. Clearly, these unscrupulous dimensions of General Musharraf's deceptive strategy have resulted in Pakistan's becoming the "new command center" of Al Qaeda, and breeding ground for Taliban, and hence primary source of instability for Karzai government and U.S. interests in Afghanistan. Whether it is 9/11 attacks, the Bali bombings, the Madrid railway bombings, the attacks on London's transport network or the Mumbai blasts, the inescapable conclusion is that Musharraf's Pakistan forms the epicenter of Osama bin Laden's unremitting terror campaign.

The United States is now reconciled to the fact that its "frontline ally" in its war on terrorism is providing sanctuary to the Al Qaeda and Taliban leadership, and at the same time successfully extracting financial assistance and political support from Washington. As the *Washington Post* columnist Jim Hoagland in his op-ed piece headlined "Fools Gold in Pakistan," described Musharraf as a "skilful political alchemist," who is "transforming a record of failure, extremism and betrayal into gold from the US treasury." Of late, Washington appears to be exploring the viability to acquiesce the "liberal and progressive" elements to play an effective role in Pakistani politics. But the White House through its edging cost-benefit assessment still considers Musharraf the best gamble and goes by its conventional wisdom that the current military government could find itself struggling for survival if it were seen domestically as a lapdog of American infidels. In turn, the General's cohorts in the army and intelligence, majority of who are open supporters of the terrorist groups, are becoming increasingly confident that they will be able to manage the situation without Washington being able to close in on the terrorist leadership. According to a Western diplomat, Pakistani intelligence agents maintain "lines of communication" with fugitive Taliban leaders, because they perceive such contacts as "an insurance policy" in the event the failure of Karzai's government and the Taliban returning to power in some form.[11]

Pakistan's long denial of terrorist camps on its territory is also coming apart in the face of evidence gathered by the United States intelligence agencies in a case aimed at prosecuting extremists who allegedly planned to attack targets in California. One Hamid Hayat, a US-born resident of California, is accused of twice attending terrorist camps near Rawalpindi, the military garrison town near Islamabad, run by the Lashkar-e-Taiba with intent to wage holy war against the US.[12] Hayat claims to have attended the camp as recently as 2003, well after 9/11 and Pervez Musharraf's pledge to dismantle the camps. The US experts have claimed that they have satellite photographs of the Pakistani camps and that they have highlighted their significance in the war against terrorism.

When a bin Laden videotape was dropped off at the Al Jazeera office in Islamabad on the eve of the Bush's November 2004 presidential elections, many American analysts veered around to the view that Osama bin Laden was actually living in comfort in some urban area of Pakistan, and not in some remote mountain cave. They viewed that most al-Qaida operatives have been captured in Pakistani cities like Karachi, Lahore and Faisalabad, not in the tribal regions in the Pakistan-Afghanistan borders. One Pakistani strategic analyst stated: "The fact that he has the courage to come out shows that he feels protected in his surroundings," and that his healthy appearance "shows that he is probably living in reasonable comfort and he is being taken care of."[13] A later discloser by the US counters terrorism officials reveal that the world's number one terrorist is in Pakistan.[14] But Washington does not want to embarrass Pakistan's military ruler Pervez Musharraf, who is considered a FATWAT–front-line ally in the war on terrorism. Experts on terrorist mastermind conclusively believe that the al Qaeda leader has been sheltered somewhere in Pakistan, and with proper knowledge and protection of the Pakistani dictator's intelligence agents. Hence, Musharraf's crackdown on the terrorist organizations and chasing of Al Qaeda leaderships has only been perfunctory.

The Stakes for the General

It seems that General Musharraf finds it advantageous to permit Al Qaeda and the jihadist Taliban to function in his country since without that threat looming large; Washington will have no use for him. And that Pakistan's ambiguities on terrorism are rooted in the strategy Musharraf adopted after September 11, 2001. While giving a strong commitment to the US on rooting out the Al Qaeda in Pakistan, the General has sought to protect the Pakistan's army's long-standing political investments in Afghanistan and Kashmir from the global war on terrorism. As a consequence, the Pakistan army has been hesitant to prevent the regrouping of the Taliban in Afghanistan and force its favourite Kashmiri militant groups to shut their jihadi factory. This inherent contradiction is now catching up with Musharraf, for the war on terrorism cannot be a partial one. It is in Musharraf's interests to ensure that there are no rivals who could offer help to the United States and that he remains as dispensable as he can. In this way, America's Afghanistan war benefits him the most.[15] From being virtually isolated by the international community and under increasing domestic pressure to prove his legitimacy, he became a U.S. coalition partner in the global war against terrorism. Ironically, this metamorphosis from 'villain' to 'natural ally' was brought about by Washington, which gave billions of dollars in assistance, readjusted billion dollars loan, waived sanctions and strengthened diplomatic ties with the General's regime because it needed Pakistan to fight the "anti-terrorists war" in Afghanistan. Now that with one more year of Bush jr. in the White House and with his war on terror continuing with greater messianic zeal, General Musharraf's political longevity is ensured, and the Pakistani dictator has emerged as the biggest beneficiary of America's Afghanistan war. Political leaders in Pakistan are also ready to support Musharraf to remain in uniform as army chief after the next general elections due in late 2007 and to back him for a second term as President of Pakistan.[16] "In the 1980s, Pakistan got a blank check from the U.S. to combat the Russians, and spent much of the check in building up the Taliban," argues journalist Christopher Hitchens. "Now it is getting another check and brand-new interest-free mortgage in order to pretend that the Taliban is its enemy. It doesn't get any better than this." One would probably be astonished at the inconsistency of this kind of U.S. foreign policy records when a civilian politician like Milosevic (whose military had been at war in Kosovo and Bosnia with Muslim forces that had links to Islamic radical movements and terrorists groups around the world) was labeled as "war criminal," while General Musharraf is praised as a "visionary leader" even though he was backed by radical anti-American forces and was an ally of a regime that helped inflict the worst terrorist attack ever on the American territory and people. America is supporting a regime that is "axiomatically Islamic, chronically violent, a terrorist training ground prone to stumble into wars with its neighbours, and run by an increasingly beleaguered man in uniform. And it already has the bomb—tested and ready to blast."[17]

With the unfolding of events after September 11, Americans should have asked themselves: Why Musharraf scampered over every issue including the deployment of American troops, agents, and private militia in Afghanistan? Why the US agents were denied access to the thousands of evacuated personnel from Kunduz and other cities after their nighttime Pakistani airlift? On what basis top American army officials and CIA agents argue that the war against terror have to be extended from Afghanistan into the Pakistani territory? Why has Musharraf refused to extradite Sheikh Omar Sayeed, prime accused in journalist Denial Pearl's murder? Why is it so that when there are terrorists' strikes in Sharm el-Sheikh in Egypt or London or New York, the whole international community point fingers at Pakistan and governments look for their arrests seeking Musharraf's help? These are but a few questions out of hundreds, where the Bush administration needs to dwell upon. Don't the American taxpayers have a right to know the destination and use of their hard-earned billions most of which are being spent in a round about way to kill their own brothers and sisters in Afghanistan, Iraq and elsewhere? Clearly, Musharraf is pursuing a policy of hunting with the American hounds while running with terrorist hares.

The Intact 'Jehadi' Factory

If General Pervez Musharraf and his cronies still claim that the government of Pakistan was not involved in whatever terrorist activities were going on in Afghanistan that is just an eye wash. So many terrorists training camps cannot function throughout the Pakistani territory without any knowledge of the governmental authority.

During his visit to Islamabad in February 2006, President Hamid Karzai presented evidence to Pakistani President Pervez Musharraf implicating Pakistan in the recruitment, training and equipping of Islamic radical suicide bombers. [18] A defiant Karzai said, "We have provided President Musharraf with a lot of very detailed information on acts of terrorism being carried out in Afghanistan, and we discussed in great detail what actions Pakistan could now take. We expect results; we expect that terrorist attacks will decrease."[19] He presented evidence to Pakistani President Pervez Musharraf implicating Pakistan in the recruitment, training and equipping of Islamic radical suicide bombers.

The dossiers given by Karzai to Musharraf also included the names and addresses of Pakistani recruiters, trainers and those who equip them with suicide vests and explosives before they are sent into Afghanistan. Much of the recruitment takes place at a radical Islamic bookshop, several mosques and madrassas in the port city of Karachi, while the training is done at safe houses in Quetta and Chaman, in Balochistan province. US satellites are gathering intelligence about Taliban activities in Pakistan rather than just concentrating on al Qaeda. According to Western diplomats, during a visit to Islamabad, Gen. John Abizaid, the head of the US Central Command showed the Pakistanis intelligence photos of Taliban training camps at an undisclosed location and asked for them to be shut down.

Musharraf, who usually is vehement in denying any kind of Pakistani connection to terrorist operations, was clearly subdued as a result of the Afghan intelligence given him. Officials from the Western countries say that the Pakistanis have allowed the Taliban to create a virtual mini-state and staging base for suicide attacks just across Afghanistan's eastern border. Suicide attacks have quintupled, from 23 in 2005 to 115 in 2006, killing more than 200 Afghan civilians.[20] There is also at least one report that Pakistani security forces have fired in support of Taliban fighters attacking Afghan posts.[21] One estimate suggests that Pakistani forces supported Taliban ground attacks with mortar fire and rocket-propelled grenades at least two dozen times in 2005 and 2006.[22]

It is a well known fact that the Pakistani ISI pursues a state policy that unashamedly uses the instrument of terror to achieve a political and strategic ends. A study shows that the country's approximately 55 terrorists' camps are still intact and that they are spread all over the country. According to an official dealing with the issue, "some of these camps are make-shift and can quickly be translocated to other parts to escape international scrutiny. Many of these camps had gone into hibernation after the US operations in Afghanistan. But they have now been revived."[23] These training camps send out *jehadis* to terror targets worldwide. For instance, one of the London suicide bombers is believed to have got his training in one such camp in Muridke, near Lahore.[24] Since the number of terrorists is substantial both against the Kashmir and Afghanistan fronts, in addition to their international networks, the tap for this militant reservoir is controlled by Islamabad. So apart from its support to Al Qaeda and Taliban's Afghanistan operation, major terrorist groups operating in and out of Pakistan is: Sipah-e-Sahaba, Sipah-e-Mohammed, Lashkar-e-Jhangvi, Hizbul Mujahiddin, Al Badr, Harkat-ul-Jihad-ul-Islami, Jaish-e-Mohammed, Lashkar-e-Taiba and Harkat-ul Ansar. So Pakistan's support to Taliban over the Afghan question should not be seen as an isolated policy. It is part of ISI's general policy. Unfortunately, this feeble management of the sources of terrorism in Pakistan has been thoroughly overlooked by Washington.

The Roads Ahead

The way out of the current stagnation is: (a) To provide opportunity to the democratic and liberal forces to grow and rise, an area where the United States can still work upon, and bring about a big difference in the cross-currents of Pakistan's domestic politics vis-à-vis the military situation in Afghanistan. (b) Washington should ensure that Musharraf shows hundred percent honesty in dismantling terrorist's infrastructure in the country, especially in the Northwest Frontier Province and Baluchistan, and initiates serious actions against the defaulters. (c) It is equally imperative on the part of Washington to guarantee complete elimination of terrorists in the Pakistan-controlled Kashmir, which serve as reservoirs for anti-U.S. jihadis in addition to their designated role as Pakistan's state-sponsored terrorists to create havoc and mayhem in the other side of the LOC on India. (d) Americans, including the multi-national forces, presently deployed in Afghanistan may have to seriously consider whether or not it is necessary to take the war on terror to Pakistani soil in order to destroy their terrorist infrastructure and training camps. The international community must understand that what is happening in Afghanistan is not part of the global terror network, but it is the other way round. The epicenter of global terrorism today is the Pakistan-Afghanistan region and its cadres are those indoctrinated by the extremist jehadi cult. (e) General Musharraf must be compelled by the international community to liquidate the jehadi elements and to act against Bin Laden, Ayman al-Zawahiri and Mullah Omar who are believed to be hale and hearty under his patronage. The US and NATO forces are in Afghanistan. India is not a friend of terror-baking Pakistan and its military, Chinese sensitivity on jehadi extremism emanating from Pakistan-Afghanistan border is well known. Iran has a proven anti-Taliban record even at a time when Teheran has to confront the Americans at international level. Russia and Central Asian opposition to this menace is also very clear. One appropriate strategy for the international community is, therefore, to apply all-round political, economic, technological and military pressure on Musharraf's Pakistan to act against terror. As Sumit Ganguly, director of Indian Studies at Indiana University in the US says, "There is an urgent need to start a campaign that would isolate Pakistan diplomatically."[25] (f) This is probably the time for Washington to look for an alternative to General Musharraf. Six years of history prove that either he is incapable or unwilling to deliver on his promise. "It's in our interest to begin to look to a post-Musharraf period and not to put all our chips on him," said Stephen P Cohen of Brookings

Institution. "The senior leadership here in Washington seems to believe that he's our only option."[26]

If the Pakistani dictator is allowed continuation of his "dirty games" in Afghanistan and India, Taliban/Al Qaeda's terror empire will also remain intact, and the threats will persist for the West and the United States. Pakistan has more than 10,000 Islamic Madrassa spread all over the country where over 1, 400 foreign students are currently enrolled. Many believe that the numbers could be higher than 4000 as many students were either Afghan refugees or foreign students enrolled into the religious schools while staying in the country on visiting visa. General Musharraf now talks about repatriating all foreign students from the Pakistani seminaries as a part of his policy to buy western good will. Some 800 Islamic militant suspects were arrested in Pakistan under a crackdown after the deadly London bombings of July 7, 2005.

If the ongoing course of anti-Taliban war is not sidetracked towards a positive direction, Musharraf will have a long tenure of presiding over a regime that promotes terrorism worldwide and espouses jihadist ideology at home. So long as elections are brazenly rigged, opposition parties are banned and Washington's uncritical support remains guaranteed, General Musharraf has little incentive to take up any of these vital challenges.

"The people of Pakistan are rather disappointed," said Mian Raza Rabbani, a senator and member of the largest political organization, the liberal-leaning Pakistan People's Party. "They have seen the United States pay a great deal of lip service supporting democracy in Muslim countries, but when we look at what is happening in Pakistan, President Bush says he shares the president's views and his democratic vision for Pakistan. For a great many, that is flawed."[27] Such an American perception only adds to anti-Americanism both in Pakistan and Afghanistan as well as shows Washington's apathetic attitude towards restoration of democracy in Pakistan.

Americans must understand that a protracted guerrilla war and an unstable Afghanistan is Musharraf's best bet to extract dollar from the US. American taxpayers would certainly not like to "reward" a nation that allies itself with regimes and groups that encourage terrorists to kill Americans. If Afghanistan does sink into a deeper quagmire for Washington, Musharraf will certainly be contented himself as a successful leader and a master strategist. So, for all practical purposes, America is fighting Musharraf in Afghanistan, and it's the Musharraf Inc responsible for the American failure so far, thanks to President Bush for dozing at the dossier of the dictator.

Notes

1. The United States is continuing to make large payments of roughly $1 billion a year to Pakistan for what it calls reimbursements to the country's military for conducting counterterrorism efforts along the border with Afghanistan, even though Pakistan has slashed patrols through the area where Al Qaeda and Taliban fighters are most active. See David E. Sanger and David Rohde, "U.S. Pays Pakistan to Fight Terror, but Patrols Ebb," *The New York Times,* 20 May 2007.
2. To understand the whole facts in a proper perspective, see Barry Bearak, "Pakistan Is..." *The New York Times Magazine,* 7 December 2003. Also see James Risen and David Rohde, "A Hostile Land Foils the Quest for bin Laden," *The New York Times,* 13 December 2004.
3. Kenneth Katzman, "Afghanistan: Post-War Governance, Security, and U.S. Policy," *CRS Report for Congress,* Congressional Research Service, The Library of Congress, Washington D.C., Report Updated 15 June 2004, p. CRS-29.

4. See Amin Saikal, "The role of outside actors in Afghanistan," *Middle East Policy,* Vol. 7, No. 4, October 2000, pp. 50-57.
5. As quoted in Barnett R. Rubin, "Saving Afghanistan," *Foreign Affairs,* Vol. 86, No. 1, January/February 2007, pp. 58-59.
6. On 25 September, 2001, Musharraf's Foreign Minister Abdul Sattar warned that any move by foreign powers "to give assistance to one side or the other in Afghanistan is a recipe for great suffering for the people of Afghanistan." Within few days, Musharraf talked about the "moderate Taliban," in a press conference with visiting U.S. Secretary of State Colin Powell in Islamabad. For a scholarly study on the subject, see William Maley, *The Afghanistan Wars,* Palgrave Macmillan, London, New York, 2000, especially chapter 11, pp. 251-283.
7. For a vivid picture of the military operation beginning October 7, 2001, see Michael E. O'Hanlon, "A Flawed Masterpiece," *Foreign Affairs,* Vol. 81, No. 3, May/June 2002, pp. 47-63.
8. For a long time after the U.S. invasion of Afghanistan, Musharraf, his Army and the powerful security agency known as ISI were directly supporting the Taliban as a matter of state policy. See Ahmed Rashid, "Islamabad's Lingering Support for Islamic Extremists Threatens Pakistan-Afghanistan Ties," *eurasianet.org* 23 July 2003.
9. David Rohde, "Questions Grow on Pakistan's Commitment to Fight Taliban," *The New York Times,* 10 September 2003.
10. Ahmed Rashid, "Taliban stepping up attacks against targets in Afghanistan," *eurasianet.org* 28 July 2003.
11. *The New York Times,* 2 September 2003.
12. Chidanand Rajghatta, "US to expose Pak terror camps," *The Times of India,* 19 February 2006.
13. As quoted in Chidanand Rajghatta, "Bin Laden is in Pakistan: US" *The Times of India,* 1 November 2004.

14. Chidanand Rajghatta, "Pak comfort for Osama?" *The Times of India,* 7 February 2006.
15. For a more detailed discussion, see Jagmohan Meher, *America's Afghanistan War: The Success That Failed,* Kalpaz Publications, New Delhi, 2004, pp. 235-241.
16. In January 2006, Punjab Chief Minister Chaudhry Pervaiz Elahi openly supported Musharraf to head the country after the next general elections. It means that the President-in-uniform will remain in power for over a decade in the current calculations. Pakistan has a political tradition of army chiefs staying on beyond their tenures.
17. Peter Preston, "A falling friendship," *The Guardian,* 8 May 2006.
18. At least 30 suicide bombing attacks, carried out by the Taliban and al Qaeda, have killed nearly 100 people in Afghanistan over a period of three months i.e. in between December 2005 and February 2006. Most of the victims have been Afghan civilians. Anti-Pakistan sentiment has been rising in Afghanistan.
19. Ahmed Rashid, "Afghan President Confronts Pakistani Counterpart Over Suicide Bombers," *Eurasianet.org,* 21 February 2006.
20. David Rohde, "Iran is Seeking More Influence in Afghanistan," *The New York Times,* 27 December 2006.
21. David E. Sanger and David Rohde, "U.S. Pays Pakistan to Fight Terror, but Patrols Ebb,"
22. *Ibid.*
23. As quoted in Rajat Pandit, "Jehadi factory working flat out," *The Times of India,* 31 July 2005.
24. *Ibid.*
25. As quoted in "Can we do an Israel ?" *The Sunday Times of India,* 23 July 2006, p. 6.
26. As quoted in Jim VandeHei and Bradley Graham, "Pakistan Braces as Bush Starts Visit," *The Washington Post,* 4 March 2006, p. A10.
27. As quoted in *The New York Times,* 4 March 2006.

Appendix-A

Text: Afghan Agreement on Broad-Based, Multi-Ethnic Government

(Interim Authority to be established December 22, 2001) (3290)

Following is the full text of the agreement signed December 4 by Afghan representatives meeting in Bonn, Germany, aimed at establishing a stable, representative government in Afghanistan following 23 years of war.

(begin text)

AGREEMENT ON PROVISIONAL ARRANGEMENTS IN AFGHANISTAN PENDING THE RE-ESTABLISHMENT OF PERMANENT GOVERNMENT INSTITUTIONS

The participants in the UN Talks on Afghanistan,

In the presence of the Special Representative of the Secretary-General for Afghanistan,

Determined to end the tragic conflict in Afghanistan and promote national reconciliation, lasting peace, stability and respect for human rights in the country,

Reaffirming the independence, national sovereignty and territorial integrity of Afghanistan,

Acknowledging the right of the people of Afghanistan to freely determine their own political future in accordance with the principles of Islam, democracy, pluralism and social justice,

Expressing their appreciation to the Afghan mujahidin who, over the years, have defended the independence, territorial integrity and national unity, of the country and have played a major role in the struggle against terrorism and oppression, and whose sacrifice has now made them both heroes of jihad and champions of peace, stability and reconstruction of their beloved homeland, Afghanistan,

Aware that the unstable situation in Afghanistan requires the implementation of emergency interim arrangements and expressing their deep appreciation to His Excellency Professor Burhanuddin Rabbani for his readiness to transfer power to an interim authority which is to be established pursuant to this agreement,

Recognizing the need to ensure broad representation in these interim arrangements of all segments of the Afghan population, including groups that have not been adequately represented at the UN Talks on Afghanistan.

Noting that these interim arrangements are intended as a first step toward the establishment of a broad-based, gender-sensitive, multi-ethnic and fully representative government, and are not intended to remain in place beyond the specified period of time,

Recognizing that some time may be required for a new Afghan security force to be fully constituted and functional and that therefore other security provisions detailed in Annex I to this agreement must meanwhile be put in place,

Considering that the United Nations, as the internationally recognized impartial institution, has a particularly important role to play, detailed in Annex II to this agreement, in the period prior to the establishment of permanent institutions in Afghanistan,

Have agreed as follows:

THE INTERIM AUTHORITY

I. General provisions

1. An Interim Authority shall be established upon the official transfer of power on 22 December 2001.

2. The Interim Authority shall consist of an Interim Administration presided over by a Chairman, a Special Independent Commission for the Convening of the Emergency Loya Jirga, and a Supreme Court of Afghanistan, as well as such other courts as may be established by the Interim Administration. The composition, functions and governing procedures for the Interim Administration and the Special Independent Commission are set forth in this agreement.

3. Upon the official transfer of power, the Interim Authority shall be the repository of Afghan sovereignty, with immediate effect. As such, it shall, throughout the interim period, represent Afghanistan in its external relations and shall occupy the seat of Afghanistan at the United Nations and in its specialized agencies, as well as in other international institutions and conferences.

4. An Emergency Loya Jirga shall be convened within six months of the establishment of the Interim Authority. The Emergency Loya Jirga will be opened by His Majesty Mohammed Zaher, the former King of Afghanistan. The Emergency Loya Jirga shall

decide on a transitional Authority, including a broad-based transitional administration, to lead Afghanistan until such time as a fully representative government can be elected through free and fair elections to be held no later than two years from the date of the convening of the Emergency Loya Jirga.

5. The Interim Authority shall cease to exist once the Transitional Authority has been established by the Emergency Loya Jirga.

6. A Constitutional Loya Jirga shall be convened within eighteen months of the establishment of the Transitional Authority, in order to adopt a new constitution for Afghanistan. In order to assist the Constitutional Loya Jirga prepare the proposed Constitution, the Transitional Administration shall, within two months of its commencement and with the assistance of the United Nations, establish a Constitutional Commission.

II. Legal framework and judicial system

1. The following legal framework shall be applicable on an interim basis until the adoption of the new Constitution referred to above:

   (i) The Constitution of 1964, a/ to the extent that its provisions are not inconsistent with those contained in this agreement, and b/ with the exception of those provisions relating to the monarchy and to the executive and legislative bodies provided in the Constitution; and ii) existing laws and regulations, to the extent that they are not inconsistent with this agreement or with international legal obligations to which Afghanistan is a party, or with those applicable provisions contained in the Constitution of

1964, provided that the Interim Authority shall have the power to repeal or amend those laws and regulations.

2. The judicial power of Afghanistan shall be independent and shall be vested in a Supreme Court of Afghanistan, and such other courts as may be established by the Interim Administration. The Interim Administration shall establish, with the assistance of the United Nations, a Judicial Commission to rebuild the domestic justice system in accordance with Islamic principles, international standards, the rule of law and Afghan legal traditions.

III. Interim Administration

A. Composition

1. The Interim Administration shall be composed of a Chairman, five Vice Chairmen and 24 other members. Each member, except the Chairman, may head a department of the Interim Administration.

2. The participants in the UN Talks on Afghanistan have invited His Majesty Mohammed Zaher, the former King of Afghanistan, to chair the Interim Administration. His Majesty has indicated that he would prefer that a suitable candidate acceptable to the participants be selected as the Chair of the Interim Administration.

3. The Chairman, the Vice Chairmen and other members of the Interim Administration have been selected by the participants in the UN Talks on Afghanistan, as listed in Annex IV to this agreement. The selection has been made on the basis of professional competence and personal integrity from

lists submitted by the participants in the UN Talks, with due regard to the ethnic, geographic and religious composition of Afghanistan and to the importance of the participation of women.

4. No person serving as a member of the Interim Administration may simultaneously hold membership of the Special Independent Commission for the Convening of the Emergency Loya Jirga.

B. Procedures

1. The Chairman of the Interim Administration, or in his/her absence one of the Vice Chairmen, shall call and chair meetings and propose the agenda for these meetings.

2. The Interim Administration shall endeavour to reach its decisions by consensus. In order for any decision to be taken, at least 22 members must be in attendance. If a vote becomes necessary, decisions shall be taken by a majority of the members present and voting, unless otherwise stipulated in this agreement. The Chairman shall cast the deciding vote in the event that the members are divided equally.

C. Functions

1. The Interim Administration shall be entrusted with the day-to-day conduct of the affairs of state, and shall have the right to issue decrees for the peace, order and good government of Afghanistan.

2. The Chairman of the Interim Administration or, in his/her absence, one of the Vice Chairmen, shall represent the Interim Administration as appropriate.

3. Those members responsible for the administration of individual departments shall also be responsible

for implementing the policies of the Interim Administration within their areas of responsibility.

4. Upon the official transfer of power, the Interim Administration shall have full jurisdiction over the printing and delivery of the national currency and special drawing rights from international financial institutions. The Interim Administration shall establish, with the assistance of the United Nations, a Central Bank of Afghanistan that will regulate the money supply of the country through transparent and accountable procedures.

5. The Interim Administration shall establish, with the assistance of the United Nations, an independent Civil Service Commission to provide the Interim Authority and the future Transitional Authority with shortlists of candidates for key posts in the administrative departments, as well as those of governors and uluswals, in order to ensure their competence and integrity.

6. The Interim Administration shall, with the assistance of the United Nations, establish an independent Human Rights Commission, whose responsibilities will include human rights monitoring, investigation of violations of human rights, and development of domestic human rights institutions. The Interim Administration may, with the assistance of the United Nations, also establish any other commissions to review matters not covered in this agreement.

7. The members of the Interim Administration shall abide by a Code of Conduct elabourated in accordance with international standards.

8. Failure by a member of the Interim Administration to abide by the provisions of the Code of Conduct

shall lead to his/her suspension from that body. The decision to suspend a member shall be taken by a two-thirds majority of the membership of the Interim Administration on the proposal of its Chairman or any of its Vice Chairmen.

9. The functions and powers of members of the Interim Administration will be further elabourated, as appropriate, with the assistance of the United Nations.

IV. The Special Independent Commission for the Convening of the Emergency Loya Jirga

1. The Special Independent Commission for the Convening of the Emergency Loya Jirga shall be established within one month of the establishment of the Interim Authority. The Special Independent Commission will consist of twenty-one members, a number of whom should have expertise in constitutional or customary law. The members will be selected from lists of candidates submitted by participants in the UN Talks on Afghanistan as well as Afghan professional and civil society groups. The United Nations will assist with the establishment and functioning of the commission and of a substantial secretariat.

2. The Special Independent Commission will have the final authority for determining the procedures for and the number of people who will participate in the emergency Loya Jirga. The Special Independent Commission will draft rules and procedures specifying (i) criteria for allocation of seats to the settled and nomadic population residing in the country; (ii) criteria for allocation of seats to the Afghan refugees living in Iran, Pakistan, and elsewhere, and Afghans from the diaspora; (iii)

criteria for inclusion of civil society organizations and prominent individuals, including Islamic scholars, intellectuals, and traders, both within the country and in the diaspora. The Special Independent Commission will ensure that due attention is paid to the representation in the Emergency Loya Jirga of a significant number of women as well as all other segments of the Afghan population.

3. The Special Independent Commission will publish and disseminate the rules and procedures for the convening of the Emergency Loya Jirga at least ten weeks before the Emergency Loya Jirga convenes, together with the date for its commencement and its suggested location and duration.

4. The Special Independent Commission will adopt and implement procedures for monitoring the process of nomination of individuals to the Emergency Loya Jirga to ensure that the process of indirect election or selection is transparent and fair. To pre-empt conflict over nominations, the Special Independent Commission will specify mechanisms for filing of grievances and rules for arbitration of disputes.

5. The Emergency Loya Jirga will elect a Head of the State for the Transitional Administration and will approve proposals for the structure and key personnel of the Transitional Administration.

V. Final provisions

1. Upon the official transfer of power, all mujahidin, Afghan armed forces and armed groups in the country shall come under the command and control of the Interim Authority, and be reorganized according to the requirements of the new Afghan security and armed forces.

2. The Interim Authority and the Emergency Loya Jirga shall act in accordance with basic principles and provisions contained in international instruments on human rights and international humanitarian law to which Afghanistan is a party.

3. The Interim Authority shall cooperate with the international community in the fight against terrorism, drugs and organized crime. It shall commit itself to respect international law and maintain peaceful and friendly relations with neighbouring countries and the rest of the international community.

4. The Interim Authority and the Special Independent Commission for the Convening of the Emergency Loya Jirga will ensure the participation of women as well as the equitable representation of all ethnic and religious communities in the Interim Administration and the Emergency Loya Jirga.

5. All actions taken by the Interim Authority shall be consistent with Security Council resolution 1378 (14 November 2001) and other relevant Security Council resolutions relating to Afghanistan.

6. Rules of procedure for the organs established under the Interim Authority will be elabourated as appropriate with the assistance of the United Nations.

This agreement, of which the annexes constitute an integral part, done in Bonn on this 5th day of December 2001 in the English language, shall be the authentic text, in a single copy which shall remain deposited in the archives of the United Nations. Official texts shall be provided in Dari and Pashto, and such other languages as the Special Representative of the Secretary-General may designate. The Special Representative of the Secretary-General shall send certified copies in English, Dari and Pashto to each of the participants.

For the participants in the UN Talks on Afghanistan:

Ms. Amena Afzali Mr. S. Hussain Anwari Mr. Hedayat Amin Arsala Mr. Sayed Hamed Gailani Mr. Rahmatullah Mousa Ghazi Eng. Abdul Hakim Mr. Houmayoun Jareer Mr. Abbas Karimi Mr. Mustafa Kazimi Dr. Azizullah Ludin Mr. Ahmad Wali Massoud Mr. Hafizullah Asif Mohseni Prof. Mohammad Ishaq Nadiri Mr. Mohammad Natiqi Mr.Aref Noorzay Mr. Yunus Qanooni Dr. Zalmai Rassoul Mr. H. Mirwais Sadeq Dr. Mohammad Jalil Shams Prof. Abdul Sattar Sirat Mr. Humayun Tandar Mrs. Sima Wali General Abdul Rahim Wardak Mr. Azizullah Wasefi Mr. Pacha Khan Zadran

Witnessed for the United Nations by:

Mr. Lakhdar Brahimi Special Representative of the Secretary-General for Afghanistan

ANNEX I
INTERNATIONAL SECURITY FORCE

1. The participants in the UN Talks on Afghanistan recognize that the responsibility for providing security and law and order throughout the country resides with the Afghans themselves. To this end, they pledge their commitment to do all within their means and influence to ensure such security, including for all United Nations and other personnel of international governmental and non-governmental organizations deployed in Afghanistan.

2. With this objective in mind, the participants request the assistance of the international community in helping the new Afghan authorities in the

establishment and training of new Afghan security and armed forces.

3. Conscious that some time may be required for the new Afghan security and armed forces to be fully constituted and functioning, the participants in the UN Talks on Afghanistan request the United Nations Security Council to consider authorizing the early deployment to Afghanistan of a United Nations mandated force. This force will assist in the maintenance of security for Kabul and its surrounding areas. Such a force could, as appropriate, be progressively expanded to other urban centers and other areas.

4. The participants in the UN Talks on Afghanistan pledge to withdraw all military units from Kabul and other urban centers or other areas in which the UN mandated force is deployed. It would also be desirable if such a force were to assist in the rehabilitation of Afghanistan's infrastructure.

ANNEX II
ROLE OF THE UNITED NATIONS DURING THE INTERIM PERIOD

1. The Special Representative of the Secretary-General will be responsible for all aspects of the United Nations' work in Afghanistan.

2. The Special Representative shall monitor and assist in the implementation of all aspects of this agreement.

3. The United Nations shall advise the Interim Authority in establishing a politically neutral environment conducive to the holding of the Emergency Loya Jirga in free and fair conditions. The United Nations shall pay special attention to

the conduct of those bodies and administrative departments which could directly influence the convening and outcome of the Emergency Loya Jirga.

4. The Special Representative of the Secretary-General or his/her delegate may be invited to attend the meetings of the Interim Administration and the Special Independent Commission on the Convening of the Emergency Loya Jirga.

5. If for whatever reason the Interim Administration or the Special Independent Commission were actively prevented from meeting or unable to reach a decision on a matter related to the convening of the Emergency Loya Jirga, the Special Representative of the Secretary-General shall, taking into account the views expressed in the Interim Administration or in the Special Independent Commission, use his/her good offices with a view to facilitating a resolution to the impasse or a decision.

6. The United Nations shall have the right to investigate human rights violations and, where necessary, recommend corrective action. It will also be responsible for the development and implementation of a programme of human rights education to promote respect for and understanding of human rights.

ANNEX III
REQUEST TO THE UNITED NATIONS BY THE PARTICIPANTS AT THE UN TALKS ON AFGHANISTAN

The participants in the UN Talks on Afghanistan hereby

1. Request that the United Nations and the international community take the necessary measures

to guarantee the national sovereignty, territorial integrity and unity of Afghanistan as well as the non-interference by foreign countries in Afghanistan's internal affairs;

2. Urge the United Nations, the international community, particularly donor countries and multilateral institutions, to reaffirm, strengthen and implement their commitment to assist with the rehabilitation, recovery and reconstruction of Afghanistan, in coordination with the Interim Authority;

3. Request the United Nations to conduct as soon as possible (i) a registration of voters in advance of the general elections that will be held upon the adoption of the new constitution by the constitutional Loya Jirga and (ii) a census of the population of Afghanistan;

4. Urge the United Nations and the international community, in recognition of the heroic role played by the mujahidin in protecting the independence of Afghanistan and the dignity of its people, to take the necessary measures, in coordination with the Interim Authority, to assist in the reintegration of the mujahidin into the new Afghan security and armed forces;

5. Invite the United Nations and the international community to create a fund to assist the families and other dependents of martyrs and victims of the war, as well as the war disabled;

6. Strongly urge that the United Nations, the international community and regional organizations cooperate with the Interim Authority to combat international terrorism, cultivation and trafficking

of illicit drugs and provide Afghan farmers with financial, material and technical resources for alternative crop production.

ANNEX IV
COMPOSITION OF THE INTERIM ADMINISTRATION

Chairman:........................... Mr. Hamid Karzai

Membership (of whom 5 will be Vice-Chairs) Department of Defence: Department of Finance: Department of Foreign Affairs: Department of the Interior: Department of Planning: Department of Commerce: Department of Mines and Industries: Department of Small Industries: Department of Information and Culture: Department of Communication: Department of Labour and Social Affairs: Department of Hajj & Auqaf: Department of Martyrs & Disabled: Department of Education: Department of Higher Education: Department of Public Health: Department of Public Works: Department of Rural Development: Department of Urban Development: Department of Reconstruction: Department of Transport: Department of Water and Electricity: Department for the Return of Refugees: Department of Agriculture: Department of Irrigation: Department of Justice: Department of Air Transport & Tourism: Department of Border Affairs: Department of Women's Affairs.

Appendix-B

Chronology of Important Events Since The Soviet Invasion of Afghanistan

1979 : Soviet Union invades Afghanistan.

1980 : Refugee exodus accelerates from Afghanistan to Pakistan and Iran.

1980 : President Jimmy Carter authorizes supply of weapons to Afghan resistance through Pakistan to fight the Soviet troops in Afghanistan.

1980 : In the State of the Union address, President Carter announces that any attempt by outside force to control the Persian Gulf region would be treated as an assault on the U.S. vital interests and subject to U.S. intervention, including military force (Carter Doctrine).

1980 : American media starts highlighting the plight of the Afghans to generate sympathy and public awareness.

1980 : United Nations General Assembly adopts resolution calling for the "immediate withdrawal of foreign troops from Afghanistan."

1981 : Javier Perez de Cuellar appointed as special representative of the U.N. Secretary General to promote Afghan peace talks.

1981 : United States signs agreement with Pakistan to supply military and economic aid, including forty F-16 fighters over the next six years, totaling US$3.2 billion.

1981 : Diego Cordovez, UN under secretary for political affairs is designated as the personal representative of the newly elected Secretary General Perez de Cuellar to promote Afghan peace talks. The Geneva talks begin.

1982 : U.S. Congress forms bipartisan Afghanistan Task Force to pressurize the Reagan administration to supply effective aid to Afghan mujahiddin. The Task Force headed by staunch supporters of the resistance like Senator Paul Tsongas and Senator Gordon Humphrey.

1982 : Soviet President Leonid Brezhnev dies, and succeeded by Yuri Andropov who stresses Soviet willingness for a political settlement of the Afghan conflict.

1983 : Andropov agrees to second round of Geneva talks. Cordovez announces settlement to be 95 percent complete.

1983 : Influential American lawmakers call for supply of effective military aid to Afghan mujahiddin.

1984 : CIA targets Soviet Central Asia through Islamic propaganda missions.

1984 : Andropov dies and replaced by Konstantin Chernenko.

1984 : U.S. Congress passes the Tsongas-Ritter resolution calling for the Reagan administration to "render effective military aid to the freedom fighters."

1985 : Chernenko dies and Mikhail Gorbachev takes over as the President and the general secretary of the Soviet communist party.

1985 : President Ronald Reagan signs National Security Decision Directive (NSDD) 166, increasing aid to Afghan mujahiddin with goal of forcing Soviet withdrawal from the country.

1985 : Fundamentalist mujahiddin leader Gulbuddin Hekmatyar, representing the resistance alliance at the United Nations, refuses to meet President Reagan.

1985 : Reagan-Gorbachev Summit at Geneva.

1986 : In his State of the Union address to the joint seating of US Congress, President Reagan pronounces his famous "roll back policy," later dubbed as Reagan Doctrine.

1986 : Gorbachev describes Afghanistan as "bleeding wound."

1986 : President Reagan meets Afghan "freedom fighters" in the Oval Office, promises more aid.

1986 : United States decides to supply the resistance with surface-to-air Stinger missiles.

1987 : United States annual assistance to the Afghan resistance rises to more than US$630 million.

1987 : President Reagan honors head of Afghan resistance in the White House.

1987 : U.S.-supplied Stinger missiles show spectacular success in destroying Soviet and Afghan aircrafts.

1988 : On 14 April, Geneva Accords are signed between Pakistan and Afghanistan as two signatories and United States and Soviet Union as two guarantors. United States declares to continue arms supply to the resistance as long as the Soviets do the same to the communist regime in Kabul, described as "negative symmetry."

1988 : The mujahiddin forms the Afghan Interim Government in Peshawar.

1988 : President Zia-ul-Haq along with U.S. ambassador to Pakistan Arnold Raphel and other American and Pakistani officials killed in air sabotage.

1989 : Soviet Union completes troop withdrawal from Afghanistan as per Geneva accords.

1990 : United States continues to insist on the change of Najibullah regime in Kabul.

1990 : Cold War between United States and Soviet Union ends, and Afghanistan reduces to a low priority area in the American thinking.

1991 : United States and Soviet Union agree to stop all military aid to their respective Afghan clients by the end of the year, described as "positive symmetry" accord.

1992 : Afghan President Najibullah appeals to the United States for help in checking the spread of Islamic fundamentalism in Central Asia.

1992 : President Najibullah resigns.

1992 : U.S. delegation visits Kabul to discuss diplomatic relations between the two countries.

1992 : Afghanistan enters into a phase of civil war.

1992 : Petroleum companies of the United States and Uzbekistan signs agreement on a fifty-fifty joint venture to develop Mingbulak oil field in Ferghana valley over a twenty-eight-year period.

1993 : Americans realize that bombing of the World Trade Center, killing six people and injuring 100, is the work of terrorists with an Afghan background.

1993 : Washington urges Islamabad to expel 'Arab Afghans' from Pakistan.

1994 : Armed Afghan/Pakistan students, emerge as Taliban, capture Afghan territory and head north toward the capital Kabul.

1994 : United States sends a State Department delegation to Kabul, Islamabad and Rome (to consult former king Zahir Shah).

1995 : Taliban advance to the outskirts of Kabul.

1995 : United States sends envoy to Jalalabad and Mazar-i-Sharif.

1996 : United States Senator Hank Brown organizes conference on Afghanistan in Washington D.C.

1996 : Senator Hank Brown visits Kabul.

1996 : Under U.S. and Saudi pressure, Osama bin Laden is expelled from Sudan, and moves to Afghanistan.

1996 : Former President Najibullah taken from United Nations compounds and hanged by Taliban in a Kabul light outpost.

1997 : Taliban delegation, headed by Mullah Wakil Ahmed, visiting the United States, meets with Assistant Secretary of State, Robin Raphel and other officials.

1997 : Osama bin Laden claims through a CNN interview that his disciples were behind the killing of 18 American soldiers in Somalia in 1993.

1997 : Taliban declare to award natural gas pipeline contract to whoever gives greater concessions to Afghanistan. The interested parties are UNOCAL (USA) and Bridas (Argentina).

1998 : Terrorist attacks on the American embassies in Kenya and Tanzania, killing over 250 people, including 12 Americans, and wounding more than 5000, traces to Osama bin Ladin's network Al Qaeda headquartered in Afghanistan.

1998 : United States launches 75 Tomahawk cruise missiles against terrorist bases and camps in eastern Afghanistan killing only 20 militants.

1999 : United States imposed economic sanctions against Afghanistan, barring Americans from trading with or investing in the country.

2000 : United States traces Al Qaeda for bombing of *USS Cole,* which claims 17 lives.

2001 : United States traces Al Qaeda for terrorist attacks in New York and Washington D.C. killing more than three thousand people.

2001 : America declares war against Taliban regime, and hunts for Bin Laden, Al Qaeda, Mullah Omar, and associates.

2001 : General Pervez Musharraf told his nation that he had to cooperate with Washington in order to "save Afghanistan and Taliban being harmed."

2001 : Bush administration successfully maneuvers the Security Council resolution 1373 and then centers around formation of a coalition against its "war on terrorism."

2001 : United States claims that 48 countries' support for the military campaign in Afghanistan.

2001 : NATO declares its full support to the American war efforts, by involving article 5 of the North Atlantic Treaty: an attack on one is an attack on all.

2001 : Kabul falls to American backed Northern Alliance.

2001 : United States detalibanizes the country and help set up an interim government under Hamid Karzai.

2001 : Afghan representatives meet in Bonn, Germany, to establish a stable representative government in Afghanistan following 23 years of war.

2002 : U.S. President George W. Bush and British Prime Minister Tony Blair declare that the war on Afghanistan was won, Al Qaeda defeated and the international anti-terrorist coalition victorious.

2002 : After heavy American casualties during Operation Anaconda in Eastern Afghanistan, United States asks Britain to help with more British troops.

2002 : A noted Pakistani weekly comes out with a proof about involvement of regular Pakistani army and

ISI with Taliban even after the September 11 attacks in the United States.

2003 : U.S. warplanes launch heavy air strikes against Taliban targets near Spin Boldak. A-10, Harrier, and B-1 aircrafts as well as AC-130 gunship and Apache helicopters participate in the air strike.

2003 : Afghan President Hamid Karzai meets President Bush in the White House. American support to Karzai continues.

2003 : Secretary of Defense Donald Rumsfeld suggested that the war in Afghanistan was in a "cleanup" phase.

2003 : About 300 Afghans, including government employees and students chanted anti-American slogans in Kabul in the first such protest since U.S. forces invaded Afghanistan to topple the fundamentalist Taliban in late 2001.

2003 : 3 German peacekeepers are killed in Kabul car bomb attack.

2003 : In a major battle since the end of Taliban regime, 40 Taliban militia and 9 government fighters are killed in Spin Boldak province near Pak-Afghan border.

2003 : Afghan resentment against the American "occupying forces" increases.

2004 : The Constitutional Loya Jirga of January 4-16, 2004, approved Afghanistan's nationally mandated constitution in 40 years.

2004 : Afghans went to the polls and Hamid Karzai became the first democratically elected President of Afghanistan.

2005 : NATO implemented its 2nd stage of ISAF expansion, taking responsibility for the security of western portion of Afghanistan.

2005 : The U.N.-backed Disarmament, Demobolization and Reintegration (DDR) programme that started in October 2003 officially came to an end on July 7, 2005.

2005 : Elections to the Afghan national assembly were held on September 18, 2005 and on December 19, 2005 the new Assembly was inaugurated.

2005 : U.S. President George W. Bush and Afghan President Hamid Karzai signed a joint declaration concerning the strategic partnership between the United States and Afghanistan.

2006 : "Building on Success: The London Conference on Afghanistan," *The Afghan Compact* was signed. It represents a framework for international co-operation in Afghanistan for the next five years.

2006 : In May, Taliban publicly executed on Badshah Khan, a local convict, in front of a large crowd in the central province of Uruzgon.

2006 : US and Afghan delegation met in Washington to begin a dialogue on governance and economic and security issues within the framework of a US-Afghan Strategic Partnership initiative launched in 2005.

2006 : The US reaffirmed the importance of its long-term commitment to Afghanistan.

2006 : Lutfullah Mashal, the former Afghan Interior Ministry Spokesman, observed that "Taliban fighters no longer rely solely on hit-and-run tactics by small groups of guerrillas. Instead, the Taliban have been concentrating into groups of more than 100 fighters to carry out frontal assaults on government security posts."

2006 : The Taliban is thought to have at least 12,000 fighters controlling areas in the provinces of Oruzgan, Helmand, Zabol and Kandahar.

2006 : Militants in the restive North Waziristan tribal region signed a "peace agreement" with Pakistani political agents pledging to halt cross-border movement and stop attacks on government installations and security forces; an implicit Pakistani endorsement of the notion that the fight against the U.S. and NATO presence in Kabul is jihad.

2006 : About 90 civilians died in armed clashes between the Taliban and NATO forces in the Panjwai District of Kandahar on October 24, causing resentment of the NATO presence.

2006 : President Karzai on December 12 unequivocally blamed the Pakistani government for fuelling Taliban insurgency stating: "if the world community does not realize the extent of Pakistan's interference in Afghanistan, and does not find a solution to the current Pakistani military intervention in Afghanistan, the flames of the fire will spread to the region and the world."

2007 : *The New York Times* reported that Pakistani forces supported Taliban ground attacks with mortar fire and rocket-propelled grenades at least two dozen times in 2005 and 2006.

2007 : *The New York Times* reported that Pakistani security forces have fired in support of Taliban fighters attacking Afghan posts.

Bibliography

BOOKS

Adamec, Ludwig W., *Afghanistan's Foreign Affairs to the Mid-Twentieth Century: Relations with the USSR, Germany and Britain,* University of Arizona Press, Tucson, 1974.

—*Afghanistan, 1900–1923: A Diplomatic History,* University of California Press, Berkeley, 1967.

Adelman, Jonathan R., *Super Powers and Revolution,* Praeger, New York, 1986.

Amstutz, J. Bruce, *Afghanistan: The First Five Years of Soviet Occupation,* National Defence University, Washington DC, 1986.

Arnold, Anthony, *Afghanistan: The Soviet Invasion in Perspective,* The Hoover Institution Press, Stanford, 1985.

—*Afghanistan's Two Party Communism: Parcham and Khalq,* The Hoover Institution Press, Stanford, 1985.

Berman, Larry, ed., *Looking Back on the Reagan Presidency,* The Johns Hopkins University Press, Baltimore, 1990.

Booth, Ken, and Dunne, Tim, ed., *Worlds in Collision: Terror and the Future of Global Order,* Palgrave Macmillan, New York, 2002.

Bowker, Mike, and Williams, Phil., *Superpower Détente: A Reappraisal,* Sage, London, 1988.

Bradsher, Henry S., *Afghanistan and the Soviet Union,* Duke Press, Durham, 1983.

Brown, Seyom, *The Faces of Power: Constancy and Change in United States Foreign Policy from Truman to Reagan,* Columbia University Press, New York, 1983.

Brzezinski, Zbigniew, *Power and Principle: Memoirs of the National Security Adviser, 1977-1981,* Farrar, Straus, Giroux, 1983.

Carter, Jimmy, *Keeping Faith: Memoirs of a President,* New York, Bantam Books, 1982.

Chadda, Maya, *Paradox of Power: The United States in South West Asia, 1973-1984,* ABC-CLIO, Barbara, 1986.

Chopra, V.D. ed., *Global Challenge of Terrorism,* Gyan Publishing House, New Delhi, 2002.

Cooley, John K., *Unholy Wars: Afghanistan, America and International Terrorism,* Pluto Press, London, 1999.

Dixit, J. N., *India's Foreign Policy: Challenge of Terrorism,* Gyan Publishing House, New Delhi, 2002.

Dupree, Louis, *Afghanistan,* Princeton University Press, Princeton, 1973.

Eliot Jr, Theodore L., and Robert L. Jr, Pfaltzgraff, ed. *The Red Army on Pakistan's Border: Policy Implications for the United States,* Pergomon, Washington DC, 1886.

—*Gorbachev's Afghan Gambit,* National Security Papers, Institute for Foreign Policy Analysis, Washington DC, 1988.

Emadi, Hafizullah, *State, Revolution and Superpowers in Afghanistan,* Greenhood Press, Greenhood, 1990.

Emerson, Steven, *Secret Warriors: Inside the Covert Military Operations of the Reagan Era,* G.P. Putnam's Sons, New York, 1988.

Ewans, Martin, *Afghanistan: A New History,* Curzon Press, Richmond, 2001.

Farr, Grant M., and Merriam, John G., ed. *Afghan Resistance: The Politics of Survival,* Westview Press, Boulder, 1987.

Fraser Tytler, Sir William K., *Afghanistan: A Study of Political Developments in Central and Southern Asia,* London, 1967.

Girardet, Edward R., *Afghanistan: The Soviet War,* St. Martin's Press, New York, 1985.

Glaus, Abdul Samad, *The Fall of Afghanistan,* Pergamon-Brassey's, Washington DC, 1987.

Goodson, Larry P., *Afghanistan's Endless War: State Failure, Regional Politics, and Rise of the Taliban,* University of Washington Press, Seattle and London, 2001.

Griffiths, John C., *Afghanistan: Key to a Continent,* Westview Press, Boulder, 1981.

Hass, Richard N., *Conflicts Unending: The United States and the Regional Disputes,* Yale University Press, New Haven, 1990.

Hamilton, Edward K., ed. *America's Global Interests; a New Agenda,* W.W. Norton & Company, New York, 1989.

Hammond, Thomas T., *Red Flag Over Afghanistan: The Communist Coup, the Soviet Invasion, and the Consequences,* Westview Press, Boulder, 1984.

Hauner, Milan & Canfield, Robert I., ed. *Afghanistan and the Soviet Union: Collision and Transformation,* Westview Press, Boulder, 1989.

Horelick, Arnold L., ed. *US–Soviet Relations: The Next Phase,* Cornell University Press, Ithaca, & London, 1986.

Hsiung, James C., & Chai, Winberg, ed. *Asia and US Foreign Policy,* Praeger, New York, 1981.

Hyland, William G., *Mortal Rivals: Superpower Relations from Nixon to Reagan,* Random House, New York, 1987.

Khalilzad, Zalmay, *The Return of the Great Game: Superpower Rivalry and Domestic Turmoil in Afghanistan, Iran, Pakistan, and Turkey,* California Seminar on International Security and Foreign Policy, Discussion Paper No. 88, Santa Monica, September 1980.

Khan, Riaz M., *Untying the Afghan Knot: Negotiating Soviet Withdrawal,* An Institute of the Study of Diplomacy Book, Duke, 1991.

Klass, Rosanne, ed., *Afghanistan: The Great Game Revisited,* Freedom House, New York, 1987.

Krickus, Richard J., *The Superpowers in Crisis: Implications of Domestic Discord,* Pergamon–Brassey, Washington, 1987.

Lavrentyev, Alexander, *USA and Asia,* Sterling, New Delhi, 1982.

Magnus, Ralph, ed. *Afghanistan Alternatives: Issues, Options and Policies,* Transaction Books, Oxford, 1985.

Magnus, Ralph H., and Naby, Eden, *Afghanistan: Mullah, Marx, and Mujahid,* Westview Press, Boulder, 1998.

Maley, William, ed., *Fundamentalism Reborn? Afghanistan and the Taliban,* Hurst & Co., London, 1998.

Meher, Jagmohan, *America's Afghanistan War: The Success That Failed,* Kalpaz Publications, Delhi, 2004.

Myers, R.H., ed. *U.S. Foreign Policy for Asia: The 1980s and Beyond,* Hoover Institution Press, Stanford, 1982.

Newell, Nancy Peabody, and Newell, Richard S., *The Struggle for Afghanistan,* Cornell University Press, Ithaca, 1981.

O'balance, Edgar, *Afghan Wars: What Britain Gave up and the Soviet Union Lost,* Brasseys, Mcmillan, 1991.

Oberdorfer, Don, *From the Cold War to a New Era: The United States and the Soviet Union 1983-1990,* Poseidon Press, New York, 1991.

Orman, John, *Comparing Presidential Behaviour: Carter, Reagan, and the macho Presidential Style,* Greenwood, New York, 1987.

Payne, Keith B., *Nuclear Deterrence in US–Soviet Relations,* Westview Press, Boulder, 1982.

Poullada, Leon B., and Poullada, Leila D.J., *The Kingdom of Afghanistan and the United States: 1828-1973,* Center for Afghanistan Studies at the University of Nebraska at Omaha, 1995.

Rais, Rasul Bakhsh, *War Without Winners: Afghanistan's Uncertain Transition after the Cold War,* Oxford University Press, Oxford, 1994.

Raymond, L. Garthoff, *Détente and Confrontation: American–Soviet Relations from Nixon to Reagan,* The Brookings Institution, Washington DC, 1985.

Reagan, Ronald, *An American Life,* Simon and Schuster, New York, 1990.

Rodman, Peter W., *More Precious than Peace: The Cold War and the Struggle for the Third World,* Charles Scribner's Sons, New York, 1994.

Rubinstein, Alvin Z., ed. *The Great Game: Rivalry in the Persian Gulf and South Asia,* Praeger, New York, 1983.

Schweizer, Peter, *Victory: The Reagan Administration's Secret Strategy that Hastened the Collapse of the Soviet Union,* The Atlantic Monthly Press, New York, 1994.

Sengupta, Bhabani, *Afghan Syndrome: How to Live with Soviet Power,* Vikas, New Delhi, 1982.

—*Afghanistan: Politics, Economics and Society, Revolution, Resistance, Intervention,* Francis Printer, London, 1986.

Shultz, George P., *Turmoil and Triumph: My Years as Secretary of State,* Charles Scribner's Sons, New York, 1993.

Tanner, *Stephen, Afghanistan, A Military History from Alexander the Great to the fall of the Taliban,* Da Capo Press, New York, 2002.

Turner, Stansfield, *Secrecy and Democracy,* Houghton Mifflin Company, Boston, 1985.

Vance, Cyrus, *Hard Choices: Critical Years in America's Foreign Policy,* Simon and Schuster, New York, 1983.

Weinbaum, Marvin G., *Pakistan and Afghanistan: Resistance and Reconstruction,* Westview Press, Boulder, 1994.

White, Ralph K., *Fearful Warriors: A Psychological Profile US–Soviet Relations,* The Free Press, New York, 1984.

Woodward, Bob, *Veil: The Secret Wars of the CIA 1981–1987,* Simon and Schuster, New York, 1987.

Yousaf, Mohammad, and Adkin, Mark, *The Bear Trap: Afghanistan's Untold Story,* Jung Publishers, Lahore, 1992.

ARTICLES

Ahady, Anwar-ul-Haq, "The Decline of the Pashtuns in Afghanistan," *Asian Survey,* Vol. 35, No. 7, July 1995.

Allan, Nigel J R, "Rethinking Governance in Afghanistan," *Journal of International Affairs,* Vol. 56, No. 2, Spring 2003.

Allan, p., and Stahel, A.A., "Tribal Guerrilla Warfare against a Colonial Power: Analyzing the War in Afghanistan," *Journal of Conflict Resolution,* Vol. 27, December 1983.

Ayoob, Mohammed, "South-west Asia after the Taliban," *Survival,* Vol. 44, No. 1, Spring 2002.

Azmi, M. Raziullah, "Afghanistan: Moscow's "Vietnam?" *Pakistan Journal of American Studies,* Vol. 7, No. 1, March 1989.

Barfield, Thomas, "The Afghan Morass," *Current History,* January 1996.

Bearden, Milton, "Afghanistan, Graveyard of Empires," *Foreign Affairs,* Vol. 80, No. 6, November/December 2001.

Bennigsen, A., "Mullahs, Mujahiddin and Soviet Muslims," *Problems of Communism,* Vol. 33, November/December 1984.

Berkowitz, Bruce, "The New Protracted Conflict: Intelligence and the War on Terrorism," *Orbis,* Spring 2002.

—"Confessions of a Soviet Muslim Rebel," *Orbis,* Vol. 32, Summer 1988.

Biddle, Stephen, "Afghanistan and the Future of Warfare," *Foreign Affairs,* Vol. 82, No. 2, March/April 2003.

Boade, William R., "The Reagan Doctrine," *Strategic Review,* Winter 1986.

Braddock, L., "Moral Unequivalence: Afghanistan is not Soviet's Vietnam," *Policy Review,* No. 45, Summer 1988.

Brown, Horald, "U.S. Security Policy in South West Asia: A case study in complexity," *Occasional Paper,* School of Advanced International Studies, Foreign Policy Institute, John Hopkins University, Washington DC, 1981.

Campbell, Kurt M., "Globalization's First War?" *The Washington Quarterly,* Winter 2002.

Chanda, N., "Reagan's Responses," *Far Eastern Economic Review,* Vol. 133, July 3, 1986.

Carpenter, Ted Galen, "The Unintended Consequences of Afghanistan," *World Policy Journal,* Vol. 11, No. 1, Spring 1994.

Cohen, S.P., "South Asia after Afghanistan," *Problems of Communism,* Vol. 34, January/February 1986.

Coldren, L.O., "Afghanistan in 1984: the fifty year of the Russo-Afghan War," *Asian Survey,* Vol. 25, February 1985.

—"Afghanistan in 1985: the sixth year of the Russo–Afghan War, *Asian Survey,* Vol. 26, February 1986.

Copson, Raymond W., and Cronin, Richard P., "The Reagan Doctrine and its prospects," *Survival*, January/February 1987.

Craffetz, D., "Afghanistan in Turmoil," *International Affairs*, Vol. 56, January 1980.

Cronin, R.P., "Afghanistan in 1988: A year of decision?" *Asian Survey*, Vol. 29, February 1989.

—"U.S. Interests, Objects and Policy Options in South West Asia," *Occasional Paper*, Strategic Studies Institute, U.S. Army War College, Carlisle Barracks, 15 January 1982.

—"Afghanistan: Soviet Invasion and U.S. Response," *Congressional Research Service (CRS)*, The Library of Congress, Washington DC, January 10, 1980.

—"Afghanistan after five years: Status of the conflict, the Afghan resistance and the U.S. role, *CRS*, The Library of Congress, Washington DC, January 1985.

—"The United States, Pakistan, and the Soviet threat to Southern Asia: Options for Congress," *CRS*, The Library of Congress, Washington DC, September 1985.

—""Military Effectiveness of the Afghan Resistance," Testimony before the Congressional Task Force on Afghanistan, *CRS*, The Library of Congress, Washington DC, August 13, 1986.

—"Afghanistan: Issues for U.S. Policy," in Contra Aid and the Reagan Doctrine, A major issue forum, *CRS*, Vol. 8, No. 3, March 1987.

—"Afghanistan after the Soviet withdrawal: Contenders for powers," *CRS*, The Library of Congress, Washington DC, March 2, 1989.

—and Miko, Francis T., "Afghanistan: Status, U.S. role, and implications of a Soviet withdrawal," *CRS*, The Library of Congress, Washington DC, April 20, 1988.

Daley, T., "Afghanistan and Gorbachev's global foreign policy," *Asian Survey*, Vol. 29, May 1989.

Davison Jr., Kenneth L., "The Geopolitics of the Soviet Withdrawal from Afghanistan," *Strategic Review*, Vol. 18, No. 1, 1990.

Delpech, Therese, "The Imbalance of Terror," *The Washington Quarterly*, Winter 2002.

Denman, D., "Afghanistan: Buffer Disappears," *Far Eastern Economic Review,* Vol. 107, January 11, 1980.

—"Win in the Great Game," *Far Eastern Economic Review,* Vol. 110, November 14, 1980.

Dorronsoro, Gilles, "Afghanistan's Civil War," *Current History,* January 1995.

Dunbar, C., "Afghanistan in 1986: the balance endures," *Asian Survey,* Asian Survey, Vol. 27, February 1987.

—"Afghanistan in 1987: a year of decision?" *Asian Survey,* Vol. 28, February 1988.

Dunn, Keith, "Soviet Constraints on South West Asia," *Occasional Paper,* Strategic Studies Institute, U.S. Army War College, Washington DC, December 7, 1981.

Dupree, L., "Afghanistan in 1983: and still no solution," *Asian Survey,* Vol. 24, February 1984.

—"The Soviet Union and Afghanistan in 1987," *Current History,* Vol. 86, No. 522, October 1987.

—"Afghanistan's Big Gamble: Part I, Historical Background of Afghan-Russian Relations," *American Universities Field Staff Reports (AUSF),* Vol. IV, No. 3, April 29, 1960.

—"Afghanistan's Big Gamble: Part II, The Economic and Strategic Aspects of the Soviet Aid," *AUFS,* Vol. IV, No. 4, May 2, 1960.

—"Afghanistan's Big Gamble: Part III, Economic Competition in Afghanistan, *AUFS,* Vol. IV, No. 5, May 9, 1960.

—"The Mountains go to Mohammed Zahir: Observations on Afghanistan's Reactions to visits from Nixon, Bulganian-Khrushchev, Eisenhower and Khrushchev," *AUFS,* Vol. IV, No. 6, May 20, 1960.

—"The Bamboo Curtain in Kabul: An American Finds Communication with the Chinese Embassy close to him," *AUFS,* Vol. IV, No. 7, July 31, 1960.

—"American Private Enterprise in Afghanistan: The Investment Climate, Particularly as it relates to one company," *AUFS,* Vol. IV, No. 9, December 1, 1960.

—"Pushtunistan: The Problems and its Larger Implications, Part I, The Complex Interrelationships of Regional Disputes," *AUFS*, Vol. V, No. 2, November 1961.

—"Pushtunistan: The Problems and its Larger Implications, Part II, The Effects of the Afghan-Pakistan Border Closure," *AUFS*, Vol. V, No. 3, November 1961.

—"Toward Representative Government in Afghanistan," Part II, *AUFS*, No. 14, 1978.

—"The Democratic Republic of Afghanistan, 1979," *AUFS*, No. 32, 1979.

—"Red Flag Over the Hindu Kush, Part V: Repressions or Security through terror purges," *AUFS*, No. 28, 1980.

—"Red Flag Over the Hindu Kush, Part VI: Repressions or Security through terror," *AUFS*, No. 29, 1980.

—"Red Flag Over the Hindu Kush, Part III: Rhetoric and Reforms, or Promises, Promises," *AUFS*, No. 23, 1980.

Eliot, T.L., "Afghanistan in 1989: stalemate," *Asian Survey*, Vol. 30, February 1990.

—"Afghanistan in 1990: Groping towards peace," *Asian Survey*, Vol. 31, No. 2, February 1991.

Felbab-Brown, Vanda, "Afghanistan: When Counternarcotics Undermines Counterterrorism," *The Washington Quarterly*, Vol. 28, No. 4, Autumn 2005.

Felton, J., "Afghanistan, human rights: Reagan, Gorbachev agree on little more than good will," *Congressional Quarterly Weekly Report*, Vol. 45, December 12, 1987.

Fromkin, Devid, "The Great Game in Asia," *Foreign Affairs*, Vol. 58, Spring 1980.

Fullerton, J., "Call to Rebellion," *Far Eastern Economic Review*, Vol. 113, September 11, 1981.

Ganguly, Sumit, "India and Pakistan in the Shadow of Afghanistan," *Current History*, April 2002.

—"Putting South Asia Back Together Again," *Current History*, December 2001.

Garfinkle, Adam, "Afghanistanding," *Orbis,* Vol. 43, No. 3, Summer 1999.

Ghufran, Nasreen, "The Taliban and the Civil War Entanglement in Afghanistan," *Asian Survey,* Vol. 41, No. 3, May/June 2001.

—"Afghanistan in 2005: The Challenges of Reconstruction," *Asian Survey,* Vol. 46, No. 1, January/February 2006.

—"Afghanistan in 2006: The Complications of Post-Conflict Transition," *Asian Survey,* Vol. 47, No. 1, January/February 2007.

Gibbs, Devid, "The Peasant as Counter-Revolutionary: The Rural Origin of the Afghan Insurgency," *Studies in Comparative International Development,* Vol. XXI, No. 1, Spring 1986.

—"Does the USSR have a 'grand strategy,'" reinterpreting the invasion of Afghanistan," *Journal of Peace Resolution,* Vol. 24, December 1987.

Haendel, Dan, "The Persian Gulf: Geopolitics Revisited," *International Security Review,* Vol. VI, No. 1, Spring 1981.

Ham, Peter van, and Kamminga, Jorrit, "Poppies for Peace: Reforming Afghanistan's Opium Industry," *The Washington Quarterly,* vol30, No. 1, Winter 2006-07.

Helliday, F., "War and Revolution in Afghanistan," *New Left Review,* No. 119, January 1980.

Hannah, N.B., "Afghanistan: The Great Gamble," *Asian Affairs,* Vol. VI, No. 3, January/February 1979.

Haqqani, H., "The Unseen Soviet Hand," *Far Eastern Economic Review,* Vol. 38, October 29, 1987.

Harrison, S.S., "Nightmare in Baluchistan," *Foreign Policy,* No. 32, Fall 1978.

—"Dateline Afghanistan: Exit Through Finland?" *Foreign Policy,* No. 41, Winter 1980/81.

—"Breakthrough in Afghanistan?" *Foreign Policy,* No. 51, Summer 1983.

—"Inside the Afghan Talks," *Foreign Policy,* No. 72, Fall 1988.

Hauner, Milan, "Forum: The War in Afghanistan," *Orbis,* Vol. 29, Spring 1985.

Hersh, Seymour M., "Watching the Warheads," *The New Yorker,* November 5, 2001.

Hoffmann, Stanley, "Reflections on Present Danger," *The New York Review,* March 6, 1980.

Hyman, A., "Invaders with a sweet tooth," *New Statesman,* Vol. 100, August 8, 1980.

Islam, Mohammad, "April 1978 Coup in Kabul and the US Response," *Pakistan Journal of American Studies (PJAS),* Vol. V, No. 1, March 1987.

—"US and the Afghan Issue," *PJAS,* Vol. VI, No. 2, September 1988.

—"US–Afghanistan Relations: A Historical Perspective," *PJAS,* Vol. IX, No. 1 & 2, Spring/Fall 1991.

Jalali, Ali A., "The Future of Afghanistan," *Parameters,* vo.136, No. 1, Spring 2006.

Johns, M., "The Lessons of Afghanistan: bipartisan support for freedom fighters pays off," *Policy Review,* No. 40, Spring 1987.

Johnson, Thomas H., and Mason, M. Chris, "Understanding the Taliban and Insurgency in Afghanistan," *Orbis,* Winter 2007.

Judah, Tim, "The Taliban Papers," *Survival,* Vol. 44, No. 1, Spring 2002.

Kamrany, Nake M., "Afghanistan under Soviet occupation," *Current History,* Vol. 81, No. 475, May 1982.

—"The Continuing war in Afghanistan," *Current History,* Vol. 85, No. 513, October 1986.

Karp, C.M., "The War in Afghanistan," *Foreign Affairs,* Vol. 64, Summer 1986.

Katz, Mark N., "Anti-Soviet Insurgencies: Growing Trend or Passing Phase?" *Orbis,* Vol. 30, No. 2, 1986.

Khalilzad, Z., "Soviet Occupied Afghanistan," *Problems of Communism,* Vol. 29, November 1980.

—"The Soviet Dilemma in Afghanistan," *Current History,* Vol. 84, No. 509, October 1985.

—"Moscow's Afghan War," *Problems of Communism,* Vol. 35, January/February 1986.

—"Afghanistan in 1993: Abandoned but Surviving," *Asian Survey,* vo.34, No. 2, February 1994.

—"Afghanistan in 1994: Civil War and Disintegration," *Asian Survey,* Vol. 35, No. 2, February 1995.

—"Afghanistan in 1995: Civil War and a Mini-Great Game," *Asian Survey,* Vol. 34, No. 2, February 1996.

—"Anarchy in Afghanistan," *Journal of International Affairs,* Vol. 51, No. 1, Summer 1997.

Kirkpatrick, J.J., "Afghanistan: Implications for peace and security," *World Affairs,* Vol. 144, Winter 1981/82.

Klass, R.T., "The Tragedy of Afghanistan," *Asian Affairs,* Vol. 7, September/October 1979.

—"Afghanistan: The Accords," *Foreign Affairs,* Vol. 66, Summer 1988.

Krakowski, Elie D., "Defining success in Afghanistan," *Washington Quarterly,* Vol. 8, No. 2, Spring 1985.

Kurth, James, "The New Protracted Conflict: The War and the West," *Orbis,* Spring 2002.

Levy, Walter J., "Oil: An Agenda for the 1980's," *Foreign Affairs,* Vol. 59, Summer 1981.

Lifschultz, Lawrence, "Afghanistan: The not-so-new rebellion," *Far Eastern Economic Review,* January 30, 1981.

Magnus, Ralph H., and Naby, Eden, "Afghanistan and Central Asia: Mirrors and Models," *Asian Survey,* Vol. 35, No. 7, July 1995.

Magnus, Ralph H., "Afghanistan in 1997: The War Moves North," *Asian Survey,* Vol. 38, No. 2, February 1998.

Maitre, H. Joachim, "Ask the Afghans," *Strategic Review,* Vol. 17, No. 1, 1989.

Malek, Martin, "Russian Policy Toward South Asia: An Update," Asian Survey, Vol. 44, No. 3, May/June 1004.

Malhuret, C., "Report from Afghanistan," *Foreign Affairs,* Vol. 62, Winter 1983/84.

Medler, James D., "Afghan Heroin: Terrain, Tradition, and Turmoil," *Orbis,* Spring 2005.

Meher, Jagmohan, "Afghanistan in Indo-Russian Strategic Calculations: The Post 9/11 Trends, *Governance and Public Policy,* Vol. 1, No. 2, September 2006.

Mehta, Jagat S., "A neutral solution," *Foreign Policy,* No. 47, Summer 1982.

Menges, Constantine, "The Diplomacy of Defeat: Are we losing Nicaragua, Angola, and Afghanistan Again?" *Policy Review,* No. 46, Fall 1988.

Miller, Steven, E., "The End of Unilateralism or Unilateralism Redux?" *The Washington Quarterly,* Winter 2002.

Mohan, C. Raja, "Geo-Politics and Energy Security," *Strategic Analysis,* Vol. 19, No. 9, December 1996.

Moreau, Ron; Hussain, Zahid, and Yousafzai, Sami, "A Risky Feud," *Newsweek,* March 20, 2006.

Moss, Robert, "What Russia Wants," *The New Republic,* January 19, 1980.

Naby, E., "Ethnic Factor in Soviet-Afghan Relations," *Asian Survey,* Vol. 20, March 1980.

Nasir, A., "New Soviet Game Plan," *Far Eastern Economic Review,* Vol. 134, November 27, 1986.

Nasir, Sohail Abdul, "Afghanistan: The more it changes..." *Bulletin of Atomic Scientists,* Vol. 59, No. 2, March/April 2003.

Nagaran, Hannah, "Afghanistan: A Marxist Regime in a Muslim Society," *Current History,* Vol. 76, No. 446, April 1979.

—"Afghan coup of April 1978: revolution and international security," *Orbis,* Vol. 23, Spring 1979.

Newell, R.S., "International Response to the Afghan Crisis," *World Today,* Vol. 37, May 1981,

—"Post-Soviet Afghanistan: the position of the minorities," *Asian Survey,* Vol. 29, November 1989.

Newman, J., "The future of northern Afghanistan," *Asian Survey,* Vol. 28, July 1988.

Overholt, W.H., "The Geopolitics of the Afghan War," *Asian Affairs,* Vol. 7, No. 4, March/April 1980.

Peake, Gordon, "From warlords to peacelords?" *Journal of International Affairs,* Vol. 56, No. 2, Spring 2003.

Pipes, Daniel, "Who is the Enemy," *Commentary,* January 2002.

Pope, R.R., "Afghanistan and the Influence of Public Opinion on Soviet Foreign Policy," *Asian Affairs,* Vol. 8, July/August 1981.

Poullada, L.B., "Afghanistan and the United States: the crucial years," *Middle East Journal,* Vol. 35, Spring 1981.

—Failure of American Diplomacy in Afghanistan," *World Affairs,* Vol. 145, Winter 1982/83.

Radu, Michael, "Terrorism After the Cold War: Trends and Challenges," *Orbis,* Spring 2002.

Rais, R.B., "Afghanistan after the Soviet withdrawal," *Current History,* Vol. 91, No. 563, March 1992.

Ram, M., "Causes of a coup," *Far Eastern Economic Review,* Vol. 107, January 11, 1980.

Ramazani, R.K., "Comments," *Orbis,* Vol. 30, Winter 1987.

Rashid, Abdul, "An Afghan Resistance Commander Looks at the War and Its Strategic Implications," *Strategic Review,* Vol. 13, No. 1, 1985.

Rashid, Ahmed, "Afghanistan: Friend of the people," *Far Eastern Economic Review,* July 20, 1995.

—"Afghanistan: Heart of Darkness," *Far Eastern Economic Review,* August 5, 1999.

—"The Taliban: Exporting Extremism," *Foreign Affairs,* Vol. 78, No. 6, November/December 1999.

—"Afghanistan: Ending the Policy Quagmire," *Journal of International Affairs,* Vol. 54, No. 2, Spring 2001.

Riphenburg, Carol J., "Post-Taliban Afghanistan: Changed Outlook for Women?" Asian Survey, Vol. 44, No. 3, May/June 1004.

Rubin, Barnett R., "Afghanistan: Back to Feudalism," *Current History,* Vol. 88, No. 542, December 1989.

—"Afghanistan: the next round," *Orbis,* Vol. 33, Winter 1989.

—"The Fragmentation of Afghanistan," *Foreign Affairs,* Winter 1989/90.

—"Afghanistan under the Taliban," *Current History*, February 1999.

—"Women and pipelines: Afghanistan's proxy wars," *International Affairs*, Vol. 73, No. 2, April 1997.

—"Saving Afghanistan," *Foreign Affairs*, Vol. 86, No. 1, January/February 2007.

Rubin, Michael, "The Teheran Temptation," *Commentary*, January 2002.

Rubinstein, Alvin Z., "Soviet Imperialism in Afghanistan," *Current History*, Vol. 79, No. 459, October 1980.

—"Afghanistan: embraced by the bear," *Orbis*, Vol. 26, Spring 1982.

—"The Soviet Union and Afghanistan," *Current History*, Vol. 82, No. 486, October 1983.

—"Afghanistan at War," *Current History*, Vol. 85, No. 509, March 1986.

—"Speculation on a National Tragedy," *Orbis*, Vol. 30, Winter 1987.

—"The Soviet Withdrawal from Afghanistan," *Current History*. Vol. 87, No. 531, October 1988.

Rumsfeld, Donald H., "Transforming the Military," *Foreign Affairs*, Vol. 81, No. 3, May/June 2002.

Saikal, Amin, "Afghanistan's Ethnic Conflict," *Survival*, Vol. 40, No. 2, Summer 1998.

—"The Role of outside actors in Afghanistan," *Middle East Policy*, Vol. 7, No. 4, October 2000.

Schultheis, Rob, "In Afghanistan: Peace Must Wait," *New York Times Magazine*, December 29, 1991.

Sheel, Ram Rahul, "Afghanistan in International Perspective," *International Studies*, Vol. 22, No. 2, April/June 1985.

Shultz, George P., "New Realities and New Ways of Thinking," *Foreign Affairs*, Vol. 63, No. 4, Spring 1985.

Smolansky, O.M., "Soviet Policy in Iran and Afghanistan," *Current History*, Vol. 80, No. 468, October 1981.

Steel, Ronald, "Afghanistan doesn't matter," *The New Republic*, February 1980.

Stern, Jessica, "Pakistan's Jihad Culture," *Foreign Affairs,* Vol. 79, No. 6, November/December 2000.

Stobdan, p., "War in Afghanistan," *Asian Strategic Review 1996-97,* Institute for Defence Studies and Analysis (IDSA), New Delhi.

—"Backing Away From Afghanistan," *Strategic Analysis,* Vol. 19, No. 9, December 1996.

—"The Afghan Conflict and Regional Security," *Strategic Analysis,* Vol. 23, No. 5, August 1999.

Strmecki, Marin, "Can the Afghan Rebels Win?" *National Review,* Vol. 38, No. 12, July 4, 1986.

Talbott, Otrobo, "Afghanistan: In the Capital of a Quagmire," *Time,* October 26, 1981.

Tarzi, Shah M., "Afghanistan in 1991: A Glimmer of Hope," *Asian Survey,* Vol. 32, No. 2, February 1992.

—"Afghanistan in 1992: A Hobbesian State of Nature," *Asian Survey,* Vol. 33, No. 2, February 1993.

Thapar, K., "Now its up to Reagan," *New Statesman,* Vol. 111, May 30, 1986.

Tomsen, Peter, "A Chance for Peace in Afghanistan: The Taliban's Days Are Numbered," *Foreign Affairs,* Vol. 79, No. 1, January/February, 2000.

—"Untying the Afghan Knot," *Fletcher Forum,* Vol. 25, Winter 2001.

Valenta, J., "Soviet invasion of Afghanistan: the difficulty of knowing where to stop," *Orbis,* Vol. 24, Summer 1980.

—"From Prague to Kabul," *International Security,* Fall, 1980.

Wafadar, K., "Afghanistan in 1980: the struggle continues," *Asian Survey,* Vol. 21, February 1981.

—"Afghanistan in 1981: the struggle intensifies," *Asian Survey,* Vol. 22, February 1982.

Wallop, Malcolm, "U.S. Covert Action: Policy Tool or Policy Hedge?" *Strategic Review,* Vol. 12, No. 3, Summer 1984.

Weinbaum, M.G., and Gautam Sen, "Pakistan Enters the Middle East," *Orbis,* Vol. 22, 1978.

Weinbaum, M.G."Pakistan and Afghanistan: The Strategic Relationship," *Asian Survey,* Vol. 31, No. 6, June 1991.

—"Afghanistan and Its Neighbours: An Ever Dangerous Neighbourhood," *Special Report,* United States Institute of Peace, No. 162, June 206.

Westad, Odd Arne, "Afghanistan: Perspective on the Soviet War," *Bulletin of Peace Proposal,* Vol. 20, No. 3, 1989.

Wright, C., "Winnable Wars," *New Statesman,* Vol. 111, March 14, 1986.

Yadav, Sanjay, "Prospects of a Non-aligned Afghanistan," *Strategic Analysis,* Vol. 12, October/March 1988/89.

Zonis, M., "Middle East Responses," *Orbis,* Vol. 30, Winter 1987.

Index

A

E

F

G

R

W

Y

Z